Miami University

The Alumni and Former Student Catalogue of Miami university

Miami University

The Alumni and Former Student Catalogue of Miami university

ISBN/EAN: 9783337365806

Printed in Europe, USA, Canada, Australia, Japan

Cover: Foto ©Paul-Georg Meister /pixelio.de

More available books at **www.hansebooks.com**

THE ALUMNI AND FORMER STUDENT

CATALOGUE

OF

MIAMI UNIVERSITY

INCLUDING MEMBERS OF

THE BOARD OF TRUSTEES

AND

FACULTY

1809-1892

OXFORD, OHIO, JUNE, 1892

Press of
The Oxford News
Oxford, Ohio

PREFATORY NOTE.

THE publication of this Alumni and Former Student Catalogue is in response to a general desire among the alumni and friends of the University to secure and preserve in accessible form a succinct account of the alumni and former students from the earliest days to the present. The work was undertaken during the year 1890 and has been resumed throughout the present year. The effort has been made to secure full and accurate accounts of all students who have ever enrolled, but on account of the great amount of work that had to be done in gathering the material for the alumni, it was impossible to give as much attention to the former students as this department should have received. Hence the list of former students concerning whom information is given is somewhat limited, but we hope that the impetus given to the work in this volume will enable us to soon collect a pretty full account of all. Many excellent sketches of graduates have been received, which, we regret to say, it is impossible to use in their entirety in a catalogue. All the material of this character that has been gathered will be kept on file, and it is hoped that in the near future we shall be able to publish a volume of early history that will give a full account of the University and her men. We desire to express our obligation and thanks to the friends who have so kindly and generously helped us in gathering this material. If any student or friend to whom this catalogue may come shall be able to give us additional information concerning deceased alumni or students, or concerning any whose address we have not been able to secure, such information will be gladly welcomed and preserved for future use.

The work of gathering the material and preparing this catalogue has been a labor of love on the part of Walter Lawrence Tobey, of the class of 1891. His gratuitous services at great expenditure of time and labor deserve grateful recognition, which we gladly give. The expense of publication has been borne by Senator Calvin S. Brice, of the class of 1863, to whose liberal generosity the University in recent years is greatly indebted.

W. O. THOMPSON.

MIAMI UNIVERSITY,
June 1st, 1892.

HISTORICAL NOTE.

THE history of Miami University covers the period of early growth and development of much of the North-west Territory. During these years her graduates have been men of character and patriotic sentiment who have been among the foremost citizens of our country. In the time of our great struggle her sons were upon nearly every battlefield. Through her commanding influence in the early history of Western life she has contributed not a little to the direction of national affairs. The reader of this catalogue will discern among her graduates names that will suggest the sweep of this influence.

The University owes her existence to a land grant made by Congress in 1788 to John Cleves Symmes, in which provision was made to establish an institution of learning. Oxford township, Butler county, was given to the University and leased for ninety-nine years under the statutory provision that the lease should be renewable forever without revaluation. The trustees are appointed by the governor of Ohio.

The first school was opened in 1815 and in 1824 the collegiate department was organized with Rev. R. H. Bishop, D. D., as its first president. The first class was graduated in 1826.

The University was closed owing to financial embarrassment from 1873 till 1885. At this time the State of Ohio made a liberal appropriation and has continued to do so from year to year. The buildings were all refitted and improved. The new chapel with its memorial windows will be attractive to all former students. The Brice Scientific Hall erected in 1891 and 1892 is now in use and is one of the best equipped buildings for scientific purposes in the State. The Faculty was increased at the opening and now has ten members.

A renewed interest is being taken in the University by all her old friends. The attendance is increasing, the State is treating us kindly and generously, the Trustees are hearty in their support, and the Faculty are a company of working men who are determined upon the best attainable results in education.

The library has now more than eleven thousand volumes and is well adapted to the needs of Faculty and students and catalogued upon the Dewey system.

The University has never been as well equipped for educational work as at the present. Superior advantages are furnished for earnest young men at a moderate cost in one of the most beautiful locations in Ohio. The climate is moderate and healthful. The alumni and friends take a just pride in the record of the University and every indication points to a future not less honorable.

BOARD OF TRUSTEES.

OFFICERS.

PRESIDENTS.

John Bigger,	1809	James McBride,	1842,	1852-59
Joseph VanHorne,	1810	John Johnston,		1843-47
William Ludlow,	1810-13	Jeremiah Morrow,		1847-52
John Reily,	1813-22	Chauncey N. Olds,		1860-62
David Purviance,	1822-24	Fergus Anderson,		1862-80
Robert H. Bishop,	1824-41	John W. Herron,		1880—
David McDill,	1841			

SECRETARIES.

James McBride,	1809-20	Robert H. Bishop, Jr.,	1855-90
Edward Newton,	1820-22	Anna J. Bishop,	1890—
Joel Collins,	1822-55		

TREASURERS.

William Murray,	1809-18	James Crawford,	1827-37
John W. McClure, Jr.,	1818-20	Jonathan Mayhew,	1837-38
Merrikan Bond,	1820-24	Peter Sutton,	1838-69
James M. Dorsey,	1824-27	Sutton C. Richey,	1869—

TRUSTEES.

Hiram M. Curry,	Champaign,	1809-15
William Ward,	Champaign,	1809-15, 1841
James Brown,	Miami,	1809-15
David H. Morris,	Miami,	1809-15
Benjamin VanCleve,	Montgomery,	1809-24
William McClure,	Montgomery,	1809-15

Benjamin Whiteman,	Greene,	1809-15
Andrew Reed,	Greene,	1809-15
John Bigger,	Warren,	1809-15
Ichabod B. Halsey,	Warren,	1809-18
John Reily,	Butler,	1809-40
Thomas Irwin,	Butler,	1809-15
John Riddle,	Hamilton,	1809-12
Joseph VanHorne,	Hamilton,	1809-12
Joshua L. Wilson,	Hamilton,	1810-12
James Findlay,	Hamilton,	1810-12, 1815-24
Daniel Symmes,	Hamilton,	1810-12
Stephen Woods,	Hamilton,	1810-12, 1821-24, 1833-42
William Ludlow,	Hamilton,	1810-12
Ogden Ross,	Hamilton,	1810-12
William Corry,	Hamilton,	1810-12, 1815-21
James Shields,	Butler,	1810-12
David K. Este,	Butler,	1812-15
Daniel Millikin,	Butler,	1812-24
Andrew Weaver,	Butler,	1812-15
Daniel Drake,	Hamilton,	1815-18
Ephraim Brown,	Hamilton,	1815-18
Matthew G. Wallace,	Butler,	1815-21
John McLean,	Warren,	1815-18
Matthias Corwin,	Warren,	1815-18
Daniel C. Cooper,	Montgomery,	1815-18
John Tatman,	Greene,	1815-18
Archibald Steele,	Champaign,	1815-24
Saul Hinkle,	Champaign,	1815-21
John H. Crawford,	Miami,	1815-18
Samuel Kyle,	Miami,	1815-21
Jacob Burnet,	Hamilton,	1815-21
David Wade,	Hamilton,	1815-21
Daniel Hayden,	Hamilton,	1815-21
Benjamin Collett,	Warren,	1815-21
James Clark,	Butler,	1815-21
Thomas B. VanHorne,	Warren,	1815-21
Joseph Canby,	Warren,	1815-21
William C. Schenck,	Warren,	1815-21

James Steele,	Montgomery,	1815-21
John Smith,	Greene,	1815-24
John Steele,	Greene,	1815-21
James Hughes,	Champaign,	1815-21
Samuel Hitt,	Champaign,	1815-24
Robert Morrison,	Miami,	1815-21
Samuel Newell,	Logan,	1815-24
Alexander Porter,	Preble,	1819-34
David Purviance,	Preble,	1819-36
Joseph S. Benham,	Hamilton,	1821-24
John C. Short,	Hamilton,	1821-24
Nathan Guilford,	Hamilton,	1821-24
Luke Foster,	Hamilton,	1821-39
Arthur Elliott,	Butler,	1821-24
James McBride,	Butler,	1821-60
Alexander Proudfit,	Butler,	1821-24
Stephen Gard,	Butler,	1821-36
William Gray,	Warren,	1821-36
Martin D. Lathrop,	Warren,	1821-24
Horace D. Chapman,	Warren,	1821-24
Joseph F. Crane,	Montgomery,	1821-24, 1830-39
David Higgins,	Clarke,	1821-30
Joshua Collett,	Warren,	1822-39
Stephen Fales,	Hamilton,	1824-36
Samson Mason,	Clarke,	1824-36
James Cooley,	Champaign,	1824-27
John Thompson,	Hamilton,	1824-34
William Graham,	Montgomery,	1824-30
Henry Bacon,	Montgomery,	1824-34
David McDill,	Butler,	1824-49
John Johnston,	Miami,	1824-50
James Galloway,	Greene,	1827-50
Michael B. Sergeant,	Butler,	1830-31
John C. Dunlevy,	Butler,	1832-34
Alvah Guion,	Miami,	1834-39
Walter Scott,	Hamilton,	1834-37
Robert C. Schenck,	Montgomery,	1835-39
Jeremiah Morrow,	Warren,	1836-54

John S. Galloway,	Clarke,	1836-39
Thomas J. S. Smith,	Miami,	1836-39
John B. Weller,	Butler,	1836-46
William Mount,	Hamilton,	1836-39
John M. U. McNutt,	Preble,	1837
William Greene,	Hamilton,	1838-39
Jesse Paramore,	Preble,	1838-60
Edwin Smith,	Montgomery,	1839-48
Peter P. Lowe,	Montgomery,	1839-57
James C. Barnes,	Montgomery,	1839-46
H. V. D. Johns,	Hamilton,	1839-42
David T. Disney,	Hamilton,	1839-40
E. D. Crookshank,	Butler,	1839-40
Hugh McMillan,	Greene,	1839-54
James Graham,	Butler,	1839-48
Elijah Vance,	Butler,	1839-54
Robert B. Millikin,	Butler,	1840-48
Pliny M. Crume,	Preble,	1840-60
George J. Smith,	Warren,	1841-48
William B. Caldwell,	Hamilton,	1842-49
Edward Woodruff,	Hamilton,	1842-60
L. L. Hamline,	Hamilton,	1843-44
Charles Anderson,	Montgomery,	1845-57
John M. Stevenson,	Montgomery,	1845-49
Charles L. Telford,	Hamilton,	1845-49
Peter Odlin,	Montgomery,	1846-57
Joseph S. Hawkins,	Preble,	1848-57
Fergus Anderson,	Butler,	1848-57, 1859-72
William R. Collett,	Warren,	1848-54
Herman B. Mayo,	Butler,	1849-50
William M. Corry,	Hamilton,	1849-60
William S. Groesbeck,	Hamilton,	1850-57, 1860-78
Chauncey N. Olds,	Franklin,	1850-78
George M. Parsons,	Franklin,	1850-51
John W. Scott,	Butler,	1850-60
Joseph G. Gest,	Greene,	1854-63
John Y. Scouller,	Preble,	1852-57, 1860-87
James F. Chalfant,	Hamilton,	1854-72

James B. King,	Butler,	1854-57
G. Volney Dorsey,	Miami,	1854-72
William R. Kinder,	Butler,	1854-59
B. P. Aydelotte,	Hamilton,	1857-65
William Beckett,	Butler,	1857—
John G. Lowe,	Montgomery,	1857-84
George W. Holmes,	Hamilton,	1857-66
Calvin G. Goodrich,	Butler,	1857-66
Robert W. Steele,	Montgomery,	1857-66
William B. Moore,	Champaign,	1858-63
Albert Galloway,	Greene,	1860-72
Richard M. Corwine,	Hamilton,	1860-71
John W. Herron,	Hamilton,	1860—
John M. Millikin,	Butler,	1860-84
Benjamin W. Chidlaw,	Hamilton,	1863—
Benjamin P. Runkle,	Champaign,	1863-72
A. H. Dunlevy,	Warren,	1865-75
J. P. E. Kumler,	Butler,	1866-75
David W. McClung,	Butler,	1866-75, 1887—
Samuel M. Smith,	Franklin,	1866-72
Thomas E. Thomas,	Montgomery,	1869-72
William J. Gilmore,	Franklin,	1871—
Alexander H. Young,	Butler,	1869-72
Otho Evans,	Franklin,	1870-75
George W. Keely,	Butler,	1869-84
William M. Dickson,	Hamilton,	1869-75
J. Reily Knox,	Darke,	1869—
Thomas Moore,	Butler,	1869-84
David T. Woodrow,	Hamilton,	1869-78
James S. Goode,	Clarke,	1869-78
James A. I. Lowes,	Ross,	1869-70
L. D. Campbell,	Butler,	1870-83
Walter S. Thomas,	Miami,	1872-84
M. W. Oliver,	Hamilton,	1872—
Samuel F. Hunt,	Hamilton,	1872—
J. McLain Smith,	Montgomery,	1872—
Joseph S. McCord,	Butler,	1872-79
L. N. Bonham,	Butler,	1872-88

H. W. Hughes,	Hamilton,	1872-90
Richard Smith,	Hamilton,	1872-86
Durbin Ward,	Warren,	1875-86
Ozro J. Dodds,	Hamilton,	1875-82
Nelson Sayler,	Hamilton,	1875—
J. H. Thomas,	Clarke,	1878-87
H. C. Lord,	Hamilton,	1878-83
Thomas Millikin,	Butler,	1878-87
James W. Owens,	Licking,	1878—
James E. Neal,	Butler,	1878-87
John B. Peaslee,	Hamilton,	1878-87
Calvin S. Brice,	Allen,	1881—
Edward L. Taylor,	Franklin,	1881—
J. W. McGregor,	Butler,	1883-89
Walter A. Dun,	Hamilton,	1884-85
John M. Withrow,	Hamilton,	1885—
Palmer W. Smith,	Butler,	1884—
Adam McCrea,	Pickaway,	1884—
Ira A. Collins,	Butler,	1884-90
John F. Neilan,	Butler,	1884—
Clark B. Montgomery,	Hamilton,	1887—
J. Elwood Morey,	Butler,	1887—
Quincy Corwin,	Montgomery,	1887—
Horace Ankeney,	Greene,	1887—
Elam Fisher,	Preble,	1887—
W. J. McSurely,	Highland,	1887—
Nelson W. Evans,	Scioto,	1888-90
T. R. Kumler,	Butler,	1889—
Alex. Sands, Jr.,	Hamilton,	1890—
H. D. Hinckley,	Butler,	1890—
Dan Millikin,	Butler,	1892—

PRESIDENTS.

*ROBERT HAMILTON BISHOP,   Minister,   Pleasant Hill, O.

A. B., Univ. of Edinburgh, 1798. D. D. Studied theology with Prof. Lawson at Selkirk, Scotland, 1798-1802. Licensed by Pres. of Perth, Scotland, June 28, 1802. Sailed with Dr. Mason to America, Sept., 1802. Pastor of Associate Presb. churches at Ebenezer and New Providence, Ky., 1803-14. Prof. in Transylvania Univ., Lexington, Ky., 1803-24. Editor of "Evangelical Record and Western Review," 1811-13. Joined the Presb. church, Oct. 1819. Pastor of McCord church, Lexington, Ky., 1819-23. President and Prof. Logic and Moral Philosophy and History in Miami Univ., 1824-41. Inaugurated March 30, 1825. Continued as Prof. of History and Political Science in Miami, 1841-45. President Farmer's Coll., 1845-55. Organized Presb. church in Oxford and Pastor, 1825-31. Author of "A Volume of Sermons," 1808; "Memoirs of David Rice," 1824; "Elements of Logic," 1833; "Sketches of the Philosophy of the Bible," 1833; "Elements of the Science of Government," 1839; "The Western Peacemaker," 1839 and numerous special sermons and addresses. Father of Rev. George B., '28, Prof. Robert H., Jr., '31, Prof. Ebenezer E., '33, and Rev. John M., '41. Born in the parish of Whittburn, Linlithgowshire, Scotland, July 26, 1777. Died, April 26th, 1855. *Vide* Scouller's Manual page 228.

*GEORGE JUNKIN,   Minister,   Philadelphia, Pa.

A. B., Jefferson College, 1813. D. D. L L. D., Miami Univ., 1854. Studied theology with Rev. Dr. Mason, New York. Pastor of Asso. Ref. Church, Milton, Pa., 1819-22. Entered Presb. Church, 1822. In charge of a Manual Labor Institution Germantown, Pa., 1830-32. President Lafayette Coll., Easton, Pa., 1832-41. President Miami Univ., 1841-44. President Lafayette Coll., 1844-48. Pres. Washington Coll., Va., 1848-60. Author of "Baptism," "The Prophecies," "Justification," "Sanctification," "Sabbatismos," "The Tabernacle," "The Vindication," "Political Fallacies," also numerous literary addresses, sermons, and a manuscript commentary on Hebrews. Father of Rev. John M. Junkin, Miami Univ., class of '41 and of Hon. George M. Junkin, Philadelphia, Miami Univ., class of '42. Born near Carlisle, Pa., Nov. 1, 1790. Died, May 20, 1868. *Vide* sketch and portrait, Presbyterian Encyclopedia, p. 389.

*ERASMUS D. MCMASTER,   Minister,   Chicago, Ills.

A. B., Union Coll., 1827. D. D. L L. D., Miami Univ., 1864. Licensed by the Reformed Presbytery of New York, June 16, 1829. Pastor Presb. Church, Ballston, N. Y., 1831-38. President Hanover Coll., Ind., 1838-45. President Miami Univ., 1845-49. Prof. Systematic Theology in Theol. Sem., New Albany, Ind., 1850-66. Prof. Theology, Northwestern Theol. Sem., Chicago, June 2,—Dec. 10, 1866. Born, Mercer, Pa., Feb. 4, 1806. Died, Chicago, Dec. 10, 1866. *Vide* sketch and portrait, Presbyterian Encyclopedia, p. 506.

xiv   MIAMI UNIVERSITY.

*WILLIAM C. ANDERSON,   Minister,   Junction City, Kan.

A. B., Washington Coll., 1824. A. M., Miami Univ., 1834. D. D., Miami Univ., 1846. Licensed by Presbytery of Washington, Pa., Dec. 13, 1827. Missionary in North Carolina, 1828-29. Agent Presb. Board, 1829-31. Pastor Presb. Church, Pigeon Creek, Pa., 1831-36. General Agent of the Western Foreign Missionary Board, 1836-37. Pastor Presb. Churches, Pittsburg, 1837-39; New Albany, Ind., 1839-43. Prof. Rhetoric Hanover Coll., 1843-44. Pastor Fort Wayne, Ind., and Washington, Pa., 1844-45. Pastor Dayton, O., 1845-49. President Miami Univ., 1849-54. Pastor San Francisco, 1854-63; Pastor Cincinnati, 1863-64; New Albany, Ind., 1864-65. Supply at Abilene and Manhattan, Kan., 1866-70. Born, Washington Co., Pa., Aug. 18, 1804. Died, Aug. 28, 1870. Father of Rev. John A. Anderson, class of '53. *Vide* sketch in Presbyterian Encyclopedia, p. 29.

*JOHN W. HALL,   Minister,   Covington, Ky.

D. D., Miami Univ., 1847. Studied theology with Dr. Gideon Blackburn and was licensed to preach by the Presbytery of West Tennessee, Oct., 1824. Evangelist in West Tenn., 1824-26. Pastor Murfreesboro, Tenn., 1826-30; Gallatin, Tenn., 1830-40. Organized and acted as President of a Female Seminary at Gallatin, 1837-40. Pastor Dayton, O., 1840-52; Huntsville, Ala., 1852-54. President Miami Univ., 1854-66. Supt. Public Schools, Covington, Ky., 1866-76. Born, Orange county, N. C., Jan. 19, 1802. Died, Jan. 6, 1886. *Vide* Presbyterian Encyclopedia, p. 293.

*ROBERT LIVINGSTON STANTON,   Minister,   Washington, D. C.

Student Literary Department Lane Seminary, 1834. D. D., Princeton, 1852. Studied theology Lane Seminary and ordained by Presbytery of Mississippi, Dec., 1839. Pastor Presb. Church, Blue Ridge, Miss., 1839-41; Woodville, Miss., 1841-43; New Orleans, La., 1843-51. President Oakland College, Miss., 1851-54. Pastor Chillicothe, O., 1855-62. Prof. Danville Theol. Sem., 1862-66. President Miami Univ., 1866-71. Editor, New York, 1870-71; "Herald and Presbyter" Cincinnati, 1872-78. Removed to Washington, D.C., 1878. Born, Griswold, Conn., March 28, 1810. Died at sea, May 23, 1885. Father of Robert B. Stanton, Denver, Colo., of the class of '71. *Vide* Presbyterian Encyclopedia p. 854.

ANDREW D. HEPBURN,   Minister,   Oxford, O.

A. B., Jefferson Coll., 1851. . D. D., Hampden Sidney, 1876. L L. D., Univ. of North Carolina, 1878. Prof. Univ. N. C., 1859-67; Prof. Miami Univ., 1868-71. President Miami Univ., 1871-73. Prof., Davidson Coll., N. C., 1874-77. President Davidson Coll., 1877-85. Prof. Miami Univ., 1885—. Author of "Manual of Rhetoric."

ROBERT WHITE MCFARLAND,   Teacher,   Oxford, O.

A. B., Ohio Wesleyan University, 1847. A. M., L L. D., Ohio Wesleyan. Teacher in public schools, 1847-50. Prof. Mathematics, Madison Coll., 1851-56. Prof. Mathematics Miami Univ., 1856-73. Prof. Mathematics and Civil Engineering, Ohio State Univ., 1873-85. President Miami Univ., 1885-88. State Inspector Railways, 1881-85. Captain and Lieutenant-Colonel 86th Ohio, 1862.

ETHELBERT DUDLEY WARFIELD,   Lawyer,   Easton, Pa.

A. B., Coll. of New Jersey, 1882. A. M. 1885. L L. B., Columbia Coll., 1885. L L. D., Miami Univ., 1891 and Coll. of New Jersey, 1891. President Miami Univ., 1888-91. President Lafayette Coll., Easton, Pa., 1891—.

WILLIAM OXLEY THOMPSON, Minister, Oxford, O.

A. B., Muskingum Coll., New Concord, O., 1878. A. M. Muskingum Coll., 1881. D. D., Muskingum, 1891. Graduated Western Theol. Sem., Allegheny City, 1882. Home Missionary and Pastor, Odebolt, Iowa, 1882-85. Pastor Longmont, Colo., 1885-91. President Longmont Coll., 1885-89. President Miami Univ., 1891—.

PROFESSORS.

*JOHN EBENEZER ANNAN,   Minister,   Lewisburg, W. Va.

A. B., Dickinson Coll., 1824. B. D., Princeton Theol. Sem., 1829. Ordained by the Presbytery of Baltimore, 1829. Prof. of Mathematics, Geography, Natural Philosophy and Astronomy, and Teacher of Political Economy, Miami Univ., 1824-28. Pastor of Presbyterian Church at Petersburg, Va., 1829-30. Died, Aug. 29, 1830.

*WILLIAM SPARROW,   Minister,   Alexandria, Va.

Former student of Columbia Coll. D. D. Ordained Deacon in the Episcopal Church, June 7, 1826, and Presbyter, June 11, 1826. Prof. of Languages, Miami Univ., 1824-25. Prof. in Kenyon Coll., 1824-41. Prof. in Theological Seminary, Alexandria, Va., 1841-74. Died, Jan. 17, 1874.

*WILLIAM H. MCGUFFEY,   Minister,   Charlottesville, Va.

A. B., Washington Coll., 1826. D. D., LL. D. Prof. of Latin, Greek and Hebrew, Miami Univ., 1826-32. Ordained a minister by the Presbytery of Oxford, 1832. Prof. of Mental Philosophy, Philology, and General Criticism, Miami Univ., 1832-36. President of Cincinnati Coll., 1836-39. President of Ohio Univ., 1839-43. Prof. in Woodward High School, Cincinnati, O., 1843-45. Prof. of Mental and Moral Philosophy, Univ. of Va., 1845-73. Author of "McGuffey's Readers." Died, May 4, 1873. *Vide*, "Miami Journal," Vol. II, No. 6.

JOHN W. SCOTT,   Minister,   Washington, D. C.

A. B., Washington Coll., 1823. A. M., Yale, 1826. D. D., Augusta Coll., 1840. Prof. in Washington Coll., 1824-28. Prof. of Mathematics, Geography, Natural Philosophy and Astronomy, and Teacher of Political Economy, Miami Univ., 1828-32. Ordained a minister by the Presbytery of Oxford, 1830. Prof. of Natural Philosophy, Chemistry and Astronomy, and Teacher of Political Economy, Miami Univ., 1832-35. Prof. of Natural Philosophy, Astronomy and Chemistry, Miami Univ., 1835-45. Prof. in Farmer's Coll., 1845-49. Principal of Oxford Female Institute, 1849-54. Prof. of Natural Science, Hanover Coll., 1860-68. Teacher, Springfield, Ill., 1868-70. Prof. in Monongahela Coll., 1874-81. Resident, Washington, D. C., since 1881.

*SAMUEL W. MCCRACKEN,   Minister,   Hopewell, O.

A. B., Miami, 1831. Prof. of Mathematics, Miami Univ., 1832-35; of Ancient Languages, 1835-37. See sketch among Alumni.

xviii   MIAMI UNIVERSITY.

*THOMAS ARMSTRONG,   Minister,   Xenia, O.

A. B., Miami, 1830. Prof. of Latin, Greek and Hebrew, 1832-35. See sketch among Alumni.

*A. T. BLEDSOE,

A. B. Prof. of Mathematics, Miami Univ., 1835-36.

*JOHN MCARTHUR,   Minister,   Indianapolis, Ind.

A. B., Jefferson Coll. A. M., and D. D., from Jefferson Coll. Studied theology under direction of the Presbytery of Beaver and licensed by the same Oct., 1827. Ordained by the Presbytery of Steubenville, Nov. 19, 1828. Pastor Ridge, O., 1828-36; Cadiz, O., 1828-37. Prof. Greek Language and Literature, Miami Univ., 1837-49. President pro. tem., Miami Univ., 1844-45. Born, Washington Co., Pa., March 5, 1803. Died, Aug. 7, 1849.

*CHAUNCEY N. OLDS,   Lawyer,   Columbus, O.

A. B., Miami, 1836. Prof. of Latin Language and Roman Literature, and Teacher of Hebrew, 1837-40. See sketch among Alumni.

*ROBERT HAMILTON BISHOP, SR.,   Minister,   Pleasant Hill, O.

Prof. of History and Political Science, 1841-45. See sketch among Presidents.

*JAMES CLEMENT MOFFAT,   Minister,   Princeton, N. J.

A. B., Coll. of New Jersey, 1835. D. D. Tutor of Greek, Coll. of New Jersey, 1837-39. Prof of Greek and Latin, Lafayette Coll., 1839-41. Prof. of Roman Language and Literature, and of Aesthetics, Miami Univ., 1841-52. Licensed a minister of the Presbyterian Church, 1851. Prof. of Latin and History, Coll. of New Jersey, 1852-54; of Greek and History, 1854-61. Helena Prof. of Church History, Princeton Theol. Sem., 1861-90. Author of "Introduction to the Study of Aesthetics;" "A Comparative History of Religions before Christ;" and "History of the Church in Scotland until the Reformation." Died, June 7, 1890.

*JOHN W. ARMSTRONG,

A. M. Prof. of Mathematics and Civil Engineering, Miami Univ., 1841-43. Died, 1856.

GEORGE WATERMAN,   Minister,   Holybourne, Eng.

A. B., A. M., Cincinnati Coll., 1840. B. D., Lane Sem., 1840-43. Prof. of Mathematics and Civil Engineering, Miami Univ., 1843-45. Prof. in Newton Univ., 1845-52. Ordained by Presbytery of Md., 1852. Supplied Independent churches in England, 1855-68. Pastor of Pres. churches, New Windsor, Md., 1868-72; Holybourne, Hampshire, England, 1872.

*THOMAS J. MATTHEWS,   Teacher,   Oxford, O.

Prof. of Mathematics and Astronomy, Miami Univ., 1845-52. Died, 1852.

*ORANGE NASH STODDARD, Teacher, Wooster, O.

A. B., Union Coll., 1834. A. M. LL. D., Monmouth, 1865. Prof. of Natural Science, Miami Univ., 1845-70; President pro. tem., 1854. Prof. of Natural Science, Wooster Univ., 1870-92. Died, Feb., 1892.

*CHARLES ELLIOTT, Minister, Easton, Pa.

A. B., Lafayette Coll., 1840. A. M. D. D., Ohio Univ., 1861. B. D., Princeton Theol. Sem., 1841. Prof. in Western Univ., 1841-49. Prof. of Greek Language and Literature, and of Logic, Miami Univ., 1849-63. Prof. of Biblical Literature and Exegesis, McCormick Theol. Sem., Chicago, Ills., 1863-82. Prof. of Hebrew, Lafayette Coll., Easton, Pa., 1882-92. Died, Feb. 15, 1892.

*ROBERT HAMILTON BISHOP, JR., Teacher, Oxford, O.

A. B., Miami, 1831. Prof. of Latin Language and Literature, Miami Univ., 1852-73 and 1885-87. See sketch among Alumni.

THEOPHILUS A. WYLIE,

A. M. D. D. Prof. of Mathematics and Astronomy, Miami Univ., 1852-55.

CHARLES HRUBY, Teacher, Bloomington, Ind.

A. M. Prof. of German and French Languages and Literature, Miami Univ., 1852-57.

ROBERT WHITE MCFARLAND, Teacher, Oxford, O.

Prof. of Mathematics, Miami Univ., 1856-73. See sketch among Presidents.

J. C. CHRISTIN,

M. D. Prof. of German and French Languages and Literature, Miami Univ., 1858-60.

JAMES Y. MCKEE,

A. B., A. M. Prof. of Greek Language and Literature, Miami Univ., 1863-66.

*ARTHUR BURTIS, Minister, Oxford, O.

A.B., Union Coll., 1827. D. D. Ordained 1835. Pastor of Pres. churches at Fort Plain, N. Y., 1835-36; Little Falls, N. Y., 1836-38; Binghampton, N. Y., 1838-39; Oxford, N. Y., 1840-45; Vernon, N. J., 1845-46; Buffalo, N. Y., 1846-57. Secretary of American and Foreign Christian Union, 1861-63. Prof. of Greek Language and Literature, Miami Univ., 1866-67. Died, March 23, 1867.

*SAMUEL H. MCMULLIN, Minister, Glendale, O.

A.B., Univ. of Pa., 1849. B. D., Princeton Theol. Sem., 1851. D. D. Ordained by the Presbytery of North River, 1856. Pastor of Presbyterian churches at Newburg, N. Y., 1856-60; Bellaire, Md., 1860-61; Smithtown, L. I., 1861-64; Philadelphia, Pa., 1865-67. Prof. of the Greek Language and Literature, Miami Univ., 1867-70. Prof. of Church History, Danville Theol. Sem., 1870-72. Pastor at Circleville, O., 1872-82; Glendale, O., 1882-89. Died, Feb. 17, 1892.

ANDREW D. HEPBURN, Minister, Oxford, O.

Prof. of Logic, Rhetoric, and the English Language and Literature, Miami Univ., 1867-71; of Philosophy and Literature, 1871-73, of English Language and Literature, 1885—. See sketch among Presidents.

C. H. CARLTON, Army Officer, Fort Meade, S. Dakota.

Prof. of Military Science and Tactics, 1869-71. Col. of the 8th U. S. Cavalry.

HENRY S. OSBORN, Minister, Oxford, O.

A. B., Univ. Pa., 1846. A. M., Univ. Pa., 1849. L. L. D., Lafayette Coll., 1856. Union Seminary class of 1849. Stated Supply one year in Rhode Island. Travelled and studied in Europe, 1851. Pastor of churches at Hanover, Va., and Belvidere, N. J. Prof. of Chemistry and Mining Engineering, Lafayette Coll., 1865-70. Prof. Natural Science, Miami Univ., 1870-73. Author of "Palestine, Past and Present," 1859; "Plants of the Holy Land," 1863; "Metallurgy of Iron and Steel," 1870; "Minerals, Mines and Mining," 1889; "Biblical History and Geography," 1891; "The Prospector's Hand Book," 1892. Also several smaller volumes. Publisher of a series of Classical and Biblical maps.

*JOSEPH MILLIKIN, Minister, Hamilton, O.

A. B., Miami Univ., 1859. Prof. of the Greek Language and Literature, Miami Univ., 1870-71. See sketch among Alumni.

JAMES D. COLEMAN,

Prof. of Greek Language and Literature, 1871-73.

HENRY SNYDER, Teacher, Oxford, O

B. S., Ohio State Univ., 1879. Taught in the Ohio Institution for the Blind at Columbus, O., 1879-84. Superintendent of same, 1884-85. Prof. of Physics and Chemistry, Miami Univ., 1885—.

OLIVER HOLBEN, Teacher, Allentown, Pa.

A. M. Prof. of the French and German Languages and Literature, 1885-88.

JOSEPH F. JAMES, Geologist and Botanist, Washington, D. C.

Prof. of Geology and Botany, Miami Univ., 1885-88.

JOHN ROBERT SITLINGTON STERRETT, Teacher, Austin, Tex.

Attended Univ. of Va. Ph. D., Univ. of Munich, Germany, 1881. Student of the American School at Athens, 1882-83. Acting Director of the same, 1883-84. Conducted an Epigraphical Journey in Asia Minor, 1884, and The Wolfe Expedition to Asia Minor, 1885. Prof. of Greek Language and Literature, Miami Univ., 1886-88. Prof. of Greek, Univ. of Texas, 1888—. Delivered a course of lectures on Grecian Life at Cornell Univ., 1891-92. Published works, "Hymni Homerici," 1881; "Inscriptions of Assos," 1885; "Inscriptions of Tralleis," 1885; "An Epigraphical Journey in Asia Minor," 397 Inscriptions, 2 Maps, 1888; "The Wolfe Expedition to Asia Minor," 651 Inscriptions, 2 Maps, 1888.

ALFRED EMERSON,   Teacher,   Ithaca, N. Y.

A. B., School of Arts, Athens, Greece, 1876. Ph. D., Univ. of Munich, Germany, 1881. Fellow, Johns Hopkins Univ., 1882–85. Prof. of Latin Language and Literature, Miami, 1887–88. Prof. of Greek, Lake Forest Univ., 1888–91. Prof. of Archæology, Cornell Univ., 1891—.

ROGER BRUCE JOHNSON,   Teacher,   Oxford, O.

A. B., Princeton, 1887. A. M. 1889. Prof. Mental and Moral Science, Miami Univ., 1888—.

WALTER RAY BRIDGMAN,   Teacher,   Lake Forest, Ills.

A. B., Yale, 1881. A. M., Miami, 1891. Tutor, Yale Coll., 1884–88. Prof. Greek, Miami Univ., 1888–91. Prof. Greek, Lake Forest, 1891—.

ARNOLD GUYOT CAMERON,   Teacher,   New Haven, Conn.

A. B., Coll. of New Jersey, 1886. A. M., same, 1888. Ph. D., same, 1891. Prof. German and French, Miami Univ., 1888–91. Asst. Prof. French, Yale, 1891—.

CHARLES WILLIAM HARGITT,   Teacher,   Rochester, N. Y.

B. S., Moore's Hill Coll. M. S. Ph. D., Ohio Univ., 1890. Prof. Moore's Hill Coll.; Prof. Biology and Geology, Miami Univ., 1888–91; Prof. Biology, Syracuse Univ., 1891—.

WILLIAM AUGUSTUS MERRILL, Teacher,   Oxford, O.

A. B., Amherst 1880. A. M., 1884. Prof. Belmont Coll., College Hill, 1885 -88; Prof. Latin, Miami Univ., 1888—.

JOSEPH VICTOR COLLINS,   Teacher,   Oxford, O.

Ph. B., Univ. Wooster, 1879. Ph. D., Wooster, 1879. Graduate Student Johns Hopkins, 1881–82 and 1883–84. Tutor Wooster Univ., 1879–80; Prof. Mathematics, Hastings College, 1883–88; Prof. Mathematics, Miami University, 1888—.

EDWARD PLAYFAIR ANDERSON, Teacher,   Oxford, O.

A. B., Univ. of Mich., 1879. A. M. Ph. D., Univ. of Mich, 1886. Student, Paris, 1880. Prof. Latin and French, McMinville Coll., 1882–84. Postgraduate student, Univ. Mich., 1884–86. Teacher Mich. Military Academy, 1887. Prof. Ohio Univ., 1888–89; Prof. Mich. Agric. Coll., 1889–91; Prof. of Modern Languages, Miami Univ., 1891—. Translator of Sorel's "Montesquieu," Simon's "Victor Cousin," and joint translator Boissier's "Madame de Sevigne." Published "The Best Letters of Madame de Sevigne," 1891.

AARON L. TREADWELL,   Teacher.   Oxford, O.

B. S., Wesleyan Univ., Middletown, Conn. M. S., Wesleyan, 1890. Assistant in Natural History, Wesleyan, 1888–91; Prof. Biology and Geology, Miami Univ., 1891—.

HERMAN LOUIS EBELING,   Teacher,   Oxford, O.

A. B., Johns Hopkins, 1882. Ph. D., 1891. Classical Instructor, German Theol. Sem., Bloomfield, N. J., 1882–86. Post graduate in Latin, Greek and Sanskrit, Johns Hopkins, 1886–91. Univ. scholar, 1888–89. Fellow in Greek, 1889–90. Teacher of Greek, Latin and French, Dr. Deichman's Gymnasium School, Baltimore, 1890–91; Prof. Greek, Miami Univ., 1891—.

INSTRUCTORS IN PREPARATORY DEPARTMENT.

[Sketches of the following may be found among the Alumni, with the exception of Williston, Lyman and Parrott.]

JOHN P. WILLISTON,	Principal,	1825-26

A. B. Yale, 1820. Died, Tunbridge, Vermont, April, 1829.

JOHN P. VANDYKE,	Associate Principal,	1826-29
JOHN S. WEAVER,	Associate Principal,	1826-29
WILLIAM F. FERGUSON,	Principal,	1829-35
WILLIAM W. ROBERTSON,	Principal,	1835-40
ROBERT H. BISHOP, Jr.,	Principal,	1840-52
DARIUS LYMAN, Jr.,	Assistant,	1851-53
MILTON SAYLER,	Principal,	1852-53
DAVID SWING,	Principal,	1853-66
A. G. CHAMBERS,	Assistant,	1853-56
JOHN T. KILLEN,	Assistant,	1856-60
ROBERT CHRISTIE,	Principal,	1866-70
JAMES A. I. LOWES,	Principal,	1870-72
HENRY B. MCCLURE,	Principal,	1872-73
THOMAS PARROTT,	Principal,	1888-90

A. B., Coll. of New Jersey, 1888. Now a student abroad.

WILBER J. GREER,	Principal,	1890—

CATALOGUE.

ALUMNI.

Class of 1826.

*SAMUEL CALDWELL BALDRIDGE,   Minister,   Shilo, Ind.

A. B., A. M. Attended Associate Reformed Theol. Sem., 1827-29. Licensed by the First Presbytery of Ohio, April 29, 1829. Ordained by same, June 3, 1830. Pastor of United Presbyterian churches in Randolph Co., Ill., 1830-36; Princeton, Ind., 1837-53; Salem, Ind., 1853-56; Providence, Ind., 1856-61; Sharon, Ind., 1863-66; Shilo, Ind., 1866-67. Father of Benjamin L., '45. Born, Adams Co., O., Feb. 18, 1801. Died, Aug. 4, 1867.

*WILLIAM MCMILLAN CORRY,   Lawyer,   Cincinnati, O.

A. B., A. M. Admitted to the bar, Columbus, O., 1832. Practised law at Cincinnati, 1832-48. Lived abroad at Paris, France, 1848-51. Member House of Representatives, Ohio, 1855-57. Founder and for several years editor of the "Cincinnati Commoner," which was established in 1865 and discontinued in 1872. Trustee of Miami Univ., 1849-60. Born, Cincinnati, Jan., 16, 1811. Died, Sept. 8, 1880. *Vide*, "Miami Journal," Vol. I, No. 8.

*Daniel L. GRAY,   Minister,   Des Arc, Ark.

A. B., A. M. Licensed by Pres. of S. Car., 1828. Ordained by same, June 1, 1829. Pastor Fairforest church, S. Car., 1829-31. Organized church in Western District of Tenn., 1832, in Jackson Co., Ark., 1833. Pastor of latter church, 1833-36. Missionary at Hudsonville, Miss., 1836-43. Pastor at Henderson, Ky., 1844-50. Agent of Board of Domestic Missions, Memphis, Tenn., 1851. Pastor at Raleigh, Tenn., 1852-55; Des Arc, Ark., 1855-61. Born, Abbeville Dis., S. Car., April 24, 1803. Died, April 16, 1862. *Vide*, "Southern Presbyterian," 1862.

*EBENEZER ERSKINE PRESSLY,   Minister,   Due West, S. Car.

A. B., A. M. Licensed as Associate Reformed Presbyterian minister, Feb. 21, 1829. Missionary in Georgia, Florida, and Alabama, 1829-30. Pastor at Due West, S. Car., 1830-53. Prof. in Theol. Sem. of Asso. Ref. Church, Due West, 1832-47. Founded Erskine College at Due West, 1839. President of same, 1839-46. President of Anderson Female Collegiate Institute, Anderson, S. Car., 1850-53. Resigned on account of ill-health. Brother of James P., '26. Died, July 26, 1860. *Vide*, "Due West Telescope," 1860.

(1)

*James Patterson Pressly,   Minister,   Due West, S. Car.

A. B., A. M. D. D., Erskine Coll. Licensed by the Second Associate Reformed Presbytery of Carolina, Feb. 20, 1829. Ordained at Generostee, S. Car., March 27, 1830. Pastor at Due West, Generostee, and Bethel, S. Car., 1830. Missionary in Georgia, Alabama, and Florida, 1831. Pastor at Prosperity and Dallas, Alabama, 1831-40. Prof. of Languages in Erskine Coll., Due West, 1840-77. Prof. of Greek Exegesis and of Systematic Theology in Erskine Theol. Sem. during the same period. Brother of Ebenezer E., '26. Died, March 30, 1877. *Vide*, Life by Rev. J. J. Bonner, Miami Univ. Library.

*James Reynolds,   Student of Theology,   Preble Co., O.

A. B. Studied theology and had completed his course when he died in April, 1829.

*James Thomson,   Minister,   Mankato, Minn.

A. B., A. M. Licensed by Presbytery of Cincinnati, Oct. 5, 1826. Ordained by same October 3, 1827. Pastor near Mt. Carmel, Ind., 1826-27. Removed to Crawfordsville, Ind., Nov., 1827, where he founded Wabash Coll. Pastor of Presbyterian church, Crawfordsville, Ind., from 1832, until his removal to Mankato, Minn., in the 60's. Brother of John S., '26, and Wm. M, '28. Born, Springdale, O., June 1, 1801. Died, Oct. 1, 1873.

*John Steele Thomson,   Minister,   Crawfordsville, Ind.

A. B., A. M. Licensed by Presbytery of Cincinnati, October 6, 1828. Ordained by same, Oct. 4, 1829. Pastor of Pres. church at Newton, Ind., 1829-31; Waveland, Ind., 1831-34. Assisted in the founding of Wabash College and became its agent. Became Prof. of Mathematics in the institution Jan. 1, 1834, which position he held until his death. Brother of James, '26, and Wm. M, '28. Born, Springdale, O., Dec. 4, 1804. Died, Jan. 3, 1843.

*John P. Van Dyke,   Minister,   · Pleasant Ridge, O.

A. B., A. M. Teacher in Grammar School, Miami Univ., 1826-28. Licensed by Presbytery of Miami, 1828. Ordained by same, June, 1829. Pastor of Pres. churches at West Union, O., 1829-52; Red Oak, O., 1852-54; Frankfort, Ind., 1854-56; Pleasant Ridge, O., 1856-62. Born, Adams Co., Pa., Oct. 18, 1803. Died, Aug. 13, 1862. *Vide*, Presbyterian Encyclopædia, p. 972.

*John Smallwood Weaver,   Minister,   Springfield, O.

A. B., A. M. Teacher in Grammar School, Miami Univ., 1826-28. Licensed by Presbytery of Miami, 1828. Ordained by same, 1830. Pastor of Pres. churches at Franklin, O., 1829-32; Sand Creek, Ind., 1832-38; Bethel, O., 1838-43; New Jersey Church, O., 1843-58; Dick's Creek Church, O., 1858-65. Served under U. S. Christian Commission of U. S. Army, 1863. Removed to Springfield, O., 1865, where he died, May 22, 1871.

*Edward Woodruff,   Lawyer,   Cincinnati, O.

A. B., A. M. Admitted to the bar, 1828. Member and President of the City Council of Cincinnati, 1834-42 and 1850-52. Member of convention to frame a new city charter for Cincinnati, 1846. Judge of Common Pleas Court of Ham. Co., O., 1852-67. One of the original corporators of the Cincinnati Law Library. Delivered address at the inauguration of Rev. E. D. McMaster as president of Miami Univ., 1845. Trustee of Miami Univ., 1842-60. Born, Philadelphia, Pa., Feb. 18, 1807. Died, Feb. 15, 1883. *Vide*, Portrait and Memoirs of Eminent Americans, p. 260.

*JAMES WORTH,   Minister,   Halsey, Ore.

A. B., A. M. Licensed by First Presbytery of Ohio, April 29, 1829. Ordained by same, June 3, 1830. Pastor of United Presbyterian churches at New Zion and Milroy, Ind., 1830-52; Lane Co., Ore., 1852-57; Eugene City, Ore., 1858-61; Brownville, Ore., 1862-74, when he retired from active ministry. Born, Salem Co., N. J., July 13, 1800. Died, July 18, 1881.

Class of 1827.

*JAMES HENRY BACON,   Lawyer,   St. Louis, Mo.

A. B., A. M. Tutor at Miam Univ., 1831-32. Studied law and practised at Dayton, O., for several years. Prof. of Languages, Pleasant Hill Academy about 1842. Removed to St. Louis, Mo., where he practised law until his death in 1860.

JOHN W. CALDWELL,   Lawyer,   Cincinnati, O.

A. B., A. M. Cadet, U. S. Military Academy, West Point, 2 years. Attended Cincinnati Law School and was admitted to the bar. Has practised continuously in Cincinnati. Chairman of the Military Committee of Ham. Co., 1860. Was Commandant of Camp Dennison at Columbus during the war, and aided in organizing Ohio's contingent for the army. U. S. Minister to Bolivia, South America, 1866-69. Address, 11 Temple Bar.

*NICHOLAS G. R. GASSAWAY,   U. S. Cadet,   Cincinnati, O.

A. B. Entered U. S. Military Academy at West Point after graduation, and while there, was attacked with hemorrhage of the lungs. Returned home and died Sept. 21, 1829.

*JOHN HOPKINS HARNEY, Teacher and Editor, Louisville, Ky.

A. B., A. M. Prof. of Mathematics and Natural Sciences, State Univ., Bloomington, Ind., 1827-32. Prof. of Mathematics and Astronomy, Hanover Coll., Hanover, Ind., 1832-36. Prof. of Natural Philosophy, Chemistry, and Geology in latter institution 1836-38. Prof. of Mathematics and Civil Engineering in the University at Louisville, Ky., 1838-44. Editor of Louisville "Democrat," 1844-68. Member of Charleston Presidential Convention, 1860. Opposed secession and was largely instrumental in keeping Kentucky in the Union. Member of State Legislature, 1861-63. Born, Bourbon Co., Ky., Feb. 20, 1806. Died, Jan. 26, 1868.

*THOMAS A. JONES,   Lawyer,   Cincinnati, O.

A. B. Admitted to the bar and practised law in Cincinnati. Died, 1830.

*JOHN MCMECHAN,   Physician,   Darrtown, O.

A. B., A. M. M. D., Ohio Medical College. Died, March 21, 1880.

*WILLIAM ANDERSON PORTER,   Lawyer,   Corydon, Ind.

A. B., A. M. Admitted to the bar, 1828. Practised law at Corydon, Ind. Judge of the Probate Court of Harrison Co., Ind., 1829-36. Member of the House of Representatives of Indiana, 1843-47. Speaker of the same, 1843-45. Born, Jan 28, 1800. Died, Jan. 24, 1884.

*ROBERT CUMMING SCHENCK, Lawyer, Washington, D. C.

A. B., A. M. Post-graduate student and tutor of French and Latin, Miami Univ., 1827-30. Studied law under Thomas Corwin and admitted to the bar, Jan. 1831. Practised law at Dayton, O. Member of Ohio House of Representatives, 1841-42. Member of Lower House of Congress, 1843-51. Appointed by President Fillmore Envoy Extraordinary and Minister Plenipotentiary to Brazil, 1851. Accredited Envoy Extraordinary to Uruguay, Paraguay, and Argentine Confederation, negotiating important treaties. Returned in 1854 and resumed the practice of law. Commissioned brigadier-general, Union Army, 1861. Assigned to Gen. Tyler's division and distinguished himself at the first battle of Bull's Run, July 21, 1861. Transferred to Gen. Rosecrans' division. Took Fremont's command and was in command of the First Corps of the Army of Va. Seriously wounded and permanently disabled at the second battle of Bull's Run, Aug. 30, 1862. Promoted to Major General for distinguished bravery. Appointed commander of Middle Department of U. S. Army, Dec. 11, 1862. Resigned command, Dec. 5, 1863, and entered Lower House of Congress, serving until 1870. Member of High Joint Commission to settle disputes between England and the United States, 1870-71. Minister to England, 1871-75. Trustee of Miami Univ., 1835-39. Born, Franklin, O., Oct. 4, 1809. Died, March 23, 1890. *Vide*, Portrait and Sketch, "Miami Student, Vol. IX., No. 6.

*JOSEPH SPENCER WALLACE, Merchant, Parkersburg, W. Va.

A.'B.!' Prepared for the ministry at Princeton Theol. Sem. and Hanover, Ind., but on account of throat trouble never preached. Engaged in flouring and milling industries at Terre Haute, Ind. Also established the first foundry in that city. Removed to Parkersburg, W. Va., 1865, and engaged in farming and fruit-growing. Born, Hamilton, O., Oct. 4, 1802. Died, Nov. 9, 1876.

Class of 1828.

*GEORGE BROWN BISHOP, Minister and Teacher, Hanover, Ind.

A. B., A.!M. Studied theology at Princeton. Ordained by Presbytery of Oxford, Nov., 1833. Pastor of Pres. church at Oxford, O., 1833-34. Prof. of Biblical Criticism and Oriental Literature in the Indiana Theol. Sem., Hanover, Ind., 1834-37. Brother of Robert H., '31; Ebenezer B., '33, and John M., '41. Born, Fayette Co., Ky., March 30, 1810. Died, Dec. 14, 1837. *Vide*, Presbyterian Encyclopedia, p. 74.

*WILLIAM F. FERGUSON, Minister and Teacher, Monmouth, Ill.

A. B., A. M. 'D. D., 1852. Master of the Grammar School, Miami Univ., 1829-35. President of Macomb Coll., Macomb, Ill. Approximate date of death, 1854.

*HENRY PRINGLE GALLOWAY, Farmer, Xenia, O.

A. B. Engaged in farming and stock raising near Xenia. Enlisted in the three month's service, 154 O. V. I., 1864. In 1874 travelled in California for his health. Brother of Albert G., '30, and James E., '44. Born, Xenia, O., Jan. 29, 1810. Died at Carlin, Nevada, July 30, 1874, while en route to his home at Xenia.

*JOHN M. GARRIGUS, Teacher, Burlington, Iowa.

A. B. Died, May 19, 1842.

*JAMES B. MARSHALL, Lawyer and Editor,

A. B., A. M. "Cannot be traced and is said to be dead. Last residence known, Columbus, O., as stated in the Triennial of 1861.

*JOHN A. MATSON,   Lawyer,   Greencastle, Ind.

A. B., A. M. Studied law at Connersville, Ind., in the office of Hon. Oliver H. Smith. Admitted to the bar 1831. Practised law at Brookville, Ind., 1833-50. Member of the Indiana House of Representatives, 1840-41. Twice nominated for Congress on the Whig ticket. Whig candidate for Governor of Indiana, 1849. Moved to Cincinnati, Feb., 1850, thence to Greencastle, Ind., Sept. 1851. Prof. of Law, Indiana Asbury Univ., for several years. Born, North Bend, O., Sept. 9, 1810. Died, July 15, 1870.

*JOHN IRWIN MORRISON,   Teacher,   Knightstown, Ind.

A. B., A. M. Founded Salem Female Institute, Salem, Ind., 1835. Member of Indiana House of Representatives from Washington Co., 1839-40. Prof. of Languages, Indiana State Univ., Bloomington, Ind., 1840-43. State Senator of Indiana, 1847-50. Delegate to Constitutional Convention of Indiana, 1850-51, and author of Section 8, which created the office of State Superintendent of Public Instruction. Treasurer of Washington Co., Ind., 1856-60. U. S. Commissioner Provost Marshal's office, 1863-65. State Treasurer of Indiana, 1865-67. Moved to Knightstown, Ind., 1872. President of Board of Trustees, Indiana State Univ., 1874-78. Trustee of Wayne township, 1878-81. Principal of Washington Co. Seminary for 20 years. Born, July 25, 1806. Died, July 17, 1882. *Vide*, American Encyclopædia, Annual 1882, p. 640.

*SAMUEL W. PARKER,   Lawyer,   Connersville, Ind.

A. B., A. M. Principal of County Seminary, Connersville, Ind., 1829-30. Studied law under Hon. Oliver H. Smith and admitted to the bar, Aug., 1831. Practised law at Connersville, Ind. Founded and edited "The Watchman," 1834-36. Member State Senate of Indiana, 1834-35; House of Representatives, 1835-36. Appointed Prosecuting attorney, 1836. Elected by Whig party as Representative Lower House of Congress, 1849; re-elected 1852. Declined a re-nomination in 1855. President of Whitewater Canal Co. and Junction Railroad Co. Born, Watertown, N. Y., Sept. 9, 1805. Died of pneumonia, Feb. 1, 1859. *Vide*, Sketch in "Miami Student," April, 1892.

*AARON HORRILL PIERSON,   Lawyer,   Natchitoches, La.

A. B. Graduated at Cincinnati Law School and engaged in practice at Natchitoches, La. Member of Constitutional Convention of La., 1861. Born, Morristown, N. J., 1811. Died, May 25, 1875.

*JAMES SIMPSON,   Physician,   Sparta, Ills.

A. B., A. M. M. D., Miami Medical Coll., Cincinnati, O., 1836. Practised medicine at Sparta, Ills. Prof. of Mathematics, Washington Coll., Penn., for several years prior to his graduation in medicine. Born, Hamilton, O., Dec. 9, 1805. Died, 1847.

WILLIAM McCLURE THOMSON,   Minister,   Denver, Col.

A. B., A. M. D. D., 1858. Attended Princeton Theol. Sem. Ordained in 1831. Served as a missionary at Syria and Palestine, 1833-49; in the Holy Land, 1850-57 and 1859-76. Author of "The Land and The Book;" "The Land of Promise;" "Travels in Modern Palestine, Illustrative of Biblical History, Manners, and Customs." Brother of James, '26, and John S, '26.
Address, 1355 Inslee street.

MIAMI UNIVERSITY.

Class of 1829.

*WILLIAM MAGAW BOYSE, Minister, Keokuk, Iowa.

A. B., A. M. Studied theology at Allegheny, Pa. Licensed by First Presbytery of Ohio, June 14, 1832. Ordained by same, Sep. 11, 1833. Pastor of United Pres. churches at Richmond and Ebenezer, Ind., 1833-53; Keokuk, Ia., 1853-61. Born, South Carolina, 1807. Died, Oct. 31, 1861.

*ROBERT CUNNINGHAM CALDWELL, Lawyer, Pensacola, Fla.

A. B., A. M. Admitted to the bar but soon gave up the practice of law to enter the U. S. Navy as an officer. Distinguished himself in the war with Mexico and in Indian wars. Died, Nov. 13, 1852.

*COURTLAND CUSHING, Lawyer, Virgin Bay, Nicaragua.

A. B., A. M. Studied law under Thomas Corwin and admitted to the bar at Madison, Ind., Sept. 3, 1832. Practised law at Madison, Ind. Attorney for Madison & Indianapolis R. R. U. S. District Attorney for Southern District of Indiana, 1841-45. Judge of Circuit Court, 1845-50. U. S. Charge d' Affaires, Ecuador, S. A., 1850-53. Agent for the Accessory Transit Co., of New York, at Virgin Bay, Nicaragua, 1853-56. Died, San Juan del Norte, Nicaragua, May 24, 1856.

*JAMES N. GAMBLE, Minister, Bellefontaine, O.

A. B., A. M. Studied theology at Allegheny, Pa., and licensed by First Presbytery of Ohio, June 14, 1832. Ordained by same, Sep. 10, 1833. Pastor of United Pres. church at Bellefontaine, O., 1833-42. Born, Xenia, O., Oct. 8, 1810. Died, Dec. 19, 1842.

*WILLIAM ADAIR HOLLIDAY, Minister, Indianapolis, Ind.

A. B., A. M. Attended Princeton Theol. Sem., 1829-32. Licensed by Presbytery of New Brunswick, N. J., 1831. Ordained at Indianapolis, Ind., 1834. Pastor Pres. church at Indianapolis, Ind., 1832-34. Home Missionary, 1834-40. Preached and taught at Crawfordsville, Rising Sun, Indianapolis, Ind., and Paris, Ky., 1840-64. Prof. of Latin in Hanover Coll., 1864-66. Brother of Robert, '38. Born, Harrison Co., Ky., July 16, 1803. Died, Dec. 16, 1866.

*RALPH PHILLIPS LOWE, Lawyer, Washington, D. C.

A. B., A. M. Studied law and admitted to the bar at Ashesville, Ala. In 1834 removed to Dayton, O., and practised there until 1840, when he moved to Muscatine, Iowa. Appointed Prosecuting Attorney for the Second Judicial district of Iowa, 1841. Appointed by Gov. Chamber General of 2nd Division of Iowa Militia, 1842. District Judge of the First Judicial district of Iowa, 1852-57. Governor of Iowa, 1858-60. Judge of the Supreme Court of Iowa, 1860-68. U. S. District Attorney, 1868-71. Appointed agent for the State of Iowa to press claim against the United States for $800,000, and removed to Washington, 1871. Brother of John G, '38. Born, Warren Co., O., Nov. 27, 1805. Died, Dec. 22, 1883. *Vide*, Sketch and Portrait, Iowa "Historical Record," Oct., 1891, in Miami Univ. Library.

*WILLIAM COWPER LYLE, Editor, Paris, Ky.

A. B., A. M. Editor of "Western Citizen," 1829-67. Treasurer of Bourbon Co., Ky., 1843-67. Brother of John A., '37. Born, Paris, Ky., Aug. 16, 1808. Died, Jan. 25, 1874.

*JOHN McDILL, Minister, S. Hanover, Ind.

A. B. Studied theology under Rev. Alexander Porter. Licensed by First Presbytery of Ohio, Dec., 1832. Ordained by Pres. of Indiana, June 22, 1835. Pastor of United Pres. church at S. Hanover, Ind., 1835-38. Father of James W., '53. Born, Preble Co., O., 1806. Died from consumption, July 27, 1840.

*JAMES REILY, Lawyer, Houston, Texas.

A. B., A. M. Admitted to the bar and practised at Houston, Texas. Represented Harris Co., Texas, in the Congress of the Republic, 1840-41. Minister to the U. S. until Texas was annexed. In command of a Texas regiment during the Mexican war, 1846-47. Appointed by President Buchanan U. S. Minister to Russia. Colonel of the 4th Texas Cavalry, C. S. A. Participated in invasion of New Mexico, 1862. Sent on a diplomatic mission to Mexico, 1862. Killed in the battle of Franklin, La., April 13, 1863, while leading his regiment with conspicuous gallantry.

*NATHANIEL COOPER WEEDE, Minister, St. Charles, Iowa.

A. B., A. M. Licensed by First Presbytery of Ohio, July 5, 1832. Ordained by Monongahela Presbytery, Nov. 13, 1833. Pastor of United Pres. churches at Bethel, Brush valley, and Blairsville, Penn., 1833-48; LaPrairie and Elmira, Ills., 1849-61. Preached but little after 1861, on account of injuries received from a fall from a horse. Born, Abbeville, S. Car., June 23, 1808. Died, Oct· 5, 1887.

Class of 1830.

*THOMAS ARMSTRONG, Minister and Teacher, Xenia, O.

A. B. Tutor of Hebrew at Miami Univ., and student of theology under Dr. Bishop, 1831-32. Licensed to preach by the Presbytery of Miami. Prof. of Latin, Greek and Hebrew, Miami Univ., 1832-35. Died at Yellow Springs, O., of consumption, Aug 27, 1835.

*ROBERT PATTERSON BROWN, Lawyer, Dayton, O.

A. B., A. M. Studied law and was admitted to the bar. Associate Justice of the Montgomery Co. court under the old constitution of Ohio. Died, Kansas City, Mo., May 4, 1879.

*WILLIAM R. COLLETT, Farmer, Lebanon, O.

A. B., A. M. Admitted to the bar, but never practised law. Trustee of Miami Univ., 1848-54. Died, July, 1860.

EBENEZER NEWTON ELLIOTT, Minister, Morning Sun, O.

A. B., A. M. Ph. D., Lewisburg Univ., Pa. L L. D., Oakland Coll., Miss. Prof. of Mathematics, Indiana State Univ., 1832-36. President of Mississippi Coll., 1836-39. Studied theology and was ordained by Southern Presbyterian church, 1840. Studied medicine but never practised except as a surgeon in the Confederate army. President of Oakland Scientific School, Oakland, Miss.; Planters' College; Ghent College; and Washington Scientific School. While in Miss. was also an extensive cotton planter. Author of "Cotton is King and Pro-Slavery Arguments," 1859. Also many newspaper articles and public addresses. Now greatly enfeebled in health and living with his nephew at Morning Sun, Preble Co., Ohio.

8   MIAMI UNIVERSITY.

*ALBERT GALLATIN GALLOWAY,   Lawyer,   Xenia, O.

A. B., A. M. Studied law at Transylvania Univ. and Cincinnati Law School. Admitted to the bar, 1835. Practised at Xenia, O. Editor of the Greene County "Gazette," 1836-38. Lived at San Francisco, Cal., 1849-53. Inspector of Customs at San Francisco, 1850-53. Resumed the practice of law, Xenia, O., 1853. Captain of Co. E, 12th O. V. I., three months' service, 1861. Secretary to Commodore Schenck, commander of U. S. Man-of-War, "Powhatan," 1865. Trustee of Miami Univ., 1860-72. Brother of Henry P, '28, and James E, '44. Born, Xenia, O., Dec. 18, 1811. Died, May 19, 1876.

*WILLIAM GREGG,   Planter,   Clinton, Miss.

A. B., A. M. After teaching a few years in Indiana, moved to Newton Co., Miss., where he served as Clerk of the Court for two terms. Afterwards moved to Clinton, Miss., and engaged in planting. Born, near Greenville, E. Tenn., April 4, 1804. Died, Aug. 9, 1862.

*JOSEPH P. HALSEY,   Teacher,   Cincinnati, O.

A. B. Tutor at Miami, 1830-31. Elected Principal of the Preparatory Department of Woodward Coll., Cincinnati, O., June 6, 1831, but died before the session opened in the fall.

*THORNTON ANTHONY MILLS,   Minister,   New York, N. Y.

A. B., A. M. D. D., Miami, 1854. Licensed by the Presbytery of Cincinnati, 1833. Pastor of Pres. churches at Frankfort, Ky., 1833-36; Cincinnati, O., 1836-48. Purchased "The Watchman of the Valley" and edited it under the name of the "Central Christian Herald," Cincinnati, O., 1848-53. Raised the funds for the erection of the Second Pres. church at Indianapolis, Ind., and served as pastor, 1853-56. General Agent of the Permanent Committee of the General Assembly of the Pres. church on Education for the Ministry, New York City, 1856-67. Born, Paris, Ky., Sept., 1810. Died, June, 1867. *Vide*, Presbyterian Encyclopedia, p. 524.

*ISAAC NEWTON SHEPHERD,   Minister,   Hennepin, Ill.

A. B. A. M., Hanover Coll., 1837. Studied theology at Hanover, Ind. Licensed by Presbytery of Miss., Oct., 1836. Prof. Mississippi Coll., Clinton, Miss., 1836-38. Pastor of Pres. church at Marion, O., 1840-62. Moved to Raleigh, Tenn., 1862, and supplied vacant churches. Born, Ripley, O., May 29, 1809. Died, July 2, 1885.

*WILLIAM B. WOODRUFF,   Minister,   Oxford, O.

A. B. Studied theology at Lane Sem., 1834-36, and Princeton Theol. Sem., 1836-37. Licensed to preach. Died, 1838.

Class of 1831.

*ROBERT HAMILTON BISHOP,   Teacher,   Oxford, O.

A. B., A. M. L L. D., Miami Univ., 1888. Prof. of Mathematics, Hanover Coll., 1832-33. Teacher of village school in Kentucky, 1834. Publisher, Oxford, Ohio., 1835-38. Instructor in the Grammar School, Miami Univ., 1838-40. Master of the Grammar School, Miami Univ., 1840-52. Prof. of Latin, Miami Univ., 1852-73 and 1885-87. During the interim between 1873 and 1885, taught one year in Farmer's College and Oxford College. Secretary of Miami Univ., 1853-90. Secretary of the Alumni Association, 1843-88. Brother of George B., '28; Ebenezer E, '33; and John M, '41. Father of George, '67, and Sylvester, '72. *Vide*, sketch and portrait, "Miami Student."

*MARCUS MARCELLUS BRIGHAM, Lawyer, Cincinnati, O.

A. B., A. M. Studied law and was admitted to the bar. Practised for several years in Mississippi, returned to Cincinnati, O., and died, 1840.

*FREEMAN G. CARY, Teacher and Horticulturist, Hamilton, O.

A. B., A. M. Proprietor and Principal of Cary's Academy, College Hill, 1833–45. Founded Farmer's College, 1845. President of the same, 1845–54. Resigned to take charge of the Horticultural department of Farmer's College, which plan was abandoned in 1861. Editor of "The Cincinnatus," 1854–61. Retired to a farm near Hamilton, O., 1861. Organizer and President of the Cincinnati Horticultural Society and also of the Butler County Horticultural Society. Brother of Samuel F, '35. Born, Cincinnati, O., April 7, 1810. Died, Aug. 26, 1888. *Vide*, Sketch by Gen. S. F. Carey, Mi-Univ. Library.

*JAMES B. CASKEY, Minister, Ripley, O.

A. B., A. M. Studied theology at Allegheny, Pa. Licensed by First Presbytery of Ohio, April 21, 1835. Ordained by same, March 25, 1836. Pastor of United Pres. churches at West Union, and Russelville, O., 1836–38; Russelville and Ripley, O., 1838–51; Ripley, O., 1851–54. Born, Rockbridge Co., Va., 1806. Died, Feb. 9, 1854.

WILLIAM R. COCHRAN, Lawyer and Farmer, Hamilton, O.

A. B. Studied law at Transylvania Univ., Lexington, Ky. Was admitted to the bar, 1834. Probate Judge of Butler Co., 1872–75. Retired. Address, South B street.

*THEOPHILUS LYLE DICKEY, Lawyer, Springfield, Ills.

A. B., A. M. L L. D. After graduation, taught common school for three years in Bourbon Co., Ky., Lebanon, O., and Millersburg, Ky. Admitted to the bar, 1835. Practised at Macomb, Ills., 1835–36; Rushville, Ills., 1836–39; Ottawa, Ills., 1839–46. Commissioned Captain, 1st Regiment, Illinois Volunteers, 1846, and served through the Mexican war. Circuit Judge, presiding in 12 counties in Illinois, 1848–52. Member of the first Republican convention held in Illinois, 1854. Removed to Chicago, Ills., at the outbreak of the Civil War, organized and was elected Colonel of the 4th Illinois Cavalry. Member of Gen. Grant's staff for two years and for some time Chief of Cavalry. Assistant Attorney-General of the U. S., 1868–69. Corporation Counsel of Chicago, 1874–75. Judge of the Supreme Court of Illinois, 1875–85. Born, Paris, Ky., Nov. 12, 1812. Died, Atlantic City, N. J., July 22, 1885.

JAMES J. FARAN, Lawyer and Editor, Cincinnati, O.

A. B., A. M. Was admitted to the bar and practised in Cincinnati, O. Member of Ohio House of Representatives, 1835–39. Speaker of the House, 1838–39. Member of Ohio Senate, 1839–43. Speaker of the Senate, 1841–43. Member of the U. S. House of Representatives, 1845–49. Mayor of Cincinnati, 1855–57. Also postmaster at Cincinnati for several years. Associate Editor of the "Cincinnati Enquirer" for several years. Address, 122 East Third street.

*CHARLES FOX LOWRY, Lawyer, St. Louis, Mo.

A. B. Admitted to the bar, 1834. Began practise at St. Louis, Mo., 1835. Died, Springfield, Ill., Nov. 1837.

*DUNCAN FARRAR KENNER,   Planter,   New Orleans, La.

A. B. Travelled through Europe, 1831-35. Studied law under Senator John Slidell, but abandoned it and became a planter. Member of Louisiana State Legislature, 1836-50. Nominee of Whig party for U. S. Senator, 1849. Member of the Constitutional Convention of Louisiana in 1844 and 1852, acting as President of the latter. Member of Confederate Congress at Montgomery, Ala., and Richmond, Va., 1861-65. Advocated Emancipation early in the War of the Rebellion. Delegate of the Confederacy to Great Britain and France, 1864. President of the N. O. Gas Co.; of the Crescent Cotton Seed Oil Co.; of the La. Sulphur Co.; and of the La. Sugar Planters' Association. Appointed by President Arthur the sole Democratic member of the U. S. Tariff Commission, 1883. Born, La., 1813. Died, July, 1887.

*DANIEL SYMMES MAJOR,   Lawyer,   Lawrenceburg, Ind.

A. B., A. M. Deputy Clerk of Dearborn Co., Ind., 1831-32. Admitted to the bar, Sept., 1832. Entered into law partnership with Hon. Amos Lane at Lawrenceburg, Ind., 1833. Joint owner and editor of the "Statesman," 1833-34. President of the Lawrenceburg branch of the Indiana State bank, 1840-44. Attorney for the Indianapolis, Cincinnati & Lafayette R. R., 1858-72. Register of Bankruptcy for Southern Indiana district, 1863-72. Born, Dearborn Co., Ind., Sept. 6, 1808. Died, Sept. 23, 1872.

*CHARLES W. MARTIN,   Minister,   South Carolina.

A. B., A. M. Studied theology and entered the ministry. Died, 1840.

*SAMUEL W. MCCRACKEN, Minister and Teacher, Hopewell, O.

A. B., A. M. Studied theology at Allegheny, Pa., 1833-34. Licensed by First Presbytery of Ohio, April 21, 1835. Ordained by same, April 20, 1836. Prof. in Miami Univ., of Languages, 1835-37; of Mathematics, 1837-40. Supplied the pastorate at Oxford, 1835-40. Pastor of United Pres. church at Hopewell, O., 1840-59. Brother of John S, '39. Born, near Cincinnati, O., 1801. Died, Sept. 10, 1859.

*WILLIAM MCLAIN,   Minister,   Washington, D. C.

A. B., A. M. D. D. Studied theology at Hanover, Ind., 1833-36. Financial Secretary and Treasurer of the American Colonization Society, Washington, D. C., 1840-73. Died, Feb. 13, 1873.

*JEREMIAH MORROW,   Minister,   Chillicothe, O.

A. B., A. M. Studied theology at Allegheny, Pa. Licensed by First Presbytery of Ohio, April 30, 1834. Ordained by same, April 21, 1835. Pastor of United Pres. churches at Fair Haven, O., 1835-42; Chillicothe, O., 1842-43. Died, July 26, 1843.

*ROBERT NALL,   Minister,   New Orleans, La.

A. B., A. M. D. D., Ogelthorpe Univ. Studied theology and ordained, Nov. 16, 1834. Pastor of Southern Pres. churches at Marion, Ala., 1834-43; Mobile, Ala., 1843-58. Evangelist of the Synod of Ala., 1858-61; Synod of Mo., 1861-62; Presbytery of East Ala., 1862-64. After that time, with approval of Presbytery, "in the field at large." Died, Dec. 28, 1885.

*WILLIAM THOMPSON, Lawyer, Memphis, Tenn.

A. B., A. M. Studied law and practised at Jackson, Miss., and Memphis, Tenn. Died about the close of the Civil War. Exact date of death unknown.

*CHARLES G. WINTERSMITH, Lawyer, Elizabethtown, Ky.

A. B., A. M. Studied law and was admitted to the bar. Practised at Elizabethtown, Ky. Member of the Kentucky House of Representatives, 1851-55. Speaker of same, 1853-55. Judge of the Court of Common Pleas, 1867-68. Grand High Priest of the order of Masons. Born, Elizabethtown, Ky., July 15, 1812. Died, Oct. 14, 1881.

Class of 1832.

*WILLIAM ELLIOTT CRANE, Lawyer, Dayton, O.

A. B. Admitted to the bar, 1835. Born, Feb. 7, 1814. Died, June 9, 1836.

*THEODORE JOHNSON, Minister, Warren Co., O.

A. B. Studied theology and ordained a Pres. minister. Died, 1840.

*HUGH McLAURIN, Jackson Co., Miss.

A. B. Died soon after graduation in no profession, 1832.

*MALCOLM J. McRAE, Politician, East Pascagoula, Miss.

A. B., A. M. Clerk of the Circuit Court, Mobile, Ala., 1833-37. Register in Chancery for Mobile, Ala., district, 1837-47. Moved to East Pascagoula, Miss., and managed a hotel for some years. Brother of John J., '34. Date of death unknown.

*BENJAMIN FRANKLIN MORRIS, Minister, Washington, D. C.

A. B., A. M. Studied theology at Lane Sem. Pastor of Congregational churches in Iowa and Illinois, 8 years; of Presbyterian churches at Rising Sun, Ind., 17 years; Connersville, Ind., 2 years. Organized a Congregational church at Lebanon, O., and served as pastor until 1861. Moved to Washington, D. C., and was engaged in the publication of "The Christian Life and Character of the Civil Institutions of the U. S." Also author of "Life of Thomas Morris," and "The Nation's Tribute to Abraham Lincoln." Born, Bethel, O., Aug. 18, 1810. Died, Springfield, O., June 28, 1867.

*JOHN CUNNINGHAM STEELE, Minister, Warrensburg, Mo.

A. B., A. M. Studied theology at Allegheny, Pa., 1834-38. Licensed by Presbytery of Ohio, April 11, 1837. Ordained by same, June 14, 1838. Pastor of United Pres. churches at Cincinnati, O., 1838-42. Prof. of Mental and Moral Philosophy and Logic in Duquesne Coll., Pittsburg, Pa., 1843-44. Pastor of U. P. churches at Indianapolis, Ind., 1849-53; Allegheny, Pa., 1855-60. Served in Christian Commission for three months in the Army of the Tennessee, 1863. Pastor of U. P. church at Warrensburg, Mo., 1872-76, 1881-89. Author of "The Genealogy of Our Savior," U. P. "Quarterly Review," Vol. I. Brother of Joseph D, '40, and Walter, '40. Born, Bourbon Co., Ky., Dec. 22, 1812. Died, Dec. 13, 1891.

*CHARLES STURDEVANT, Minister and Teacher, Larned, Kan.

A. B., A. M. Entered ministry. Pastor of Pres. churches at Lawrenceburg, Ind., and Elizabethtown, O., 1836-38. Organized the First Pres. church at Richmond, Ind., and was its pastor, 1838-41. Resigned on account of ill-health and travelled for three years in the South. Pastor of Pres. church at Connersville, Ind., 1844-46. General Agent for the Board of Domestic Missions. Pastor at Hamilton, 2 years. Principal of a Boarding School at Springfield, O., for many years. Died, 1886.

*JOHN LOVE TORREY, Lawyer, Grand Gulf, Miss.

A. B., A. M. Studied law and admitted to the bar at Port Gibson, Miss. Died, Port Gibson, Miss., about 1840.

*WILLIAM DICKEY TURNER, Minister, Bloomington, Ind.

A. B., A. M. Studied theology at Oxford, O., and Allegheny, Pa. Licensed by the First Presbytery of Ohio, April 21, 1835. Ordained by Indiana Presbytery, June 16, 1836. Pastor of the United Pres. church at Bloomington, Ind., 1836-69. Resigned on account of blindness. Brother of Thomas, '32. Born, Anderson Co., S. Car., Aug. 6, 1806. Died, Aug. 6, 1883.

*THOMAS TURNER, Minister, West Union, White Co., Ill.

A. B., A. M. Studied theology at Allegheny, Pa. Licensed by First Presbytery of Ohio, April 21, 1835. Ordained by Associated Reformed church of the South, 1836. Pastor of Asso. Ref. Pres. churches at Hopewell, Ga., 1835-54; West Union, White Co., Ill., 1857-59. Lived at Dalton, Ga., 1861-65. Returned to White Co., Ill., 1865, and acted as a missionary the rest of his life. Brother of William D., '32. Born, Anderson District, S. Car., April 7, 1808. Died, April 26, 1890.

*JAMES LITTLE YOUNG, Minister, Bethany, Miss.

A. B., A. M. Attended theological seminary at Allegheny, Pa. Ordained, 1836. Pastor of Associate Reformed Pres. churches at Bethel, Laurensville and Providence, S. Car., 1836-51; Hopewell, Miss., 1854-56; Bethany, Miss., 1854-67. Died, Jan. 31, 1867.

*HENRY H. WALL, Planter, Woodville, Miss.

A. B. An extensive planter in Wilkinson Co., Miss. Born, 1811. Died, March 18, 1892.

Class of 1833.

CHARLES ANDERSON, Lawyer, Kuttawa, Lyon Co., Ky.

A. B., A. M. L L. D., Miami Univ., 1890. Admitted to the bar, 1835. Practised law at Dayton, O., 1836-46. Prosecuting attorney of Montgomery Co. State Senator for Warren and Montgomery Cos., 1844-46. Travelled abroad, spring and summer of 1845. Practised law at Cincinnati, O., 1846-58. Removed on account of health to San Antonio, Texas, 1858, and engaged in horsebreeding. Declined appointment as Assistant Secretary of State by President Buchanan, 1860. Declared an alien enemy of Texas. Escaped to the North and organized the 93rd O. V. I. Colonel of same, 1861-63. Severely wounded at the battle of Stone River, Dec. 31, 1862. Elected Lieutenant-Governor of Ohio, 1863, and upon the death of Gov. Brough, succeeded to the Governor's chair. Has since lived in Lyon Co., Ky. Delivered an address before the Alumni of Miami Univ., 1840; before the Literary Societies of Kenyon Coll., 1849; Funeral Oration on Henry Clay, Cincinnati, O., Nov. 2, 1852. Trustee of Miami Univ., 1845-57. *Vide* Portrait and Sketch, "Miami Journal," Vol. II, No. 2.

MIAMI UNIVERSITY. 13

*WILLIAM ANDERSON,   Physician,   Laurens, S. Car.

A. B., A. M.   M. D., Transylvania Univ., 1837. Practised near Temple of Health, S. Car., 1837–39; Laurens, S. Car., 1839–51; Cartersville, Ga., 1851–65; Russel Co., Ala., 1865–69; Laurens, S. Car., 1869–81. Judge of Probate Court of Laurens Co., 1876–77. Treasurer of same, 1877–79. Born, near Due West, S. Car., Aug. 7, 1810. Died, June 10, 1881.

*EBENEZER BROWN BISHOP,   Teacher,   Paris, Ills.

A. B., A. M.   Superintendent of Public Schools, Hamilton, O., and principal of Edgar Academy, Paris, Ills. Brother of George B, '28; Robert H, '31; and John M, '41. Died, Jan. 4, 1877.

*JAMES R. BONNER,   Minister,   Lima, O.

A. B., A. M.   Studied theology at Allegheny, Pa. Licensed by First Presbytery of Ohio, April 22, 1836. Ordained by same, June, 1838. Pastor of United Pres. churches at Xenia, O., 1838–45; Canonsburg and Lima, O., 1851–59. Died, March 8, 1870.

*DENNIS W. BUCKLEY,   Texas.

A. B.   Died soon after graduation in Texas, having chosen no profession.

BENJAMIN WILLIAMS CHIDLAW,   Minister,   Cleves, O.

A. B., A. M.   D. D., Hanover Coll., 1886. Studied theology at Oxford. Licensed by the Presbytery of Oxford, April, 1835. Ordained by same, May 26, 1836. Pastor of Pres. church at Glendower, O., 1836. Sunday School Missionary since 1838. Chaplain of 39th O. V. I., 1861–62. Served in the Christian Commission, 1863–65. Trustee of Miami Univ. since 1863. Trustee of Ohio Reform School for Boys, 1866–87. Visitor to West Point since 1889. Author of "The Story of My Life," 381 pp. *Vide*, same, Miami Univ. Library; also portrait and sketch, "Miami Journal," Vol. II, No. 8.

*BENJAMIN FRANKLIN CLARK,   Minister,   N. Chelmsford, Mass.

A. B., A. M.   B. D., Lane Seminary, 1837. Ordained, 1839. Pastor of Pres. church at N. Chelmsford, Mass., 1839–69. Member of the Mass. State Senate. Born, Lyndeborough, N. H., Feb. 23, 1808. Died, May 28, 1879.

*RICHARD HENRY COKE,   Lawyer,   Louisville, Ky.

A. B., A. M.   Admitted to the bar and practised at Springfield, Ky., 1836–40. Member of the Kentucky House of Representatives, 1838–40. Removed to Louisville, Ky., 1840. Delivered address before Erodelphian Literary Society, Aug. 9, 1837. Born, Springfield, Ky., Aug. 12, 1815. Died, May 18, 1845.

*SAMUEL GALLOWAY,   Teacher and Lawyer,   Columbus, O.

A. B., A. M.   L L. D., Ind. Asbury Univ., 1860. Student, Princeton Theol. Sem., 1835–36. Teacher, Hamilton, O., 1836–37. Teacher in the Department of Languages, Miami Univ., 1837–38. Prof. of Ancient Languages, Hanover Coll., 1839–40. Admitted to the bar and practised at Hillsboro, O., 1843–44. Elected Secretary of State and removed to Columbus, 1844. Commissioner of Schools. Member of Lower House of Congress from Franklin Co., O., 1856–58. Born, Gettysburg, Pa., March 22, 1812. Died, April 7, 1872.

LYMAN HARDING, Teacher, Cincinnati, O.

A. B., A. M. Taught private school until 1869. Clerk in Cincinnati post-office, 1869-91.

*GEORGE N. HASLETT, Student of Theology, Anderson Co., S. C.

A. B. Attended Western Theol. Sem., 1834-35. Died during his course in the Seminary.

*JOHN WARDLAW HEARST, Physician, Cedar Spring, S. Car.

A. B., A. M. M. D., Medical Coll. of S. Car., 1836. Practised at Cedar Spring, Abbeville Co., S. Car. Member of S. Car. House of Representatives, 1846-56. Surgeon in Confederate army. Born, Cedar Spring, S. Car., Oct. 3, 1813. Died, June 5, 1873.

*DAVID K. MCDONALD, Minister, Cincinnati, O.

A. B., A. M. Attended Western Theol. Sem., 1833-36. Licensed, 1836. Pastor of Presbyterian churches at Hopewell and Somerset, O., 1837-42; Cincinnati, O., 1842-49. Died, Dec. 19, 1849.

*JOHN A. MEEKS, Minister, Findlay, O.

A. B., A. M. Studied theology at Oxford. Pastor of Pres. churches in Indiana, 1836-37; and at Bellefontaine, O.; Piqua, O.; Greenville, O.; Bell Centre, O.; and Findlay, O. Died, July 6, 1886.

*FRANCIS REA, Physician, Washington, O.

A. B., A. M. M. D., Jefferson Med. Coll. Practised at Bloomfield, Zanesville and Washington, Guernsey Co., O. Member of the Ohio House of Representatives, 1858-60. Born, Harrison Co., O., April 17, 1808. Died, Feb. 9, 1890.

*JAMES ROSAMOND, Minister, Memphis, Tenn.

A. B., A. M. Died, 1888.

*JAMES FRENCH SAWYER, Minister, Allegheny, Pa.

A. B., A. M. Studied theology at Allegheny, Pa. Licensed by First Presbytery of Ohio, April 21, 1835. Ordained by same, April 20, 1836. Pastor of the United Pres. church at Springfield, O., 1837-48. Born, Piqua, O., Jan. 7, 1810. Died, July 1, 1849.

*DAVID MILLS STEWART, Minister, Rushville, Ind.

A. B., A. M. Licensed by Presbytery of Oxford, Oct., 1835. Pastor of Pres. churches at Rushville, Ind., 1836-54; Pleasant Grove, Ind., 1854-59; Stated Supply of Homer church, 1859-82. Served in Christian Commission 1862-63. Wounded at Vicksburg, Miss. Member of Indiana State Legislature, 1864-70. Trustee of Hanover Coll., 1845-56, and 1877-86. County Examiner of Rush Co., Ind., 6 years. Stated Clerk of White Water Presbytery from its organization until 1886. Died, Aug. 26, 1890.

*JOHN WILSON, Minister, Monticello, Ark.

A. B., A. M. Studied theology at Allegheny, Pa. Licensed by Associate Reformed Presbytery of Ohio, April 24, 1835. Ordained, April 24, 1837. Missionary in Alabama, Mississippi, Georgia and North Carolina, 1835. Pastor of Asso. Ref. Pres. churches at Salem and Sardis, Tipton Co., Tenn., 1837-65; Monticello, Ark., 1867-69. Born, S. Car., July 13, 1805. Died, Jan. 26, 1883. *Vide*, Sketch in "Asso. Ref. Pres., March 15, 1883.

*WILLIAM C. WOODS, Lawyer, Hamilton, O.

A. B. Admitted to the bar, 1835 and began practice at Hamilton, O. Died, Aug. 15, 1836.

WILLIAMSON WRIGHT, Lawyer, Logansport, Ind.

A. B., A. M. Admitted to the bar and began practice of law at Logansport, Ind. Member of Indiana State Senate, 1840-43. Attorney for Logansport & Pacific R. R., 1854-56; Logansport & Eel River R. R., 1854-56. Vice-President of Cincinnati, Logansport & Chicago R. R., 1854-56.

Class of 1834.

*DAVID H. BRUEN, Lawyer, Dayton, O.

A. B., A. M. Died, 1853.

EBENEZER WATERS BULLARD, Minister, Kill Buck, N. Y.

A. B., A. M. Lane Seminary, 1834-36. Licensed by the Congregational church, 1837. Ordained, Aug. 8, 1838. Pastor of Congregational churches at Fitchburg, Mass., 1838-52; Royalston, Mass., 1852-71; Hampstead, N. H., 1871-76. Member of Mass. House of Representatives, 1864-65. Address, Kill Buck, Cataraugus Co., N. Y.

*ROBERT COLLIN CLARK, Lawyer, Sacramento, Cal.

A. B., A. M. Admitted to the bar and practised at Winchester, Ky., 1837-50; St. Louis, Mo., 1850-52; Sacramento, Cal., 1852-83. Member of California State Senate, 1860-62. County and Superior Judge, 1863-83. Born, Winchester, Ky., 1814. Died, Jan. 27, 1883.

*JOHN M. CRABB, Minister, Bryan, O.

A. B., A. M. Auburn Seminary, 1834-36. Licensed May 15, 1838. Ordained, 1839. Pastor of Pres. churches at New Lexington, O., 1839-41; Lima, O., 1842-47; Montpelier, O., 1851-52; William's Centre, O., 1853-55; Bryan, O., 1856-59. Born, Garrard Co., Ky., 1804. Died, March, 17, 1859.

*HERMAN J. GROESBECK, Lawyer, Covington, Ky.

A. B., A. M. Admitted to the bar and practised at Covington, Ky. Died, 1849.

WILLIAM SLOCUM GROESBECK, Lawyer, Cincinnati, O.

A. B., A. M. LL. D., Miami Univ., 1869. Admitted to the bar, 1836. Has practised continuously in Cincinnati, O. Member of the Constitutional convention of Ohio, 1851. Member of Commission to modify the laws of Ohio, 1852. Member of the U. S. House of Representatives, 1857-59. Member of the Peace Congress, 1861. Member of the State Senate, 1862. Delegate to National Union Convention, Philadelphia, 1866. Counsel for President Johnson in the Impeachment trial, 1868. Nominated for President of the U. S. by a branch of the Liberal Republicans, 1872. Representative of the U. S. to the International Monetary Congress, Paris, France, 1878. Was Prof. in the Cincinnati Law school for many years. Trustee of Miami Univ., 1850-57 and 1860-78.

JAMES K. HITCHCOCK, Lawyer, Mont Clair, N. J.

A. B. Admitted to the bar, 1836. Retired.
Address, Mont Clair, South Orange P. O.

*LEVI LAPHAM, Farmer, Mechanicsburg, O.

A. B. Lived at Mechanicsburg, O., until 1854; Van Buren Co., Iowa, 1854–56; Mechanicsburg, O., 1856–77. Made a tour of the West and sojourned on Mt. St. Helena, 1877–80. Returned to Mechanicsburg, 1880. Born, Mechanicsburg, O., April 23, 1810. Died, Dec. 14, 1887.

*WILLIAM HALL MCAULEY, Minister, Stockton, Ala.

A. B., A. M. B. D., Princeton Theol. Sem., 1836. Ordained by Presbytery of New Brunswick, 1840. Missionary at Futterghur and Furrukhabad, India, 1840–50; Georgia and Alabama, 1851–52. Stated supply at Uniontown, Ala., 1853–67; Shell Creek, Ala., 1853–59; Pisgah, Ala., 1859–70; Columbiana and Scott's Grove, Ala., 1870–73; Shelby Iron Works, 1873–76; Stockton, Monroeville, and Scotland, 1877–85. Born, Montgomery Co., N. Car., Dec. 1, 1811. Died, Jan. 21, 1885.

*SAMUEL MCCLEERY, Lawyer, Fairfield Co., O.

A. B., A. M. Admitted to the bar and practiced law at Peru, Ind. Returned to his father's home in Fairfield Co., O., on account of illness, 1843. Born, Lancaster Co., Pa., Sept. 18, 1813. Died, Sept. 1, 1843.

*JOSEPH MCCRERY, Minister, Allenton, Ala.

A. B., A. M. Minister in the Associate Reformed Pres. church in the South. Killed by the explosion of the steamboat, "Lucy Walker," on the Mississipi river, while en route to his pastorate at Allenton, Ala., from the meeting of the synod at Ebenezer, Ky., 1844.

*JOHN A. MCKESSON, Wilkes Co., N. Car.

A. B. Died soon after graduation. Exact date unknown.

*ALEXANDER MCKINNEY, Physician, Versailles, Ky.

A. B. M. D. Date of death unknown.

*JOHN JOHNSON MCRAE, Lawyer, Balizi, Honduras.

A. B., A. M. Admitted to the bar. Served in both branches of the Mississippi Legislature. Speaker of the House, two terms. Appointed to the U. S. Senate by Governor Guion, of Miss., to fill the unexpired term of Jefferson Davis, Dec. 9, 1851, and served until March 4, 1852. Governor of Miss., 1854–58. Member of U. S. House of Representatives, 1859–61, when the Southern representatives withdrew. Member of Confederate House of Representatives, 1862–65. Removed to British Honduras, 1865. Brother of Malcom J., '32. Born, Wayne Co., Miss., 1810. Died, May 30, 1868.

*JOHN HENRY MILLER, Minister, Pontotoc, Miss.

A. B., A. M. Studied theology at New Albany, Ind. Licensed by the Southern Pres. church. Oct. 18, 1849. Ordained by same, Oct. 18, 1850. Pastor of Southern Pres. churches at Wellington, Tallahatchie Co., Miss., 1850–51; Pontotoc, Miss., 1851–63; Harmony church, 1857–63. Member of the Legislature of Miss., 1842. Captain, Major and Colonel in the C. S. A., 1861–63. Killed March 22, 1863.

JOSEPH GLASS MONFORT, Minister and Editor, Cincinnati, O.

A. B., A. M. D. D., Centre Coll., 1853. LL. D. Studied theology, Indiana Theol. Sem., 1835-36. Established and edited the "Presbyterian Herald," Louisville, Ky., 1836-37. Licensed by Presbytery of Oxford, Sep., 1837. Ordained, 1838. Pastor of Pres. churches at Hamilton, O., 1838; Greensburg and Sand Creek, Ind., 1839-42. Agent of Theol. Sem., New Albany, Ind., 1842-44. Pastor at Greensburg, Ind., 1844-55. Since 1855, editor of the "Presbyterian of the West," subsequently "The Presbyter," and in 1869, the name was changed to "Herald and Presbyter." For many years a member of the Church Extension Committee, and of the Board of Domestic and Foreign Missions of the Pres. church. Trustee of Hanover Coll., 1847-84. Trustee of Lane Seminary, 1870—. Treasurer of same, 1871-83. Member of the Joint Committee on Reunion of the Pres. churches, 1866.

JAMES ALEXANDER NELSON, Teacher, Paris, Ills.

A. B., A. M. Principal of Pres. Academies at Charleston, Ind., 1836-37; Hillsboro, O., 1837-45; Connersville, Ind., 1845-49; Paris, Ills., 1849-54. General business man, Paris, Ill., 1854-81. Chief clerk of U. S. Assessor in the 15th Illinois Congressional District, 1861-65. Retired from active business, 1881.

WILLIAM W. ROBERTSON, Minister, Fulton, Mo.

A. B., A. M. D. D., Westminster Coll. Tutor Miami Univ., 1833-34. Master of the Grammar School, Miami Univ., 1835-40. Licensed by Presbytery of Oxford, 1836. Ordained by same, 1837. Pastor of the Pres. churches at Fulton and Concord, Mo., 1841-51; Fulton, Mo., 1851-60; Concord, Mo., 1860-68. Removed to Fulton and acted as Agent for Westminster Coll., 1868-73. Established and was president of a Female Seminary at Fulton, Mo., 1850-60. Conducted a Female Seminary at Concord, Mo., 1864-68. One of the founders of Westminster Coll., 1859. One of the originators and sustainers of the Synodical Coll., for Young Ladies, Fulton, Mo. Author of the "Life of Rev. David Coulter," 551 pp. Also author of "The History of the Synod of Missouri."

*JARED M. STONE, Minister and Teacher, Old Du Quoin, Ills.

A. B., A. M. D. D., Miami Univ., 1873. Licensed by the Presbytery of Oxford, April, 1836. Ordained by the same, Oct., 1837. Stated supply of the Pres. church, Connersville, Ind., 1837-41. Pastor of Pres. church at Springdale, O., 1842-50. Prof. of Languages, Anderson's Coll. Inst., New Albany, Ind., 1850-51; of Natural Science, Hanover Coll., 1851-56. Acting President of Iowa State Univ., 1856-58. Stated Supply of Pres. church at Principal of Academy, Princeville, Ills., 1858-63. Pastor of Pres. church and Old Du Quoin, Ills., 1871-76. Born, Milford, Conn., Oct. 4, 1808. Died, Oct. 10, 1876.

*THOMAS EBENZER THOMAS, Minister, Cincinnati, O.

A. B., A. M. D. D., Wabash Coll., 1850. Teacher at Rising Sun, Ind., 1834-35; Franklin, O., 1835-36. Licensed by Presbytery of Oxford, Oct., 1836. Ordained by Pres. of Cincinnati, July, 1837. Pastor of Pres. churches at Harrison, O., 1837-38; Hamilton, O., 1838-49. President of Hanover Coll., Ind., 1849-54. Prof. of Biblical Literature and Exegesis, New Albany Theol. Sem., 1854-57. Stated Supply of Pres. church, New Albany, Ind., 1857-58; Pastor at Dayton, O., 1858-71. Prof. of New Testament Greek and Exegesis, Lane Theol. Sem., Cincinnati, O., 1871-75. Trustee of Miami Univ., 1869-72. Born, Chelmsford, Eng., Dec. 23, 1812. Died, Feb. 3, 1875.

ANTHONY THORNTON, Lawyer, Shelbyville, Ills.

A. B., A. M. Admitted to the bar, 1836. Delegate to Illinois Constitutional Convention, 1848. Member of Illinois Legislature, 1850. Member of U. S. House of Representatives, 1865-67. Judge of the Supreme Court of Illinois, 1870-73.

DAVID T. WOODROW, Merchant, Cincinnati, O.

A. B. Trustee of city waterworks, Cincinnati, O., for one term. Trustee of Miami Univ., 1869-78. Now in very feeble health.

Class of 1835.

*WILSON BLAIN, Minister and Editor, Union City, Ore.

A. B., A. M. Studied theology at Allegheny, Pa. Licensed by the Presbytery of Chillicothe, April 18, 1838. Ordained by same, Oct. 17, 1839. Pastor of United Pres. churches at Hebron, Porter Co., Ind., 1842-47. Removed to Oregon City, Ore., 1848. Organized and pastor of A. R. P. churches at Oregon City, 1848-50; Union Point, Linn Co., Ore., 1853-61. Member of Oregon Legislature three years. Editor of "Spectator" for several years. Born, Ross Co., O., March 2, 1813. Died, Feb. 22, 1861.

*LUCIUS A. BRIGHAM, Lawyer, Cincinnati, O.

A. B., A. M. Admitted to the bar. Date of death unknown.

*JOHNSTON EATON BRIGHT, Minister, Jackson, Tenn.

A. B., A. M. D. D., Andrew Coll., Tenn. L L. D. and Ph. D., Southwestern Univ. Principal of Academies, Rising Sun, Ind., 1835-36; Burlington, Ia., 1836-37; Female Sem., Brownsville, Tenn., 1837-52. Licensed by Western District Presbytery, 1838. Ordained, 1839. Pastor of Pres. church at Brownsville, Tenn., 1839-52. President of I. O. O. F. Coll., and Pastor of Pres. church at Trenton, Tenn., 1852-62; President of Minden Coll., La., 1862-71. Organized and had charge of the Pres. Female Coll., Jackson, Tenn., 1871-78. Born, Norfolk, Va., April 22, 1807. Died, Oct. 1878.

*JAMES M. BROWN, Teacher, Rockville, Ind.

A. B., A. M. Assistant teacher, Preparatory Department, Miami Univ., 1835-36. Teacher of Academy, Rockville, Ind., 1837-41. Died in the spring of 1841.

*WILLIAM B. CALDWELL, Lawyer, Cincinnati, O.

A. B., A. M. Admitted to the bar, 1837, and practised law, Cincinnati, O. Law firm, Caldwell & Cary. Attorney-General, State of Ohio. Judge of Common Pleas Court of Hamilton Co.; Associate Justice, Supreme Court of Ohio; Chief Justice of Supreme Court of Ohio. Trustee of Miami Univ., 1842-49. Died, 1878.

SAMUEL FENTON CARY, Lawyer and Lecturer, College Hill, O.

A. B., A. M. L L. B., Cincinnati Law School, 1837. Practised at Cincinnati, O. Pay-Master General of Ohio under Governors Bartley and Bebb. Collector of Internal Revenue, First District of Ohio, 1865. Member of U. S. House of Representatives, 1867-69. Has lectured in 32 states, the British Provinces of America, and England, Ireland, Scotland, and Wales. Editor of "National Temperance Offering," 1859. Address, College Hill, Hamilton Co.

*WILLIAM DENNISON, Lawyer, Columbus, O.

A. B., A. M. Admitted to the bar and practised law at Columbus. State Senator of Ohio, 1848–50. Delegate to Republican Presidential Conventions, 1856 and 1864. Chairman of the latter. Governor of Ohio, 1860–64. Appointed by President Lincoln U. S. Postmaster-General, 1864. Resigned, 1866. President of Columbus and Xenia R. R. Born, Cincinnati, O., Nov. 23, 1815. Died, June 15, 1882.

*DANIEL GILMER, Minister, Sandoval, Ills.

A. B., A. M. Pastor of Pres. churches at Greenland, O.; Camden, O.; Sardinia, O.; Red Oak, O.; and Sandoval, Ills. One of the framers of the Free Synod of Cincinnati. Died in the fall of 1860.

*GEORGE A. GREGG, Minister, Bellefontaine, O.

A. B., A. M. Entered ministry of the Pres. church. Pastor of Pres. church at Bellefontaine, O., 1845–54. Died, Jan. 18, 1854.

*HORATIO J. HARRIS, Lawyer, Vicksburg, Miss.

A. B., A. M. Admitted to the bar in Mississippi. State Auditor of Miss. for several years. Died, 1859.

WILLIAM SMITH HUMPHREYS, Teacher, Otisville, N. Y.

A. B., A. M. Conducted an Academy at Ripley, O., for many years. Now retired.

*BOWLING S. LEATHERS, Lawyer, Covington, Ky.

A. B. Admitted to the bar and died soon afterwards.

*WILLIAM D. MATSON, Farmer, Boone Co., Ky.

A. B. Lived near Fern Bank, O., 1835–55; in Boone Co., Ky., 1855 until death. Died in 1882 or '83.

*COLIN MCKINNEY, Minister, Ripley, Tenn.

A. B., A. M. Attended Lane Sem., 1835–36. Ordained by Presbytery of Oxford, March 20, 1838. Served as pastor in Indiana. Joined the Southern Pres. church and supplied pastorates in Mississippi and Tennessee. Born, Danville, Ky., April 20, 1809. Died, Aug. 9, 1873.

*SAMUEL JUDSON MOREHEAD, Lawyer, Brown's Wells, Miss.

A. B., A. M. Tutor of Mathematics, 1834–35. Admitted to the bar, 1837. Practised at Gallatin, Miss., 1837–57. Attorney for the Grand Gulf Bank, 1838–45. Entered into the Commission business, New Orleans, La., 1857. Member of La. Legislature, 1861–65. Captain of Militia, C. S. A. Resumed practice of law, 1866. Removed to Brown's Wells, Miss., 1878. Born, Hagerstown, Md., 1807. Died, May 2, 1891.

*JEREMIAH HUNT PEIRCE, Lumber Merchant, Dayton, O.

A. B. Manufacturer and dealer in lumber. Born, Dayton, O., Sept. 8, 1818. Died, May 6, 1889.

*JOSEPH PORTER,   Minister,   Lodiana, India.

A. B., A. M. Sailed as a missionary to India, 1835. Ordained by the Presbytery of Lodiana, India, Oct., 1837. Joint author of a "Punjabi" dictionary. Born, Derby Plains, O., Jan. 5, 1808. Died, Nov. 21, 1853. *Vide*, "The Foreign Missions of the Pres. church," pp. 275-279.

*WILLIAM H. ROGERS,   Minister,   Kansas City, Mo.

A. B., A. M. Licensed by Presbytery of Chillicothe, Sept. 11, 1837. Ordained, 1838. Pastorates in Ohio, Indiana and Illinois. Spent 49 years with Home Mission churches. Chaplain of the 69th O. V. I., 1861-65. Born, Greenfield, O., Oct. 26, 1808. Died, Aug. 31, 1886.

*WILLIAM S. ROGERS,   Minister,   Oxford, O.

A. B., A. M. Sailed as missionary to India, Nov., 1835. Ordained by Presbytery of Lodiana, India, Oct., 1837. Returned to U. S., 1843. Stated supply of Pres. church at Oxford, O. 1843-44. Agent of the Board of Foreign Missions, 1844-54. Agent for the building of the Oxford Female Coll. S. S. of Pres. churches at Camden, O.; Harmony, O.; College Corner, O.; and Shelby, O. Born, Greenfield, Jan. 14, 1809. Died, Aug. 20, 1873.

*HARVEY BAIRD SHEPHERD,   Physician,   Lawrence, Kan.

A. B. M. D. Practised at Branoby, O. Moved to California, 1849, and elected Probate Judge. Moved to Lawrence, Kan., 1862. Born, 1816. Died, Jan. 8,1864.

*WILLIAM SILLARS,   Lawyer,

A. B., A. M. Cannot be traced, but is said to be dead.

*EDMUND SMITH,   Physician,   Dayton, O.

A. B., A. M. M. D. Practised at Dayton, O. Died, Aug. 15, 1851.

JOHN A. SMITH,   Lawyer and Banker, Hillsboro, O.

A. B., A. M. Admitted to the bar. Member of Ohio Legislature, 1841-42. Member of Ohio Constitutional Conventions, 1851 and 1873. Member of U. S. House of Representatives, 1869-73. President of the First National Bank of Hillsboro.

*WILLIAM BRICE SPENCE,   Minister,   Sidney, O.

A. B., A. M. Principal of Acadamies, Oxford, O., 1835-37; New Albany, Ind., 1837-40. Ordained by Presbytery of Sidney, June, 1842. Pastor of Pres. churches, Sidney, O., 1842-64; Chatham, Ills., 1865-69; Pleasant Run, O., 1869-80. Honorably retired, 1880, and lived at Sidney, O. Born, Loveland, O., April 9, 1807. Died, Feb. 6, 1892.

*NIVISON WATKINS,   Lawyer,   Tenn.

A. B., A. M. Admitted to the bar and practised at Goochland, Va. Removed to Tennessee in 1842 and died there soon afterwards.

*THOMAS WHALLON, Minister, Oak Park, Ills.

A. B., A. M. Attended Theol. Sem., Hanover, Ind. Licensed, 1838. Ordained, 1842. Pastor of Pres. churches at Rossville, O., 1838-41; Richmond, Ind., 1841-45; Rising Sun, Ind., 1845-47; Putnamsville, Ind., 1847-55; Renssalaer, Ind., 1855-59; Tipton, Ind., 1859-65; Lexington, Ind., 1865-72; Vevay, Ind., 1872-78. Chaplain of 101st Indiana Vol. Inf., 1863. — — Born, July 14, 1812. Died, April 11, 1891.

*EDWARD WEEKLY WRIGHT, Minister, Allegheny, Pa.

A. B., A. M. D. D. Attended Theol. Sem., Allegheny, Pa., 1836-38. Licensed by the Presbytery of Logansport, Ind., 1837. Ordained by same, Oct. 5, 1839. Pastor of Pres. churches at Plymouth and Rochester, Ind., 1839-40; Lafayette, Ind., 1840-45; Delphi, Ind., 1846-65. Agent for the Pres. Board of Education, 1845-46. Born, Lancaster, O., April 23, 1817. Died, Sept. 17, 1866.

Class of 1836.

*JAMES BIRNEY, Lawyer, Bay City, Mich.

A. B., A. M. Assistant Teacher in Grammar School, Miami Univ., 1836-38. Graduated in law at Yale and practised in Cincinnati. Moved to Bay City, Mich., 1857. Member of Michigan State Senate, 1858-59. Lieutenant-Governor and acting Governor of Mich., 1860-62. Circuit Judge, 1862-66. Established "The Bay City Chronicle," 1873; subsequently merged into the "Tribune." Appointed Centennial Commissioner for Mich., 1872; Minister Resident of the U. S. to The Hague, Holland, 1875-82. Born, Danville, Ky., Jan. 7, 1817. Died, May, 1888.

*JOHN MASON CROTHERS, Lawyer, Oswego, Ills.

A. B., A. M. Admitted to the bar, 1840. Practised law at Oswego, Ills. Clerk of the Court of Kendall Co., Ills., two terms. Member of Illinois Legislature, one term. Born, Greenfield, O., April 17, 1817. Died, Greenfield, O., March 22, 1860.

ALEXANDER DUNLAP, Physician, Springfield, O.

A. B., A. M. M. D., Cincinnati Med. Coll., 1839. Prof. of Surgical Diseases of Women, Starling Med. Coll., Columbus, O., 1873-83. Address, 190 South Fountain Avenue.

*ALBERT MUNROE FLETCHER, Student of Law, Cincinnati, O.

A. B. Attended the Cincinnati Law School. Born, Cincinnati, O., May 18, 1817. Died, Sept. 11, 1840.

*CHARLES FOSTER, Lawyer, Davenport, Ia.

A. B. Admitted to the bar and practised in Iowa. State Senator from Washington Co., Ia., 1858-59. Was Major of the 11th Iowa Volunteers, U. S. A., and was mortally wounded at the battle of Atlanta, Ga., July 22, 1864. Died soon afterwards in the hospital at Cincinnati, O.

*GEORGE BURDER GRAHAM, Lawyer, Autauga Co., Ala.

A. B. Admitted to the bar, 1839. Brother of James W., '36. Born, N. Car., 1816. Died, March 13, 1839.

JAMES WHITEFIELD GRAHAM,   Minister,   Tampa, Fla.

A. B., A. M. Admitted to the bar, 1839. Practised law in Autauga, Ala., 1839–48. Teacher of schools, Lowndesboro, Ala., 1849–60. County Superintendent of Instruction, Lowndes Co., Ala., 5 years. Judge of a State Court of Ala., 1861–69. Principal of Female Coll., Lowndesboro, Ala., 1869–71. Licensed by the Presbytery of South Ala., 1871. Stated Supply of Southern Pres. churches at Good Hope and Lowndesboro, Ala., 1871–76; Oxford, Miss., 1876–81; Ripley, Miss., 1881–86; Braidentown, Fla., 1886–92. Brother of George B, '36.

*WILLIAM HOLMES,   Planter and Teacher,   Holmwood, Miss.

A. B., A. M. Teacher in Canton, Miss., 1836–38. Admitted to the bar, 1838, but never practised. Moved to Holmwood, near Post Gibson, Miss., 1839 and engaged in planting. Erected an academy on his farm and prepared boys for college. Born, Washington Co., Pa., 1812. Died, Aug. 3, 1859.

*HUGH LANCASTER,   Lawyer,   Hamilton, O.

A. B. Admitted to the bar. Died about 1843.

JOHN MCCOY,   Manufacturer,   Independence, Mo.

A. B., A. M. Has been engaged as a merchant and manufacturer.

*LAUGHLIN MCDONALD,   Minister,   New Hope, S. Car.

A. B., A. M. Studied theology at Due West, S. Car., 1836–38. Licensed by the Second Presbytery of the Associate Reformed Pres. church of the South, Oct. 5, 1838. Ordained by same, Dec. 10, 1839. Pastor of Asso. Ref. Southern Pres. churches at Tirzah and Union, S. Car., 1839–51; Union, S. Car., 1851–53; Neely's Creek and Union, S. Car., 1853–70; New Hope, S. Car., 1870–74. Born, Hart Co., Ga., Oct. 3, 1810. Died, March 26, 1874. *Vide*, History of Union Church, S. Car., pp. 58–67.

*CHAUNCEY NEWELL OLDS,   Lawyer,   Columbus, O.

A. B., A. M. L L. D., Marietta Coll., 1869. Prof. of Latin Language and Roman Literature and Teacher of Hebrew, Miami Univ., 1837–40. Admitted to the bar and practised law at Chillicothe, O. Member of Ohio House of Representatives, 1848–49; State Senator, 1850–51. Removed to Columbus, O., 1856. Attorney-General of Ohio, 1865. Attorney for Panhandle R. R., 1868–88. Trustee of State Insane Asylum, 1866–76; of Lane Seminary, 1872–90; of Miami Univ., 1850–78. Died, Feb. 11, 1890.

*CHARLES D. POPE,   Louisville, Ky.

A. B. Died a few years after graduation.

*ANDREW ROSS,   Physician,   St. Louis Co., Mo.

A. B. M. D., Kemper Coll., 1848. Teacher at Oxford, Miss., 1838–39. Practised in St. Louis Co., Mo. Born, Bourbon Co., Ky., Dec. 4, 1807. Died, Jan. 16, 1854.

MIAMI UNIVERSITY.   23

*SAMUEL MITCHELL SMITH,   Physician,   Columbus, O.

A. B., A. M.   M. D., Ohio Med. Coll. and Jefferson Med Coll. Practised medicine at Columbus, O. Physician to State Insane Asylum and Penitentiary. Surgeon-General of Ohio, 1862-64. Prof. of Obstetrics and Diseases of Women and Children, Starling Med. Coll., Columbus, O.; later of Theory and Practice; Dean of Faculty. President of the Board of Trustees of Central Ohio Lunatic Asylum. Member of the Board of Trustees of Miami Univ., 1866-72. President of the Ohio State Medical Society. Died, Dec. 5, 1874.

*WINDSOR AUGUSTUS SMITH,   Minister,   Cincinnati, O.

A. B., A. M.   B. D., Lane Sem., 1839. Pastor of Pres. churches at Columbus, Ind.; Lawrenceburg, Ind.; Belpre, O.; Madison, Ind., 1840-53; Oxford, N. H., 1853-60; Cincinnati, O., 1860-61. Born, Mass., Sep. 16, 1809. Died, Walnut Hills, Cincinnati, O., April, 1861.

*CHARLES LOOMIS TELFORD,   Lawyer,   Cincinnati, O.

A. B., A. M. Prof. of Belles-Lettres, Cincinnati Coll., 1837. Admitted to the bar, 1839, and practised law at Cincinnati, O. Appointed Prof. in the Law department of Cincinnati Coll., 1846. Trustee of Miami Univ., 1845-49. Born, Troy, O., Nov. 27, 1817. Died, Aug. 5, 1849.

*JOHN BAYLOR TEMPLE,   Lawyer,   Louisville, Ky.

A. B., A. M. L L. B., Transylvania Univ., 1838. Practised law at Russelville, Ky., 1838-70. Auditor of Logan Co., 2 years. President of the Military Board of Kentucky, 1861-62. Removed to Louisville, Ky., 1870. Vice-President of the Southern Mutual Insurance Company, 1870-73; President of the same, 1873-86. Trustee of Center Coll., Ky. Delivered an address before the Erodelphian Literary Society of Miami Univ. Born, Russelville, Ky., 1815. Died, May 27, 1886.

THOMAS PATTERSON TOWNSLEY,   Merchant,   Xenia, O.

A. B. Has been engaged in mercantile business all his life. Father of James P., '71.

*JEROME TWITCHELL,   Minister,   Houston, Texas.

A. B., A. M. Entered the ministry of the Old School Presbyterian church. Pastor of church at Houston, Texas. While en route from Houston, Texas, to New Orleans, La., he was lost on board the "Nautilus," which sunk in mid-ocean, Aug., 1856.

*JAMES B. WALLER,   Lawyer,   Chicago, Ills.

A. B., A. M.

OLIVER SPENCER WITHERBY,   Lawyer,   San Diego, Cal.

A. B., A. M. Admitted to the bar and began practice of law at Hamilton, O. Prosecuting Attorney of Butler Co., 1843-47. Quartermaster and Commissary of U. S. Commission to run boundary line between U. S. and Canada, 1848-49. Settled at San Diego, Cal., 1849. Member of California Legislature, 1849-50. District Judge of First Judicial District, 1850-53. Collector of Customs, 1853-57. Lieutenant of the First Ohio Volunteers in the Mexican war. President of the San Diego National Bank. Address, 1106 D street.

Class of 1837.

*JAMES H. ANDERSON,   Minister,   William's Centre, O.

A. B., A. M. Entered the ministry of the Pres. church. Principal of Maumee Pres. Academy, 1850–53. Brother of David S., '43. Died, Jan. 31, 1853.

*JACOB BURNET,   Lawyer,   Cincinnati, O.

A. B., A. M. Admitted to the bar, 1839, and practised at Cincinnati, O. Judge of the Common Pleas Court of Hamilton Co., 1871–81, Died, March 27, 1889.

*ROBERT DUNCAN,   Lawyer,   Fayette, Miss.

A. B., A. M. Admitted to the bar and practised law at Fayette, Miss. Died some time during the war. Brother of John H, '40.

*MICHAEL EFFINGER,   Physician,   Lancaster, O.

A. B., A. M. M. D., Univ. of Pennsylvania, 1841. Practised at Lancaster, O. Born, Lancaster, O., Dec. 1819, Died, Jan. 5, 1890.

PEREGRINE D. FOSTER, Merchant, Glenwood, Mills Co., Iowa.

A. B. Has been continuously engaged in mercantile work.

*HORACE HENRY GOODMAN,   Lawyer,   Cincinnati, O.

A. B., A. M. Admitted to the bar, 1839. Practiced law at Cincinnati, 1839–50. Removed to New York, 1850, and practised there until 1875. Judge-Advocate of the U. S. Navy under Presidents Lincoln and Johnson. Lost his mind and was confined at the College Hill Sanitarium, where he died, May 16, 1880.

*GILBERT GORDON,   Minister,   Orlando, Fla.

A. B., A. M. Studied theology at Erskine Theol. Sem. Ordained, 1840, Pastor of Presbyterian churches, Bath Co., Ky., 1840–54; Louisville, Ky., 1854–74. On account of failing health, removed to Orlando, Fla. Brother of Neal M, '37, and Thomas B, '40. Died, Aug. 10, 1887,

*JOHN MCDANIEL GORDON,   Minister,   Fairfax, Ia.

A. B., A. M. Studied theology at Allegheny and Oxford. Licensed by Presbytery of Springfield, April 22, 1840. Ordained by same, Sept. 8, 1841. Pastor of United Pres. churches at Piqua, O., 1841–50; Berlin, Ills., 1854–60; Harmony, Ills., 1862–69; Stated Supply at Fairfax, Ia., 1869–71. Financial agent of Monmouth Coll., 1860–62. Born, Xenia, O., Dec. 8, 1813. Died, Sept. 28, 1871.

*NEAL MACDOUGAL GORDON,   Minister,   Keene, Ky.

A. B., A. M. Studied theology at the Erskine Theol. Sem. Licensed by Pres. church, Oct. 8, 1840. Pastor of Pres. churches in Jessamine and Shelby Cos., Ky., 1841–71. Author of "The Purpose of the Book of Psalms"; also a poem entited "Alleghan." Brother of Gilbert, '37, and Thomas B, '40. Died, March 19, 1871.

*ALLEN TRUMAN GRAVES, Minister and Teacher, Plainfield, N. J.

A. B., A. M. Ordained by Presbytery of Western District, April 7, 1843. Stated Supply of Pres. churches at Huntingdon, Tenn., 1841-43; Trenton, Tenn., 1843-51; Bethel, Miss., 1852-55. Assistant Editor of the "Presbyterian Herald," 1855-58. Teacher in Plainfield, N. J., 1858-70. Served in U. S. Christian Commission, 1864. Born, Saratoga Co., N. Y., June 25, 1809. Died, Dec. 5, 1878.

*WILSON CAMPBELL HOLLYDAY, Minister, Greenfield, O.

A. B., A. M. Licensed by the Presbytery of Chillicothe, Sept. 12, 1839. Ordained by same, June, 1841. Pastor of Pres. churches at Salem and Newton, O., 1841-56; Eddyville, Kirkville, Chariton, Oceola and Whitebreast, Iowa, 1863-80. Teacher at St. Mary's, O., West Point and Albia, Iowa, 1856-63. Organized and built eight churches while in Iowa. Removed to Greenfield, O., 1880. Brother of Robert H, '38. Died, May 13, 1889

*JAMES B. HOWELL, Lawyer and Editor, Keokuk, Iowa.

A. B., A. M. Admitted to the bar and practised law at Newark, O. Moved to Kosaque, Iowa, 1842. Editor of "Des Moines Valley Whig." Removed to Keokuk, Iowa, 1849, and edited the "Daily Gate City. Delegate to Republican Presidential Convention, 1856. Appointed U. S. Senator to fill the unexpired term of James W. Grimes, 1870, and served until 1871. Appointed by President Grant as one of the three commissioners to examine and report on claims for stores and supplies that had been taken or furnished the U. S. A. in the seceded states, and served until 1880 on this commission. Born, Morristown, N. J., July 4, 1816. Died, June 17, 1880.

ROBERT MCGILL LOUGHRIDGE, Minister, Waco, Tex.

A. B., A. M. D. D., Miami Univ., 1886. Princeton Theol. Sem., 1837-38. Ordained as a missionary evangelist to the Muskokee Indians by the Presbytery of Tuscaloosa, Ala., Oct. 15, 1842, and has been engaged in this work ever since. Superintendent of Mission schools. Author of "Christ's Mode of Baptism," in English and Muskokee Language, 1882; A Translation of Hymns and Books of the Bible into Muskokee; A Dictionary of the Muskokee Language in two parts, English-Muskokee, Muskokee-English.

*JOHN ALEXANDER LYLE, Physician, Paris, Ky.

A. B., A. M. M. D., Transylvania Univ., 1842. Practised medicine at Paris, Ky., 1842-65. Editor of the "Citizen," 1844-45. Director of Danville Theol. Sem., 1853-65. Brother of William C., '29. Born, Paris, Ky., March 5, 1817. Died, May 22, 1865.

CHARLES THOMPSON MCCAUGHAN, Minister, Winterest, Ia.

A. B., A. M. D. D., Monmouth Coll. Studied theology at Allegheny and Oxford. Licensed by First Presbytery of Ohio, April 22, 1840. Ordained by Pres. of Springfield, Oct. 13, 1841. Pastor of Asso. Ref. church at Sidney, O., 1841-57. Principal of Urbana Female Sem., 1856-59; Mansfield Academy, Pa., 1861-64. Pastor at Winterset, Ia., 1865-82. Author of "History of the Asso. Ref. Presbytery of Springfield," 1880.

*DUNCAN MURPHY, Lawyer, California.

A. B. Admitted to the bar and practised at Claiborne, Ala. Went to California in 1849. Died at Sea, 1852.

GEORGE MCLELLAN PARSONS, Lawyer, Columbus, O.

A. B., A. M. Admitted to the bar and practised at Columbus. Member of the Ohio House of Representatives, 1856–57. Trustee of Miami Univ., 1850–57. Now retired.

*SAMUEL REBER, Lawyer, St. Louis, Mo.

A. B., A. M. Admitted to the bar, 1839 and practised at Lancaster, O. Moved to St. Louis, Mo., 1843. Judge of the Court of Common Pleas, 1857–66; of the Circuit Court, 1866–68. City Counsellor of St. Louis, two years. Prof. in the Law School of Washington Univ., St. Louis, for many years. Born, Lancaster, Ohio., 1813. Died at Cincinnati, O., while on a visit, Dec. 1, 1879.

*MOSES RUSSELL, Minister, Clifton, O.

A. B., A. M. Attended Western Theol. Sem., 1838–39. Licensed by Presbytery of Miami, 1840. Ordained by same, 1840. Pastor of Pres. church at Clifton, Greene Co., O., 1840–64. Born, Xenia, O., Feb. 29, 1812. Died, March 22, 1864.

*WILLIAM DAVID SAYER, Lawyer, Port Gibson, Miss.

A. B., A. M. Admitted to the bar, 1843. Practised at Port Gibson, Miss. Died, April, 1853.

*ROBERT CALENDAR SMITH, Minister and Teacher, Macon, Ga.

A. B., A. M. Ordained by Presbytery of Alabama and preached at Eufaula, Ala., until 1847. Prof. of Mental and Moral Philosophy, Ogelthorpe Coll., Milledgeville, Ga., 1847–62. Pastor of Pres. church at Macon, Ga. Died, May 23, 1874.

WILLIAM M. SMITH, Lawyer, New York, N. Y.

A. B., A. M. Admitted to the bar, 1851, and has practised many years in New York City. Lived abroad at Paris, France, for several years. Address, 207 West 44th Street.

WILLIAM STANBERY, Lawyer, Pekin, Ills.

A. B. Admitted to the bar, 1840. President of the Pekin Gas Co. Address, 338 Buena Vista Avenue.

ALFRED THOMAS, Government Clerk, Washington, D. C.

A. B., A. M. Clerk in the Treasury Department.

*A. M. WHITE, Teacher, Clinton, Miss.

A. B., A. M. Engaged in teaching at Clinton, Miss., and is said to have died there about 1845 or '46.

*JOHN MORGAN WOODBRIDGE, Merchant, Marietta, O.

A. B., A. M. Attended Theol. Sem. at Yale and licensed to preach and was pastor of a Pres. church, near Marietta, O., for a short time. Abandoned the ministry on account of throat trouble and engaged in mercantile business. Volunteer Paymaster of U. S. A., 1862–63. Died, 1871.

*JOHN NORIS YOUNG, Minister and Teacher, Due West, S. Car.

A. B., A. M. L L. D., Erskine Coll., 1891. Attended Erskine Theol. Sem. Licensed to preach by the Second Presbytery of the Associate Reformed church of the South, Oct. 8, 1840. Prof. of Mathematics and Natural Philosophy, Erskine Coll., 1839–81. Treasurer of Erskine Coll., 40 years. Member of State Legislature of S. Car., one term. Born, Abbeville Co., S. Car., Feb. 17, 1813. Died, Oct. 31, 1891.

Class of 1838.

*JOHN W. BELL, Lawyer and Banker, Hillsboro, O.

A. B. Admitted to the bar, 1840 and practised at Hillsboro until 1856, when he abandoned law to enter the banking business. Clerk of the Court, 1852–54. Born, Hillsboro, O., Feb. 17, 1817. Died, June 30, 1859.

*JOSEPH YOUNG BOYD, Teacher and Farmer, Bolivar Co., Miss.

A. B., A. M. Taught in West Tennessee, 1838–42; Northern Miss., 1842–47; Somerville, Tenn., 1847–52; Hickory Withe, Tenn., 1852–61. Abandoned teaching and engaged in farming in Bolivar Co., Miss. Born, Newberry Co., S. Car., Dec. 7, 1815. Died, June, 1874.

*VIRGIL MILTON DUBOSE, Lawyer, Tex.

A. B. Admitted to the bar. Approximate date of death, 1852.

JOHN MCKEE GRAHAM, Minister, South Pasadena, Cal.

A. B., A. M. Attended Theol. Sem. at Allegheny, Pa., and Oxford, O., 1838–42. Licensed by First Presbytery of Ohio, April 15, 1841. Ordained by same, June 22, 1842. Pastor of United Pres. churches at Mt. Pleasant, O., 1842–47; Broadalbin, N. Y. 1847–57; Elmira, Ills., 1857–65; Harrison, Ia., 1876–79. Resides at South Pasadena without charge. Brother of Wm. M., '38.

*WILLIAM MILLS GRAHAM, Minister, Spring Grove, Ills.

A. B., A. M. Attended Theol. Sem. at Allegheny, Pa., and Oxford, O. Licensed by the First Presbytery of Ohio, April 15, 1841. Ordained by Ills. Pres., 1844. Pastor of United Pres. churches at Union and Sparta, Ills., 1844–47; Virginia Grove and Harrison, Ia., 1850–60; Spring Grove, Ills., 1860–63. Brother of John M., '38. Born, Todd Co., Ky., March 5, 1814. Died, Dec. 5, 1863.

ROBERT H. HOLLYDAY, Minister, Findlay, O.

A. B., A. M. Licensed by Presbytery of Chillicothe, Sept. 9, 1840. Ordained by Presbytery of Sidney, 1842. Pastor of Pres. churches at West Liberty, O., 1841–42; Findlay, O., 1842–54. Has also served Rock Hill, Bellaire, Enon Valley, Arcadia, Fostoria, and North Bethel, all in Ohio. Was agent and trustee of Wooster Univ. Author of "Centennial History of the Pres. church in Northern Ohio and Lima Presbytery," 1888. Brother of Wilson C, '37.

*JAMES FRANKLIN JOHNSTON, Teacher, San Antonio, Tex.

A. B., A. M. Died, 1885.

*GILBERT KENNEDY,   Lawyer and Editor,   Dayton, O.

A. B., A. M. Admitted to the bar. Practised law, Dayton, O., until 1861, when he moved to Wapakoneta, O. Editor of a Wapakoneta Weekly Paper, 10 or 12 years. Removed to Dayton, 1881. Born, Dayton, O., Dec. 2, 1816. Died, July 30, 1884.

*JOHN FINLEY KERR,   Minister,   Oswego, Ind.

A. B., A. M. Studied theology at Allegheny, Pa., and Oxford, O. Licensed by Chillicothe Presbytery, April 22, 1841. Ordained by Indiana Pres., 1843. Pastor of United Pres. church at Oswego, Ind., 1843–51. Born, Brown Co., O., 1813. Died, Oct. 21, 1851.

JOHN GILBERT LOWE,   Lawyer,   Dayton, O.

A. B., A. M. Admitted to the bar and has practised law at Dayton, O. Colonel, 131st O. V. I., 100 days' service, U. S. A. Trustee of Miami Univ., 1857–84. Brother of Ralph P, '29. Law office, 136 East Third Street.
Address, 127 South Main Street.

*JOHN MCCAGUE,   Lawyer,   Ripley, O.

A. B., A. M. Studied for the ministry and licensed to preach, but compelled to abandon it on account of ill-health. Afterwards engaged in the practice of law. Born, Sept., 1816. Died, Sept. 19, 1879.

DAVID MCCAW,   Teacher and Farmer,   Columbia, Tenn.

A. B., A. M. Teacher of Public School, Blackstocks, S. Car., 1839–41. Tutor, Erskine Coll., Due West, S. Car., 1841–43; Prof. of Latin, 1843–47. Principal of English and Classical School, Jefferson Co., Ga., 1847–49. Engaged in farming and has taught at intervals since 1850.

THOMAS MILLIKIN,   Lawyer,   Hamilton, O.

A. B., A. M. Admitted to the bar, 1841, and has practised continuously at Hamilton, O. Attorney for C., H. and D. R. R., and C. C. C. and I. R. R. Trustee of Miami Univ., 1878–87.
Address, 113 South Second Street.

*JAMES WALLACE PARKS,   Lawyer,   St. Charles, Mo.

A. B., A. M. Taught school, four years. Admitted to the bar, Nov., 1843, and died a few months afterwards. Brother of William H. '38, and Robert H, '39.

WILLIAM HUMPHREY PARKS,   Minister,   St. Louis, Mo.

A. B., A. M. Admitted to the bar, 1843, and practised a few years at St. Charles, Mo. Licensed by the New School Pres. church, 1848. Ordained and pastor at St. Louis, Mo., 1848–58. On account of his bad health, has not been in the active ministry since 1858. Joined the Southern Pres. church, 1866. Brother of James W. '38, and Robert H. '39.
Address, 1122 Chambers Street.

*GEORGE S. REA,   Minister,

A. B., A. M. Entered the ministry of the Pres. church and preached at Lewisville, Ind., 1843–44. Cannot be traced since then, but is said to be dead.

JOHN P. REYNOLDS, Lawyer, Chicago, Ills.

A. B., A. M. Admitted to the bar and has practised in Chicago, Ills. Secretary of the Illinois State Board of Agriculture, 1860-71. President of same, one term. Secretary of the Inter-state Industrial Exposition, 1873-91. President of the Illinois State Sanitary Commission, 1861-65. State Commissioner to Universal Exposition, Paris, France, 1867. Chief Inspector of Grain, Chicago, 1887—. President of the Illinois Commission to the Centennial Exposition, 1876. Director-in-chief of the Illinois Board of World's Fair Commissioners for the World's Columbian Exposition.
Address, 468 La Salle Avenue.

*FRANCIS D. RIGDON, Lawyer, Atlanta, Ga.

A. B., A. M. Admitted to the bar. Date of death unknown.

MILTON AUGUSTUS SACKETT, Minister, Cleveland, O.

A. B. Ordained at West Liberty, O., 1843. Pastor of Pres. churches at West Liberty, O., 1843-44; Circleville, O., 1845-52; Walnut Hills, Cincinnati, O., 1853-58; Mt. Vernon, O., 1858-62. Principal of Mt. Pleasant Academy, 1852-53; Urbana Collegiate Institute, 1863-66; Family Boarding School for boys, Cleveland, O., 1867-84. Retired, 1884.
Address, 40 Cornell Street.

*HENRY SNOW, Lawyer, Cincinnati, O.

A. B., A. M. Prof. of Ancient Languages, Woodward Coll., Cincinnati, O., 1839-40. Admitted to the bar and practised at Cincinnati, O. Died, 1880.

JOHN STUART WILLIAMS, Lawyer and Farmer, Mt. Sterling, Ky.

A. B., A. M. Admitted to the bar, 1840, and practised law until 1845 at Paris, Ky. Served through the Mexican war, first as Captain of an independent company attached to the Sixth Infantry, 1845; Colonel of the Fourth Regiment, Kentucky Vol., 1846-47. Distinguished bravery at Cerro Gordo, gave him the title of "Cerro Gordo" Williams. Member of Kentucky Legislature, 1851-53; 1873-75. Entered the Confederate service as Colonel in 1861, and was made Brigadier-General, April, 1862. U. S. Senator, 1879-85. Now engaged in farming at Mt. Sterling.

Class of 1839.

*JAMES BARNETT, Minister, Emporia, Kan.

A. B., A. M. D. D. Studied theology at Oxford. Licensed by First Presbytery of Ohio, April, 1842. Ordained by same, July 23, 1844. Sailed as a missionary to Palestine, Jan., 1845. Missionary in Damascus, 1846-54; Cairo, Egypt, 1854-75. Returned to U. S. and labored as home missionary at Emporia, Kan. Born, Hanover, Pa., June 16, 1817. Died, Oct. 2, 1884.

*MARTIN C. BENNETT, Oxford, O.

A. B. Died soon after graduation.

*JACOB BUTLER, Lawyer, Chicago, Ills.

A. B., A. M. Admitted to the bar, 1841. Practised at Muscatine, Iowa, for many years. Member of Iowa Legislature, 1863-64. Speaker of the House. Date of death unknown.

*JACKSON DUFF, Minister, Center Ridge, Kan.

A. B., A. M. Studied theology at Oxford, O. Licensed by the First Presbytery of Ohio, April 5, 1843. Ordained in Illinois, June 27, '44. Pastor of United Pres. churches at Harrison and Virginia Grove, Iowa, 1844-47; Scotch Ridge, O., 1853-69; Home Missionary, 1869-86. Born, Garrard Co., Ky., Sept 24, 1814. Died, Feb. 9, 1886.

PHILEMON BEECHER EWING, Lawyer, Lancaster, O.

A. B., A. M. L L. D, Univ. of Notre Dame, 1878. Admitted to the bar and has practised continuously at Lancaster, O. Appointed by Governor Tod Judge of the Common Pleas Court, 1862. Also engaged in the banking business and in the development of the Hocking Valley coal fields. Now retired.

*JAMES ROBINSON GIBSON, Minister, Manchester, O.

A. B., A. M. Ordained, Oct., 1841. Pastor of the Pres. churches at Decatur, O., 1841-46; Ripley, O., 1846-53; Frankfort, O., 1853-67; Eckmansville, O., 1867-71; Manchester, O., 1871-75. Father of James K, '69, Born, Washington Co., Pa., Oct. 28, 1809. Died, March 30, 1881.

SAMUEL BETTS HALLEY, Merchant, Silverton, O.

A. B., A. M. Studied theology but abandoned it on account of ill health. Engaged in steam boating and railroading.

*RUFUS K. HARRIS, Washington, D. C.

A. B. Approximate date of death, 1844.

*JAMES D. HOCKER, Richmond, Ky.

A. B. Died soon after graduation. Approximate date of death, 1841.

JOHN REILY KNOX, Lawyer, Greenville, O.

A. B., A. M. Taught school in Mississippi, 1841-42. Admitted to the bar and practised at Greenville, O., 1843-52; Dayton, O., 1852-56; has practised in Greenville, O., since 1856. Presidential elector, 1860. A founder of the Beta Theta Pi fraternity, 1839. Trustee of Miami Univ., appointed, 1869; term expires, 1893. Law firm, Knox, Martz & Rupe.

*DAVID LINTON, Lawyer, Pleasantown, Kan.

A. B., A. M. L L. B, Cincinnati Law School, 1841. Prosecuting attorney of Clinton Co., O., 1845-47. Member of Ohio State Senate, 1851-55. Probate Judge of Linn Co., Kan., 1867-69. A founder of the Beta Theta Pi fraternity, 1839. Died, Aug. 10, 1889.

ANDREW MANSPEAKER, N. Car.

A. B., A. M. Cannot be traced.

JOHN CLELAND MAXWELL, Physician, Lebanon, Ky.

A. B., A. M. M. D., Transylvania Univ., 1842. Has practised in Lebanon, Ky. Acting Assistant Surgeon and Surgeon of the Board of Enrollment, U. S. A., 1861-65. Examining Surgeon of Pensions, for many years.

MIAMI UNIVERSITY. 31

*JOSEPH WRIGHT MCCAGUE, Merchant, Chillicothe, O.

A. B., A. M. Admitted to the bar and practised law at Ripley, O., until 1844, when he abandoned the profession and engaged in the dry goods business at Chillicothe, O. Born, Sinking Springs, O., Aug. 5, 1818. Died, April 3, 1881.

SAMUEL F. MCCOY, Lawyer, Chillicothe, O.

A. B., A. M. Admitted to the bar. Probate Judge, 1852-61.

*JOHN STEELE MCCRACKEN, Minister, Xenia, O.

A. B. Studied theology at Allegheny, Pa., and Oxford, O. Ordained by First Presbytery of Ohio, Aug. 23, 1843. Stated supply of United Presbyterian church at Kenton, O., 1843-46; pastor of same, 1846-51. Gave up active work on account of broken health. Brother of Samuel W, '31. Born, Cincinnati, O., April 25, 1804. Died, April 1, 1863.

*JOSEPH MILLER, Lawyer, Chillicothe, O.

A. B., A. M. Admitted to the bar and practised at Chillicothe, O. Member of U. S. House of Representatives, 1857-59. Appointed U. S. District Judge and died while in that capacity in Nebraska, 1862.

*WILLIAM ALEXANDER MOORE, Banker, Midway, Ky.

A. B., A. M. President of Midway Deposit Bank; of Midway Paper Mill Co., 1874-78. Died, 1885.

*HENRY FOLSOM PAGE, Lawyer, Circleville, O.

A. B. Admitted to the bar. Presidential elector for Ohio, 1864. Member of the Ohio Constitutional Convention, 1873. Died, Oct. 27, 1891.

*ROBERT HARRIS PARKS, Lawyer, St. Charles, Mo.

A. B., A. M. Admitted to bar, 1843, and practised at St. Charles, Mo. Member of Missouri State Senate, 4 years. Brother of James W., '38, and William H., '38. Died in the fall of 1889.

*DAVID PRESSLY, Minister, Brighton, Tenn.

A. B., A. M. D. D., Erskine Coll. Attended Erskine Theol. Sem., 1840-42. Ordained, 1842. Pastor of Associate Reformed churches of the South at Starkville, Miss., 1843-85; Brighton, Tipton Co., Tenn., 1885-91. Died, July 29, 1891.

*MICHAEL CLARKSON RYAN, Lawyer, Hamilton, O.

A. B., A. M. L L. B., Cincinnati Law School, 1842. Practised at Hamilton, O. Prosecuting attorney of Butler Co., 1848-52; Clerk of the Court, 1852-58. Delegate to the National Democratic Convention, 1856. Commissioned Colonel of the 50th O. V. I., 1861. A founder of the Beta Theta Pi fraternity. Died, Oct. 23, 1861.

*RICHARDSON C. SAUNDERS, Planter, Sweet Home, Tex.

A. B., A. M. Planter in Madison Co., Miss., until 1871. Member of Miss. State Legislature, 2 terms. Moved to Sweet Home, Tex., 1871. Member of Texas State Legislature, 1 term. Died, July 27, 1889.

L. ORESTES SMITH,

A. B., A. M. Went South after graduation and began teaching. Can not be traced.

GEORGE HORTAIN STEWART, Physician, Cincinnati, O.

A. B. M. D., Ohio Med. Coll., 1844. Has practised at Frankfort, O., and Newport, Ky. Also a druggist. Address, Tusculum, Cincinnati, O.

*GEORGE SWAN, Student of Law, Columbus, O.

A. B. Commenced the study of law and died before he was admitted to the bar.

*GEORGE W. SWAN, Minister, Philadelphia, Pa.

A. B. Died, 1884. This information is taken from the catalogue of 1885-86.

THOMAS F. SWIM,

A. B. Came to college from Beaver Co., Pa. Can not be traced.

*WILLIAM M. TAYLOR, Lawyer, Crockett, Tex.

A. B. Admitted to the bar and practised for some time at Houston, Tex. Grand Master of the Grand Lodge of Masons. Delegate to Masonic convention held in Baltimore, Md., Oct., 1871, and died while in attendance at this convention. Author of a book on Masonry, entitled, "Taylor's Monitor."

JOHN WALLACE, Minister, Ione, Cal.

A. B. Entered the ministry.

*JAMES MATHEWS YOUNG, Minister, Harrell's Cross Roads, Ala.

A. B., A. M. Attended Erskine Theol. Sem., 1840-42. Ordained at Prosperity, Ala., 1843. Pastor of Asso. Ref. Pres. church of the South at Harrell's Cross Roads, Dallas Co. Ala., 1842-66. Brother of John C., '39, and Samuel O., '39. Died, May, 1866.

JOHN CLARK YOUNG, Lawyer, Corsicana, Tex.

A. B. Admitted to the bar, 1841. Brother of James M., '39, and Samuel O., '39.

*SAMUEL OLIVER YOUNG, Physician, Houston, Tex.

A. B. M. D., Charleston, S. Car., Med. Coll., 1842. Brother of James M., '39, and John C., '39. Died, Nov. 10, 1847.

Class of 1840.

*JOHN BARR, Farmer, Columbus, O.

A. B., A. M. Approximate date of death, 1850.

*WILLIAM W. BELLVILLE, Physician, Woodbridge, Cal.

A. B. M. D. Died, 1871.

*JOHN R. BLOUNT, Merchant, Springfield, O.

A. B. Followed mercantile pursuits. Died, 1849.

MITCHELL MATTHEWS BROWN, Minister, New Wilmington, Pa.

A. B., A. M. Studied theology at Oxford, O. Licensed by First Presbytery of Ohio, May, 1844. Ordained by Pres. of Ills., Oct. 16, 1846. Pastor of United Pres. church at Springfield, Ills., 1849–54; Principal of Union Academy, Sparta, Ills.; of the Female Sem., Bloomington, Ind.; and President of Lincoln Coll., Greenwood, Mo. Has lately been supplying Home Missionary work in the U. P. church. Author of a tract, "Come to Jesus."

*JOHN MILTON CAMPBELL, Minister, Cape Palmas, Africa.

A. B. Attended Lane Theol. Sem., 1840–43. Ordained as a minister in the Pres. church, Nov. 8, 1843. Sailed as a missionary to Africa, Jan. 1, 1844. Died, March 18, 1844.

*ELIPHALET P. COLE, Teacher, Southern Ind.

A. B., A. M. Was engaged in teaching. At one time Principal of the Female Seminary, Bloomington, Ind. Died in the southern part of Indiana, 1889.

*WILBUR CONOVER, Lawyer, Dayton, O.

A. B., A. M. Admitted to the bar and practised law at Dayton, O. Died, Oct. 3, 1881.

*WILLIAM BRADFORD CRAWFORD, Minister, Buechel, Ky.

A. B. B. D., Princeton Theol. Sem., 1842. Licensed by the Second Presbytery of New York, April 30, 1844. Stated supply of Pres. churches at Bladensburg, Md., 1844–45; Mt. Vernon, Ky., 1846–49; Harrodsburg, Ky., 1849–60. Retired to a farm near Buechel, Jefferson Co., Ky. Born, Boyle Co., Ky., 1817. Died, Nov. 1, 1886.

*ROBERT C. DAMERON, Physician, Vicksburg, Miss.

A. B. M. D. Died about the close of the war.

JOHN HOLT DUNCAN, Lawyer, Houston, Tex.

A. B. Admitted to the bar. Chief Justice of Bexar Co., Tex., 1857–62. Captain in the C. S. A., 1862–63. District Judge of Texas, 1864–65. City Attorney of Houston, Texas, 1877–79. Brother of Robert, '37. A founder of the Beta Theta Pi fraternity.

*JOHN ELDER, Farmer, Kan.

A. B. Lived at Camden, O., and removed to Kansas. Died, 1889.

*THOMAS BOSTON GORDON, Lawyer, Nicholasville, Ky.

A. B., A. M. Principal of Academy, Decatur, Ga., 1841-42. Admitted to the bar, 1842. Judge of Bath Co., Ky., 1854-58. Brother of Neal M, '37, and Gilbert, '37. A founder of the Beta Theta Pi fraternity. Died, Jan. 25, 1891.

JOHN JAY JOHNS, Farmer, St. Charles, Mo.

A. B. Moved from Mississippi to St. Charles, Mo., 1844, and was engaged in farming near that city until a few years ago. Now retired and living in the city of St. Charles, Mo. Held the office of School Commissioner.

*HENRY HUNTER JOHNSON, Minister, St. Edward, Neb.

A. B., A. M. Studied theology at Allegheny, Pa. Licensed by Presbytery of Chillicothe, April 20, 1843. Ordained by Illinois Presbytery, Sept., 1844. Pastor of Asso. Ref. churches at St. Louis, Mo., 1845-47; Sugar Creek, O., 1848-51; Dayton, O., 1851-56; East Boston, Mass., 1857-58. Entered the Reformed Dutch church, 1858, and was pastor of Hastings-on-the-Hudson, 1861-65; Leyden Centre, Ills., 1867-80. Born, Chillicothe, O., June 24, 1819. Died, Jan. 18, 1881.

*JAMES W. JOHNSON, New Orleans, La.

A. B. Died soon after graduation.

SAMUEL TAYLOR MARSHALL, Lawyer, Keokuk, Ia.

A. B., A. M. Teacher of Latin, West Point, Ia., 1844. Sergeant-at-arms of the Iowa Legislature, 1846-48. Editor of the "Nipantuck," the first daily paper in Keokuk, Ia., 1855. Father of Robert M, '69. A founder of the Beta Theta Pi fraternity. Law firm, S. T. Marshall & Sons. Address, 730 Grand Avenue.

*DAVID D. MARTIN, Physician, Vicksburg, Miss.

A. B. M. D. Died about the close of the war of the Rebellion.

*GEORGE ELLIS PUGH, Lawyer, Cincinnati, O.

A. B., A. M. Admitted to the bar and practised at Cincinnati, O. Captain of the Fourth Ohio Inf. in the Mexican war. Member of the Ohio Legislature, 1848-49. City Solicitor of Cincinnati, 1850. Attorney-General of Ohio, 1851. U. S. Senator, 1855-61. Born, Cincinnati, O., Nov. 28, 1822. Died, July 19, 1876.

*JOSEPH DRAKE STEELE, Minister, Warsaw, Mo.

A. B. Studied theology at Allegheny, Pa., and Oxford, O. Licensed by Monongahela Presbytery, Mar. 26, 1844. Ordained by Iowa Presbytery, June 24, '57. Spent many years in missionary work in Iowa. Resided at Warsaw, Mo., for many years, teaching and preaching. Brother of John C, '32, and Walter, '40. Born, Xenia, O., Aug. 30, 1820. Died, May 15, 1882.

*ROBERT WILBUR STEELE, Philanthropist, Dayton, O.

A. B., A. M. Commenced the study of law, but abandoned it on account of ill-health. Member of the Board of Education of Dayton, 1842-72; president of the same, 1860-72. Founder of the Dayton Library Association, 1847, and of the Dayton Public Library, 1888. Member of the Board of State Charities, 1866-71. Member of the Montgomery Agricultural Association and had charge of the first State fair in Dayton, 1853. One of the organizers of the 93rd O. V. I. Member of the Board of Trustees of Miami Univ., 1857-66. Born, Dayton, O., July 3, 1819. Died, Sept. 24, 1891. *Vide*, Sketch in "Miami Student," Vol. XI, No. 1.

*WALTER STEELE, Student of Theology, Steele's Ford, Ky.

A. B. Attended Theol. Sem. Allegheny, Pa., 1841-43. Brother of John C, '32, and Joseph D, '40. Died, June 7, 1844.

*JAMES GEORGE SMITH, Farmer, Lebanon, O.

A. B., A. M. A founder of the Beta Theta Pi fraternity, 1839. Died, Aug., 1849.

*RICHARD H. SMITH, Teacher, Columbia, Tenn.

A. B. Date of death unknown.

*Robert W. WILSON, Minister, Bloomingburg, O.

A. B., A. M. Studied theology at Lane Sem. and Oxford, O. Licensed by Oxford Presbytery, 1842. Ordained by same, 1843. Pastor of Pres. churches at Bethel, Butler Co., O., 1842-47; Bloomingburg, O., 1851-65. Teacher in Salem Academy, 1847-51. Served in the Christian Commission, U. S. Army, 1864. Born, Washington, Ky., July 12, 1821. Died, 1865.

*WILLIAM P. YOUNG, Grain Merchant, Hamilton, O.

A. B. Died, 1862.

Class of 1841.

GEORGE L. ANDREW, Physician, La Porte, Ind.

A. B., A. M. M. D., Ohio Med. Coll. 1845. U. S. Examining Surgeon since 1876. Sanitary Inspector, U. S. Sanitary Commission, 1861-64. Medical Examiner for all the principal life insurance companies operating in Indiana. Member of American Medical Association and of the American Academy of Science.

*JOHN MASON BISHOP, Minister, Oxford, O.

A. B., A. M. B. D., Lane Sem., 1844. Ordained by LaPorte Presbytery, April, 1845. Pastor of Pres. churches at Plymouth, Ind., 1844-46; New Albany, Ind., 1846-50; Bedford, Ind., 1850-60; Bloomington, Ind., 1860-67; Rockville, Ind., 1867-72; Lebanon, Ind., 1872-79; Covington, Ind., 1879-83; Rockfield, Ind., 1883-88. Resided at Oxford, 1888-90. Trustee of Western Female Sem. and of Lane Theol. Sem. until his death. Brother of George B. '28, Robert H. '31, and Ebenezer E, '33. Born, Lexington, Ky., April 2, 1819. Died, Dec. 26, 1890.

*JOHN L. BRANHAM, Lawyer, Frankfort, Ky.

A. B. Admitted to the bar but died soon afterwards.

PERSIUS BARNET CALHOUN, Lawyer and Farmer, Austin, Tenn.

A. B. Admitted to the bar, 1842. Practiced law and acted as land agent, Austin, Tex., 1859–66. A farmer in Wilson Co., Tenn., since 1866. Contributor to the U. S. Chief Signal Service for 23 years.

*LUCIUS CHESTERFIELD CHURCHILL, Physician, San Francisco.

A. B., A. M. M. D. Practised medicine at Marshall, Ills., Memphis, Tenn., and San Francisco, Cal. Date of death not known.

*JOHN GILCHRIST, Minister, Boggstown, Ind.

A. B., A. M. Licensed by the Presbytery of Clinton, Miss., 1843. Principal of Academy, Clinton, Miss., 1842–44. Agent of the American Tract Society in Miss., 1844–45. Ordained by Presbytery of Oxford, 1845. Pastor of Pres. churches at Brookville, Ind., 1845–47; Dunlapsville, Ind., 1847–56; Boggstown, Ind., 1858–63. Brother of James, '42. Born, Scotland, April 10, 1814. Died, April 8, 1863.

*GEORGE W. GOWDY, Minister, Xenia, O.

A. B., A. M. Studied theology at Oxford, O., and Edinburgh, Scotland. Licensed by Presbytery of Springfield, 1848. Ordained by same, 1850. Pastor of United Pres. churches, Vernon, Wis., 1850–54; Columbus, O., 1856–58; Fairview, O., 1863–67. Was Principal of McKeesport, Pa., Academy. Co-editor of the "Presbyterian Witness" for several years. Born, Xenia, O., June 23, 1823. Died, Sept. 21, 1869.

CHARLES HENRY HARDIN, Lawyer and Banker, Mexico, Mo.

A. B., A. M. Admitted to the bar and practised law at Fulton, Mo., 1843. Circuit Attorney, 1848–52. Member of the Missouri Legislature, 1852–58. Member of Commission to Revise the Statutes of Missouri, 1855. Member of the Missouri Senate, 1860–62 and 1872–74. Governor of Missouri, 1875–77. Founded Hardin Female Institute, Mexico, Mo., 1873. Trustee of William Jewell Coll., 1870–89; of Lincoln Institute, 1875–76; President of the Board of Directors of Hardin Female Institute since 1873. A founder of the Beta Theta Pi fraternity, 1839. *Vide*, Sketch and Portrait, "Miami Journal," Vol. 1, No. 8.

*JOHN MILLER JUNKIN, Physician, Easton, Pa.

A. B., A. M. M. D., Jefferson Med. Coll. Surgeon of the 9th Pa., Cavalry, 1861–64. Brother of George, '42. Died, Jan. 18, 1889.

JAMES LONG, Teacher, Washington, D. C.

A. B., A. M. Studied law but never practised. Has been engaged in teaching and as Superintendent of Schools. Editor of Richmond, Ind, "Jeffersonian" 1846. Brother of Robert K., 44. Now retired. Address, 900 K Street, N. W.

JAMES ANDREW IRWIN LOWES, Teacher, Portsmouth, O.

A. B., A. M. Studied theology and ordained as a Pres. minister. Principal of Salem Academy, 1847–70; of Grammar School, Miami Univ., 1870–72; Superintendent of Schools at New Richmond, O., and Portsmouth, O., 7 years. Is now Prof. of Languages in the Portsmouth High School. Trustee of Miami Univ., 1869–70.

DAVID MACK, Lawyer, Carthage, Ills.

A. B., A. M.

*WILLIAM S. MARTIN, Physician, Saltillo, Mexico.

A. B. M. D., Transylvania Univ., 1845. Killed by a rival physician in Saltillo, Mexico, 1860.

BENJAMIN MILLS, Minister, Meade, Kan.

A. B., A. M. D. D. Attended Lane Theol. Sem. and was ordained in 1844. Supplied several pastorates at various places. Admitted to the bar, 1854, and practised law in Kentucky for some time. Resumed ministerial work. Pastor of Pres. churches at St. Louis, Mo., 1870-74, Shelbyville, Ills., Sidney, Iowa, and now at Meade, Kan. Brother of John, '41.

*JOHN MCFARLAND MILLS, Physician, Shelbyville, Ills.

A. B. M. D., Louisville Med. Coll. Practised medicine at Frankfort, Ky., 1847-74, when he removed to Shelbyville, Ills. Commissioner of State Prisons in Kentucky, 1867-74. President of the Ky. State Med. Association. Captain of the Governor's Guard, U. S. Army, 1861. Colonel of the 31st Ky. Vol. Inf., U. S. A., 1862-65. Brother of Benjamin, '41. Died, March 17, 1884.

*SAMUEL MCCLELLAND MOORE, ' Lawyer, Chicago, Ills.

A. B., A. M. L L. D., Wooster Univ. Admitted to the bar, 1842, and practised at Covington, Ky. Judge of the Ninth Judicial Circuit of Ky., 1856-62. Removed to Chicago, Ills. Appointed Judge of Superior Court of Cook Co., Ills. Term expired, 1873. Elected to the same judgeship, 1873, and served until 1880. Chancellor of the Superior Court during this period. Died, April 25, 1885.

WILLIAM HENRY MOORE, Minister, Brookville, Ind.

A. B., A. M. Ordained at New Albany, Ind., Nov. 17, 1846. Pastor of Pres. churches at Jeffersonville, Ind., 1845-49; Rising Sun and Dillsboro. Ind., 1849-55; Harrison, O., 1855-57; Rising Sun, Ind., 1857-60; Reading, O., 1860-65; Gettysburg, O., 1865-67; Covington, O., 1867-69; Mt. Jefferson, O., 1869-81; Mt. Carmel, Ind., 1881-83; Dillsboro, Ind., 1885-91. Now retired.

ARTHUR RALPH NAYLOR, Minister, Perth Amboy, N. J.

A. B., A. M. Ordained by Presbytery of Cincinnati, 1844. Has labored continuously in the Pres. church, until within the last few years. Served in the U. S. Christian Commission during the war of the Rebellion. Father of James M, '66. Now retired.

*JOHN OGLE, Lawyer and Planter, Waterproof, La.

A. B. Admitted to the bar. Died, 1857.

ALEXANDER PADDACK, Lawyer, Cincinnati, O.

A. B., A. M. Admitted to the bar and has practised continuously in Cincinnati, O. Probate Judge of Hamilton Co., O., 1861-64. Law office, 17½ West Third street.
Address, East Walnut Hills.

38   MIAMI UNIVERSITY.

*ROBERT LUDLOW YANCY PEYTON, Lawyer, Harrisonville, Mo.

A. B. Admitted to the bar. State Senator of Mo., 1858-61. Colonel in the Missouri State Guard, 1861. U. S. Senator from Mo., 1862-63. Died at Bladen Springs, Ala., in the fall of 1863.

*JOHN J. SCOTT, Minister, Lewisville, Ind.

A. B., A. M. Licensed and ordained as a Pres. minister. Pastor of Ebenezer and Cambridge City Pres. churches, 1851-55. Mysteriously murdered, March 8, 1855.

SAMUEL SHELLABARGER, Lawyer, Washington, D. C.

A. B., A. M. L L. D., Miami Univ., 1891. Admitted to the bar, 1846, and practised law at Springfield, O. Member of Ohio Legislature, 1851-53. Member of the U. S. House of Representatives, 1861-63; 1865-69, and 1871-73. U. S. minister to Portugal, 1869-71. Appointed by President Grant as a member of the U. S. Civil Service Commission. Attorney for the Union Pacific R. R.

CALVIN FLETCHER VANCE, Lawyer, Memphis, Tenn.

A. B., A. M. Admitted to the bar and has since been engaged in active practice in Memphis. Secretary and Treasurer of the Miss. and Tenn. R. R. Co., 1853-66. Was attorney for the same road for many years. At present attorney for the Illinois and Central R. R. Co.

Class of 1842.

*JAMES J. BERRY, Lawyer, Sangamon Co., Ills.

A. B., A. M. L L. B., Transylvania Univ., 1844. Practised law for many years at Lake Providence, La. Approximate date of death, 1873.

*WILLIAM EDWARD BLACKBURN, Lawyer, Lake Providence, La.

A. B. Admitted to the bar and practised law at Lake Providence, La. Killed in a duel at Spring Station, Ky., 1849.

JAMES LAW BUELL, Minister, Hutchinson, Kan.

A. B., A. M. Studied theology at Canonsburg. Licensed by Miami Presbytery, July 1, 1846. Ordained by same, July 8, 1847. Pastor of United Pres. churches at Kenton, O., 1847-61; Tranquillity, Ia., 1864-68. Was principal of Traer Academy, Iowa.
Address, 219 E. Third Avenue.

*JOHN ARMSTRONG COLLINS, Lawyer, Lake Providence, La.

A. B., A. M. Admitted to the bar and practised law at Lake Providence, La. Died, New Orleans, La., June 10, 1850.

BENJAMIN CORY, Physician, San Jose, Cal.

A. B., A. M. M. D., Medical Coll. of Ohio, 1845. Member of the California Legislature, 2 years. Physician and surgeon for the Santa Clara Co. Hospital for several years. Trustee of the State Normal school for 10 years. Brother of James M, '48, and Andrew J, '55.
Address, 97 South First Street.

*THOMAS CRAVEN,   Minister,   College Hill, Ind.

A. B., A. M. Was a minister in the Baptist church and had preached for several years before entering college. Spent the last fourteen years of his life in founding and supporting the Eleutherian College at College Hill, Jefferson Co., Ind. Father of John G, '45. Died, 1860.

JOSEPH R. DAVIS,   Lawyer,   Biloxi, Miss.

A. B. A. M. (Honorary), by a Southern College. Admitted to the bar. Was State Senator of Mississippi and a general officer of the C. S. A.

JAMES GILCHRIST,   Minister,   Vernon, Ind.

A. B., A. M. Attended Theol. Sem., New Albany, Ind. Ordained by Whitewater Presbytery, 1848. Pastor of Pres. churches at Mt. Carmel, Ind., 1848–60; Union and Sardinia, Ind., 1860–65; Acton and Bethany, Ind., 1865–70; Scipio, Oak Grove, Sugar Creek, Shenandoah, and Dover, Ind., 1870–75; Los Angeles Presbytery, Cal., 1875–83; Stated supply in Indiana, 1883–90. Retired since 1890. Brother of John, '41.

*JOHN GOBLE,   Minister,   West Cairo, O.

A. B. Ordained as a minister in the Cumberland Pres. church and supplied pastorates in the South. Born, Washington Co., Pa., April 5, 1817. Died, March 11, 1888.

*ARCHIBALD WILLIAM HAMILTON,   Lawyer,   Mt. Sterling, Ky.

A. B., A. M. LL. B., Harvard, 1844. Member of the Kentucky Legislature, 1851–53. Died, 1854.

*JAMES SAMUEL HIBBEN,   Merchant,   Indianapolis, Ind.

A. B., A. M. Merchant at Rushville, Ind., and Indianapolis, Ind. Died, Oct. 17, 1877.

*WILLIAM HUNTER,   Minister,   Hebron, O.

A. B. Attended Western Theol. Sem., 1842–44. Licensed by Presbytery of Ohio, June 18, 1844. Ordained by Presbytery of Donegal, Nov. 3, 1845. Pastor of Pres. churches at Cedar Grove, O., 1845–49; Hopewell, O., 1852–68; Hebron, O., 1869–70. Died, Oct. 3, 1870.

*DANIEL WILKINSON IDDINGS,   Lawyer,   Dayton, O.

A. B., A. M. Admitted to the bar, 1844. Mayor of Dayton, 8 years. U. S. Register in Bankruptcy, 13 years. Paymaster of Ohio troops, 1861–62. Attorney for C. C. C. and I. R. R., 16 years. Died, Dec. 24, 1885.

WILLIAM JAMISON,   Lawyer,   Columbus, O.

A. B., A. M. Admitted to the bar, 1846. Probate Judge of Franklin Co., O., 1855–58.
Address, 121 South Sixth street. Also, Jamison, Ky.

GEORGE JUNKIN,   Lawyer,   Philadelphia, Pa.

A. B., A. M. LL. D., Rutgers Coll., 1890. Admitted to the bar, Mar. 18, 1848. Vice-Provost of the Law Academy of Philadelphia, 12 years. Nominee of the Independent Republican party for Judge of the Supreme Court, 1882. Son of President George Junkin.
Address, 1334 Chestnut street.

*DANIEL McCLEARY, Merchant, Dayton, O.

A. B. Lieutenant in U. S. A., Mexican war. Died, Vera Cruz, Mexico, June 23, 1847.

ADAM McCREA, Insurance Agent, Circleville, O.

A. B., A. M. Studied law but never admitted to the bar. Was engaged in mercantile pursuits for many years. Life Director of the Board of Foreign Missions, Pres. church; also of the American Bible Society. Trustee of Miami Univ. since 1884.

*MATTHEW McDONALD, Lawyer, Abbeville, S. Car.

A. B. Admitted to the bar, 1843. Clerk of the Court of Common Pleas, Abbeville Co., S. Car., 1852–76. Orderly Sergeant, C. S. A., 1862–63. Born, Abbeville, S. Car., Mar. 13, 1820. Died, June 12, 1876.

*SAMUEL TAPLIN MORRIS, Minister, Montgomery, Ala.

A. B., A. M. Attended Erskine Theol. Sem., and entered the ministry of the Asso. Ref. Pres. church of the South. Died, Sept. 16, 1848.

*WILLIAM F. MOSGROVE, Urbana, O.

A. B., A. M.

ARNALDO F. PACK, Lawyer,

A. B., A. M. Student of Law, Cincinnati Law School, 1843. Came to college from Madison Co., Miss. Can not be traced.

*JOHN F. PATTON, Rome, Ga.

A. B. Date of death unknown.

*WILLIAM W. PATTON, Minister, Cedar Springs, S. Car.

A. B., A. M. Attended Erskine Theol. Sem. and was ordained as a minister in the Asso. Ref. church. Joined the United Presbyterian church, April 10, 1849, and had received a call to St. Louis, Mo., when he was attacked with cholera and died, Sept., 1849.

*WILLIAM Y. PATTON, Lawyer and Planter, Crystal Springs, Miss.

A. B. Admitted to the bar and practised law at Gallatin, Miss., for several years. Removed to Crystal Springs, Miss., and engaged in planting. Date of death unkown.

*JOHN ARNOTT REILEY, Minister, East Feliciana, La.

A. B., A. M. B. D., Princeton Theol. Sem., 1843. Licensed by Newton Presbytery, May 16, 1844. Ordained, Nov. 18, 1845. Pastor of Pres. churches at Knowlton and Blairstown, N. J., 1845–54; Knowlton, N. J., 1854–64; East Feliciana, La., 1866–78. Born, Bucks Co., Pa., May 3, 1816. Died, Sept. 30, 1878.

GEORGE KNOX SHEIL, Lawyer, Salem, Ore.

A. B. Admitted to the bar. Member of U. S. House of Representatives, 1861–63.

JOSEPH STOUT, Physician, Ottawa, Ills.

A. B. M. D., Cincinnati Med. Coll., 1845. Address, 1004 Paul street.

*JAMES E. TIFFANY, Minister, Oxford, O.

A. B., A. M. Engaged in teaching for a few years after graduation and then entered the ministry. Died, about 1850.

WILLIAM S. TURRELL,

A. B. Engaged in teaching after graduation and was at Richmond, Ind., 1843. Can not be traced.

ISAAC VANAUSDAL, Merchant, Dayton, O.

A. B. Firm name, I. & C. VanAusdal, Importers of and Dealers in Carpets and House Trimmings, 23 South Main street. Address, Dayton View.

Class of 1843.

*DAVID S. ANDERSON, Minister, Perth Amboy, N. J.

A. B., A. M. Principal of Academy, Williams Center, O., 1853–55. Pastor of Presbyterian churches at Defiance, O.; Delta, O.; Byran O., and Eagle Creek, O. Died at the home for disabled ministers at Perth Amboy, N. J., April 2, 1886. Brother of James H, '37.

*CHARLES BARNES, Teacher, Madison, Ind.

A. B., A. M. Superintendent of city schools at New Albany, Ind., 1855–67; Madison, Ind., 1853–55 and 1867–70. Born, Lancaster, Ky., April 14, 1822. Died, Feb. 22, 1870.

*LAFAYETTE WASHINGTON CHALFANT, Lawyer, Felicity, O.

A. B. Admitted to the bar. Died, 1847.

*JOHN ROGERS CLARK, Lawyer, Maysville, Ky.

A. B. Admitted to the bar, May 11, 1846. Master Commissioner of Mason Co. (Ky.) Court. Born, Mason Co., Ky., April 29, 1826. Died, Jan. 10, 1865.

ENOCH GEORGE DIAL, Lawyer, Springfield, O.

A. B., A. M. Admitted to the bar. Was president of the Springfield Female College, 4 years. Judge of the Probate Court, 1870–76. Member of the Ohio Legislature, 1879–81.

MIAMI UNIVERSITY.

*THOMAS HAIRE, Lawyer, Cincinnati, O.

A. B. Admitted to the bar. Died, 1846.

JOHN SHERZER HITTELL, Journalist, San Francisco, Cal.

A. B. Was editor of the "Alta Californian." Member of the California Legislature, 1863-64. Author of "Resources of California," seven editions; "History of San Francisco;" "Evidences Against Christianity." Address, 1216 Hyde street.

*VERSALIUS HORR, Lawyer, Urbana, O.

A. B. Clerk of the Court of Champaign Co., 1867-76. Captain, Co. I., 66th O. V. I., U. S. A., 1863. Ohio Military Agent at Louisville, Ky., until 1866. Died, April 29, 1885.

*JAMES W. KERR, Butler Co., O.

A. B. Died, 1843.

WILLIAM BENNET MOORE, Statistician, Washington, D. C.

A. B., A. M. Deputy Fourth Auditor and Acting Fourth Auditor of the U. S. Treasury Department, 1865-81. At present statistician to Registrar of vital statistics of District of Columbia. Trustee of Miami Univ., 1858-63.
Address, Health Department.

EDWARD BRUCE STEVENS, Physician, Lebanon, O.

A. B., A. M. M. D., Ohio Med. Coll., 1846. Assistant Surgeon, U. S. A., 1861-65. Prof. of Materia Medica, Miami Medical Coll., Cincinnati, O., 1865-73; Prof. of Materia Medica, Syracuse Univ., New York, 1873-77. Editor of the "Obstetric Gazette," Cincinnati, O., 1878-83. Delivered annual address before the Miami Union Literary Society, Miami Univ., 1846; before the Alumni Association of Miami Univ, 1848.

*JOHN C. THOMPSON, Teacher, Greenfield, O.

A. B., A. M. Principal of Greenfield (O.) Seminary. Died, 1859.

J. C. TOMLINSON,

A. B. Came to college from Claiborne Co., Miss. Cannot be traced.

*JOHN VAN EATON, Minister, York, N. Y.

A. B., A. M. D. D. Studied theology at Oxford, O. Licensed by Presbytery of Springfield, April, 1846. Ordained by Pres. of Caledonia, Oct. 3, 1849. Pastor of United Pres. churches at Rochester, N. Y., 1849-53; York, N. Y., 1853-80. Born, Xenia, O., Dec. 31, 1817. Died, Clifton Springs, N. Y., March 5, 1880.

*SILAS BAILEY WALKER, Sidney, O.

A. B. Died, 1873.

MIAMI UNIVERSITY. 43

*JOHN MATTHIAS WAMPLER, Minister, Cincinnati, O.

A. B., A. M. Studied theology at Oxford, O. Licensed by the Presbytery of Oxford, April, 1845. Ordained by the Pres. of Indianapolis, Aug. 1848. Pastor of Pres. churches at Shelbyville, Ind., 1847-48; Monticello, Ind., 1848-56. Co-editor of the "Presbyterian of the West," subsequently the "Herald and Presbyter," Cincinnati, O., 1856-70. Pastor of Harmony church, near Oxford, O., 1870-81. Resumed editorial work on the "Herald and Presbyter," 1881-85. Born, Littlestown, Pa., Jan. 20, 1811. Died, Dec. 11, 1885.

JAMES PARK WRIGHT, Minister, Iola, Kan.

A. B., A. M. Studied theology at Oxford. O. Licensed by First Ohio Presbytery, April 21, 1846. Ordained by Michigan Presbytery, May 4, 1850. Pastor of United Pres. churches at Lafayette, Ind., 1849-50; Providence, O., 1850-54; Cedarville, O., 1855-59; Jordan's Grove, Ills., 1860-61; Tipton, Ind., 1862-65; Salem, Ind., 1868-72; Mulberry, Mo., 1873-75; Wakarusa and Auburn, Kan., 1879-81. Teacher at Bloomington, Ind., and Batavia, Ills., 1867. In Freedman's work, Nashville, Tenn., 1876-78. Pastor of Pres. churches, Prairie Home, Ills., 1882-86; Robinson, Ills., 1887; Neosha Falls, Kan., 1888; Pleasanton, Kan., 1889. Retired since 1890.

Class of 1844.

*JOSEPH EVANS ANTHONY, Lawyer, Springfield, O.

A. B. Admitted to the bar and practised law in Springfield, O. Born, Springfield, O., Jan. 26, 1824. Died, Sept. 8, 1847.

WILLIAM BECKETT, Manufacturer, Hamilton, O.

A. B., A. M. Admitted to the bar, 1846. Has been engaged in the manufacture of paper since 1848. Delegate to the Republican Presidential convention, 1860. Trustee of Miami Univ. since 1857. Brother of David C, '60. *Vide*, portrait and sketch, "Miami Journal," Vol. II., No. 8. Address, Fifth and Dayton streets.

*M. A. BROWN, Circleville, O.

A. B. Died about 1846.

*JOHN TREON DUBOIS, Physician, Carlisle, O.

A. B. M. D., Cincinnati Med. Coll., 1846; Jefferson Med. Coll., 1847. Died, March 11, 1849.

JAMES EDMUND GALLOWAY, Merchant, Xenia, O.

A. B. Member of the Montana Legislature, 1866-67. Now retired. Brother of Henry P, '28, and Albert G, '30. Address, Detroit street.

*DAVID HANES, Teacher, Xenia, O.

A. B. Taught school at Rising Sun, Ind., 1844-45; Somerville, Ala., 1845-47; Wheeling, W. Va., 1847-48. Born, Washington Co., Md., June 9, 1820. Died, Dec. 11, 1848.

44   MIAMI UNIVERSITY.

JOHN MCCAMPBELL HERON,   Minister,   Jamestown, O.

A. B., A. M. Studied theology at Oxford. O. Licensed by Springfield Presbytery, May, 1846. Ordained by Caledonia Pres., May 17, 1848. Pastor of United Pres. churches at York, N. Y., 1848-52; Lisbon, N. Y., 1856-57; Burlington Green, N. Y., 1857-58; Thompsonville, Conn., 1858-61; Hartford, Conn., 1864-67. Since then identified with the Board of Home Missions, Philadelphia, Pa., until 1892. Author of "Pocket Manual," and several published sermons.

JAMES DONALDSON LIGGETT,   Minister,   Detroit, Mich.

A. B., A. M. Licensed and ordained. Pastor of Congregational churches at Leavenworth, Kan., 1859-70; Hiawatha, Kan., 1872-78. Editor of "Peninsular Freeman", 1849-51; Xenia (O.) "News," 1852-58. Principal of the Detroit (Mich.) Home and Day school.
Address, 715 Fourth Avenue.

*ROBERT KYLE LONG,   Physician,   Americus, Ind.

A. B. M. D., Western Reserve Coll. Brother of James, '41. Died, 1850.

*SPENCER C. LYONS,   Teacher,   Oxford, O.

A. B. Died, Feb. 19, 1845.

*ALEXANDER W. MCCLANAHAN,   Minister,   Decatur, O.

A. B., A. M. Studied theology at Oxford, O. Licensed by the Presbytery of Chillicothe, 1847. Ordained by the same, 1848. Pastor of United Pres. churches at Decatur, O., 1848-55; Illinois, 1855-57; Decatur, O., 1857-62. Born, West Union, O., Nov. 28, 1821. Died, Oct. 29, 1862.

*WILLIAM SHOTWELL,   Lawyer,   Cadiz, O.

A. B. Admitted to the bar, 1847. Died, Dec. 1, 1849.

*JAMES TORBERT,   ·   Circleville, O.

A. B. Died about 1847.

Class of 1845.

BENJAMIN LOGAN BALDRIDGE,   Minister,   Messina, Cal.

A. B., A. M. Licensed by the Presbytery of Indiana, May, 1848. Ordained by Presbytery of Michigan, Jan. 10, 1851. Pastor of United Pres. churches at Centreville, Mich., 1851-57; Leavenworth, Kan., 1857-66. Chaplain of the Kansas State prison, 2 years. Superintendent of Public Instruction for the city and county of Leavenworth, Kan., 6 years. Appointed Chaplain of U. S. Army, with the rank of Captain, 1876. Retired, 1886.
Address, Messina, San Bernardino Co.

*WILLIAM S. BURROWS,   Lawyer,   Cincinnati, O.

A. B., A. M. Admitted to the bar, Connersville, Ind., Sept. 28, 1846. Editor of a Connersville newspaper for a few years. Removed to Cincinnati, O., 1857, and practised there. Also at the same time conducted a large malt business at Franklin, O. Brother of Thomas A., '47. Born, Franklin, O., 1824. Died, Franklin, O., July 11, 1872.

PASCAL H. CHAMBERS,

A. B., A. M. Came to Miami from Louisville, Ky. Can not be traced.

JOHN GILL CRAVEN,   Minister and Teacher,   Beloit, Kan.

A. B., A. M. Attended Western Baptist Theol. Sem., Covington, Ky. Ordained. 1847. Pastor of the Baptist churches at College Hill, Ind., 1848-61; High Forest and Hamilton, Minn., 1861-63; Mankato, Minn., 1863-67; Pella, Ia., 1867-68. Principal of Eleutherian Institute, College Hill, Ind., 1848-61; of Irving Institute, Irving, Ia., 1869-79. Has since been engaged in Biblical work. Son of Thomas, '42.

*CHARLES DEWEY,   Lawyer,   Fremont, Ia.

A. B., A. M. Admitted to the bar and practised at Terre Haute, Ind. Subsequently removed to Charleston, Ind. Republican candidate for Common Pleas Judge, 1856. Removed to Fremont, Ia., 1859. Born, Charleston, Ind., April 17, 1825. Drowned while swimming in the Missouri river, June 8, 1859.

*JOHN MICHAEL ERLOUGHER,   Physician,   Sims, Ind.

A. B., A. M. M. D., Ohio Med. Coll., 1848. School examiner of Howard Co., Ind., 1855-57. Member of the First Medical Board of Howard Co. Born, July 16, 1817. Died, Sept. 8, 1883.

WASHINGTON FITHIAN,   Physician,   Paris, Ky.

A. B., A. M. M. D. Surgeon of the 14th Ky. Vol. Cavalry, 1861-65.

*JAMES ADAIR FRAZIER,   Minister,   Damascus, Syria.

A. B., A. M. Studied theology at Oxford, O. Licensed by the Michigan Presbytery, April, 1848. Ordained by same, June, 1849. Pastor of the United Pres. church at Martin, Mich., 1849-50. Sailed as a missionary to Syria, Dec. 12, 1850. Returned, 1853. Sailed a second time, Sept. 30, 1854. Returned, 1861. Sailed a third time, Oct. 25, 1862. Born, West Union, O., Jan. 17, 1819. Died, Aug. 30, 1863.

*JAMES SAMUEL GOODE,   Lawyer,   Springfield, O.

A. B., A. M. Admitted to the bar, Jan., 1848. Mayor of Springfield, 1854-56. Prosecuting Attorney of Clarke Co., 1857-68. Judge of the Court of Common Pleas, 1875-85. President of the Mad River National Bank for many years. Trustee of Miami Univ., 1869-78. Died, April 10, 1891.

SAMUEL GRAVES,   Teacher and Farmer,   Rantout, Ills.

A. B., A. M. Engaged in teaching for 21 years in Ohio, Alabama, and Illinois. Author of numerous magazine and newspaper articles. Address, Rantout, Champaign Co.

JOHN WILLIAMSON HERRON,   Lawyer,   Cincinnati, O.

A. B., A. M. L L. D., Miami Univ., 1890. Admitted to the bar, 1848, Cincinnati, O. Member of the Constitutional Convention of Ohio, 1873-74. U. S. Attorney for the Southern District of Ohio since 1889. Member of the Board of Trustees of Miami Univ., since 1860. President of the same since 1880. Law firm, Herron, Gatch & Herron, 62 and 64 West Third Street. *Vide*, sketch and portrait, "Miami Journal," Vol. II, No. 8. Residence address, 69 Pike Street.

*CHARLES HILTS, Lawyer, Cincinnati, O.

A. B., A. M. Admitted to the bar and practised at Cincinnati, O. Died, Dec. 21, 1891.

FIELDING R. A. JETER, Teacher and Farmer, Brookville, Ind.

A. B., A. M. Principal of the Franklin Co. (Ind.) Seminary, 2 years; teacher in common schools, 20 years. Member of the Indiana House of Representatives, one term. Now engaged in farming.

CLARKE KENDALL, Minister, Xenia, O.

A. B., A. M. Studied theology at Oxford, O. Licensed by Springfield Presbytery, April, 1848. Ordained by Lake Presbytery, June 20, 1850. Pastor of United Pres. church at Buffalo, N. Y., 1849–72; of Pres. churches at Bloomingburgh, O., 1872–78; Salem, O., 1878–79. Now retired.

JAMES DOUGLAS KIRKPATRICK, Cotton Factor, Charleston, S. C.

A. B., A. M. L L. B., Harvard Law School, 1848. Never practised, but at once engaged in the business of cotton factor. Served in the C. S. Army.

*WILLIAM CHALMERS LAUGHEAD, Student of Theology, Xenia, O.

A. B. Entered the Theol. Sem. of the Asso. Pres. church, Canonsburg, Pa., Oct., 1845. Taught in Tennessee, 1846–47. Died, Jan. 22, 1849.

*EDWARD CLINTON MERRICK, Washington, D. C.

A. B., A. M. Tutor in the Ohio Wesleyan Univ., 1846–49. Ordained as a minister, Sept., 1849. Pastor of Methodist Episcopal churches at Miamisburg, O., 1849–50; Logan, O., 1850–51. Principal of Coolville (O.) Academy, 1852–54. Prof. of Mathematics and Natural Philosophy, McEndree Coll., Lebanon, Ills., 1854–55. Tutor in Ohio Wesleyan Univ., 1855–57. Resumed preaching for 6 years. Removed to Washington, D. C., 1863, and was there connected with the Internal Revenue, Interior, and Agricultural departments. Author of the Monthly and Annual Agricultural reports. Assistant editor of the Washington "Chronicle" for several years; also of the Washington "World." Died, Dec. 5, 1880.

*ROBERT C. MURPHY, Government Clerk, Washington, D. C.

A. B. Charge at Shanghai, China, for several years previous to the war of the Rebellion. Colonel of the 8th Wisconsin Vol. Inf., 1861–63. Employed in the Department of Agriculture and in the Registry Division of the Washington P. O. Approximate date of death, 1883.

*HENRY CLAY NOBLE, Lawyer, Columbus, O.

A. B., A. M. Admitted to the bar and practised at Columbus, O. Trustee of the Ohio Institution for Education of the Blind, 1866–78. Delivered the Centennial Historical Address, Columbus, O., July 3, 1876. Died, Dec. 12, 1890.

JOSEPH STEWART O'CONNOR, Lawyer, San Antonio, Tex.

A. B. Admitted to the bar, Palmyra, Mo., 1847. Practised at Gonzales, Tex., until 1890, when he removed his law office to San Antonio, Tex. Residence Address, Gonzales, Tex.

JACOB WARWIC OGLE, Farmer, Prairieton, Ind.

A. B., A. M. M. D., Rush Med. Coll., Chicago, Ills., 1863, but never practised. Has been engaged in farming.

*JOHN ORR, Teacher, Xenia, O.

A. B., A. M. Prof. of Languages, Macon Masonic Coll., Tenn.; also president of the same until the beginning of the Civil War, when he removed to Xenia. Clerk of the Court, Greene Co., O., 1862–80. Died, Dec. 30, 1883.

*ROBERT STEVENSON, Teacher, Dayton, O.

A. B., A. M. Engaged in teaching a private school, Dayton, O. Died, Aug. 25, 1860.

*ALGERNON SYDNEY SULLIVAN, Lawyer, New York, N. Y.

A. B.; A. M. Admitted to the bar, 1849. Practised law at Cincinnati, O., 1849–57. Corporate member of the Historical Society of Cincinnati. Delegated by the citizens of Cincinnati to receive Louis Kossuth, 1851. Removed to New York City, 1857. Assistant District Attorney of New York City, 1870-73. Public Administrator of New York City, 1875–85. President of the Southern Society of New York and Vice-President of the Ohio Society of New York. President of the Board of Trustees of New York College of Music. Born, Madison, Ind., April 5, 1826. Died, Dec. 4, 1887.

BENJAMIN CHESTNUT SWAN, Minister, Metropolis, Ills.

A. B., A. M. D. D., Miami Univ., 1888. B. D., Western Theol. Sem., 1848. Licensed by the Oxford Presbytery, June, 1850. Ordained by same April, 1851. Pastor of Pres. churches at Winchester and South Salem, O., 1850–52; Carthage, Ills., 1852–60; Shawneetown, Ills., 1860–68; Carmi, Ills., 1868–77; Enfield, Ills., 1877–83; Harrisburg, Ills., 1883–88; Metropolis, Ills., since 1888. Moderator of the Synod of Illinois, 1876 and 1885. Stated Clerk of Cairo Presbytery since 1876. Term expires, 1894. Chaplain, 131st Ills. Vol. Inf., 1862–63. *Vide*, sketch in Dr. Norton's "History of Presbyterianism in Illinois."

*HENRY TAYLOR, Lumber Merchant, Lafayette, Ind.

A. B. Member of Indiana Legislature, 1870–74. Trustee of Purdue Univ., 1860–70. Died, Oct. 16, 1884.

*FRANCIS M. WELLS, Lawyer, Easton, Penn.

A. B. Died, 1887.

Class of 1846.

HENRY ALSTON BOOTH, Minister, Santa Ana, Cal.

A. B., A. M. Attended Princeton Theol. Sem. Ordained, 1849. Pastor of Des Peres and Feefee Pres. churches, St. Louis Co., Mo., 1849–54; Feefee and Bonhomme churches, 1854–57; Bonhomme church, 1857–85. Retired, 1885.

WILLIAM CARSON, Physician, Cincinnati, O.

A. B., A. M. M. D., Univ. of Pennsylvania, 1850. Physician to St. John's Hospital, Good Samaritan Hospital, Cincinnati Hospital and Episcopal Hospital for Children. Author of a series of articles on diseases of the lungs in Vol. III of Pepper's System of Medicine. Brother of James, '53. Address, 138 East Third street.

WILLIAM H. CHRISTY, Lawyer, Jacksonville, Fla.

A. B., A. M. Admitted to the bar, 1858. Brother of Robert, '47. Address, 57 West Adams street.

*JAMES CLARK, Lawyer, New York, N. Y.

A. B., A. M. L L. B., Cincinnati Coll., 1848. Judge of the Court of Common Pleas, 2nd District of Ohio, 1855-58. Contributor to the New York "Ledger," 1865-82. Died, 1882.

*WILLIAM M. DICKSON, Lawyer, Cincinnati, O.

A. B., A. M. L L. B., Harvard Law School, 1850. Appointed Judge of the Common Pleas Court, Hamilton Co., 1859. Retired from active practice, 1867, and travelled abroad. Trustee of Miami Univ., 1869-75. Killed in an inclined railway accident, October, 1889.

ISAIAH FARIES, Minister, Minneapolis, Minn.

A. B., A. M. Pastor of Pres. churches at Beulah, N. Y., 1852-58; Phelps, N. Y., 1859-65; Minneapolis, Minn., 1878-82. Retired. Address, 327 South Seventh street.

*CHARLES WARD GILMORE, Lawyer, Chillicothe, O.

A. B., A. M. Prosecuting Attorney of Ross Co., O., 1855-67; City Solicitor of Chillicothe, O., 1868-73. Died, Oct. 31, 1873.

*DANIEL D. JONES, Lawyer, Brookville, Ind.

A. B. Admitted to the bar, 1849. Prosecuting Attorney of Franklin Co., Ind. Died, Jan. 1, 1861.

JOSEPH BLOOMFIELD LEAKE, Lawyer, Chicago, Ills.

A. B., A. M. Admitted to the bar, Jan. 16, 1850. Member of the House of Representatives of Iowa, 1861-62. Member of the Iowa Senate, 1862-65. Captain, Co. G, 20th Iowa Vol. Inf., U. S. A., 1862. Lieutenant-Colonel of same, 1862-65. Brevet-Colonel and Brevet-Brigadier-General, U. S. Volunteers, March, 1865. Prosecuting Attorney of Scott Co., Ia., 1866-71. President of the Board of Education, Davenport, Ia., 1868-71. U. S. Attorney for the Northern District of Illinois, 1879-84. Attorney for the Board of Education, Chicago, Ills., 1887-91. Address, 218 Cass Street.

*HENRY L. MCGUIRE, Minister, Richmond, Ind.

A. B., A. M. Attended Princeton Theol. Sem. Pastor of Pres. church at Richmond, Ind., 1852-53. Died, Sept. 4, 1853.

*GAVIN RILEY MCMILLAN, Minister, Cedarville, O.

A. B., A. M. Pastor of Pres. churches at New Castle, Pa., 1851-59; Brooklyn, N. Y., 1859-62. Principal of the Union Female Seminary, Xenia, O., 1863-64. Died, Jan. 9, 1865.

ISAAC W. MONFORT, Minister, Denver, Col.

A. B., A. M. Licensed by the Whitewater Presbytery, Sept. 11, 1850. Pastor of Pres. churches at Liberty, Ind., 1850-59; Independence, Kan., 1877-81; Athens, O., 1882-89. Stated supply at Pleasant Ridge, O., 1860; Greenfield and Tipton, Ind., 1867-70; Minneapolis, Minn., 1871-72; Cambridge City, Ind., 1874-75; Pueblo, Col., 1876; Denver, Col., 1877. Chaplain of the 52nd Ind. Vol. Inf., U. S. A., 1861-62. Military and Claim Agent for Indiana, Washington, D. C., 1863-66. Western Secretary of the American Tract Society, 1873. Retired, 1889. Address, 2435 Grant Avenue.

MARION MORRISON, Minister, Starkville, Miss.

A. B., A. M. D. D., Monmouth Coll. Licensed by the Chillicothe Presbytery, April 30, 1849. Ordained by the same, Aug. 21, 1850. Pastor of United Pres. church, Tranquillity, O., 1850-56. Prof. of Mathematics, Monmouth Coll., 1856-62. Editor of the "Western United Presbyterian," 3 years. Chaplain, 9th Ills. Vol. Inf., U. S. A., 1863-64. Pastor of U. P. churches at Fairfield, Ills., 1866-70; College Springs, 1871-76; Mission Creek, Neb., 1878-91. Author of the "Life of Rev. David McDill," 1874, and "History of the Ninth Regiment, Illinois Volunteers."

*HARVEY JOAB SHIRK, Lawyer, Peru, Ind.

A. B., A. M. Admitted to the bar, 1850. Attorney for the First National Bank, Peru, Ind. Died, Sept. 12, 1889.

*WARREN STAGG, Minister, Chicago, Ills.

A. B., A. M. B. D., Lane Sem., 1849. Died, 1862.

*ROBERT EWING STEWART, Minister, Sugar Creek, O.

A. B., A. M. Licensed by the Indiana Presbytery, April 4, 1849. Ordained by the same, April 8, 1850. Pastor of United Pres. churches at Vienna and Shiloh, Ind., 1850-55; Sugar Creek, O., 1856-60. Born, New Richmond, O., Dec. 23, 1825. Died, Oct. 16, 1860.

*HIRAM STRONG, Lawyer, Dayton, O.

A. B., A. M. Admitted to the bar, 1849. Practised law at Dayton, O. Lieutenant-Colonel, 93rd Ohio Vol. Inf., U. S. A., 1861-62. Colonel of the same, 1862-63. Mortally wounded at the battle of Chickamauga, Sept. 19, 1863. Died, Nashville, Tenn., Oct. 7, 1863.

*David ALEXANDER WALLACE, Minister, Wooster, O.

A. B., A. M. D. D. LL. D. Licensed by the Second Ohio Presbytery, April 10, 1849. Ordained, June 3, 1851. Pastor of United Pres. churches at Fall River, Mass., 1851-54; East Boston, Mass., 1854-56; Monmouth, Ills., 1856-68; Henderson, Ills., 1874-75; Wooster, O., 1878-83. President of Muskingum Coll., 1846-49; of Monmouth Coll., 1856-78. Trustee of Wooster Univ. and Allegheny Theol. Sem. Born, Guernsey Co., O., June 16, 1826. Died, Oct. 21, 1883.

Class of 1847.

JOHN CLINTON BONHAM, Minister, Westport, Mo.

A. B., A. M. Teacher in Bonham's Seminary, St. Louis, Mo., 1863-72. Pastor of the First Baptist churches at Decatur, Ills., 1872-76; Kansas City, Mo., 1876-79. Resigned on account of ill-health. Brother of Louis N, '55.

MIAMI UNIVERSITY.

*THOMAS ASHTON BURROWES,   Teacher,   Springfield, O.

A. B., A. M. Organized the Cincinnati Female Seminary and served as Principal, 1850-60. Moved to Springfield and engaged in the insurance business. Died, May 7, 1889.

ROBERT CHRISTY,   Lawyer,   Washington, D. C.

A. B., A. M. Admitted to the bar, Hamilton, O., 1853. Member of the Ohio House of Representatives, 1857-58. Author of "Proverbs and Phases of All Ages." Brother of Wm. H, '46. Address, 1606 Seventeenth street W. N. W.

LAWRENCE GANO HAY,   Minister,   Minneapolis, Minn.

A. B., A. M. D. D., Olivet Coll., 1876. B. D.. Princeton Theol. Sem., 1850. Ordained, Trenton, N. J., 1850. Sailed, Aug. 8, 1850, as missionary to India. Superintendent of Mission Press at Allahabad, India, 1850-58. Returned to this country, 1858, and lectured in the principal cities of the U. S. Organized the 9th Pres. church, Indianapolis, Ind. President of Coates Coll., Terre Haute, Ind., 1885-88. Address, 45 Fifteenth street, N.

*JEROME T. GILLET,   Minister,   Madison, Ind.

A. B. Drowned at sea, 1850.

*JOHN MCMILLAN,   Minister,   Philadelphia, Pa.

A. B., A. M. D. D., Washington and Jefferson Coll. Studied theology in Philadelphia, Pa., and Edinburgh, Scotland. Pastor of Pres. churches at Dundee, Ills.; Allegheny, Pa.; Mount Pleasant, Pa.; and Philadelphia, Pa. Brother of Gavin R, '46, and Robert, '54. Died, Nantucket Island, 1884.

WILLIAM.JOHN MOLYNEAUX,   Lawyer,   New York, N. Y.

A. B., A. M. Admitted to the bar, 1849. Practised in Charleston, S. Car., for several years. Removed to New York, 1888.

MELANCTHON WADE OLIVER,   Lawyer,   Cincinnati, O.

A. B. A. M. Judge of the Common Pleas Court, Hamilton Co., 1856-66. Member of the Ohio Legislature, 1873-75. Alderman of the city of Cincinnati, 1880-82. Trustee of Miami Univ., since 1872. *Vide*, sketch and portrait, "Miami Journal," Vol. II, No. 8. Address, Price Hill.

*WILLIAM K. OSBORNE,   Teacher,   San Francisco, Cal.

A. B., A. M. Principal of a Classical School at San Francisco, Cal., 1852-57. Died, 1858.

*ALEXANDER STERRETT,   Minister,   Kansas City, Kan.

A. B., A. M. B. D., New Albany Theol. Sem., 1850. Ordained by the Presbytery of Evansville, Ind., 1851. Pastor of Pres. churches at Harmony Landing, Ky., 1850-51; Evansville, Ind., 1851-65; Washington, Ind., 1871-72; Terre Haute, Ind., 1872-79. Home Missionary at Manhattan, Kan., 1865-69; Wamego, Kan., 1880-82; Kansas City, Kan., 1882-83. Born, Wayne Co., Ind., Sept. 28, 1821. Died, Sept. 25, 1885.

CHARLES STEWART, Manufacturer, Easton, Pa.

A. B., A. M. M. D., Univ. of Penn., 1853, but never practised. Director of the Thomas Iron Co., Hokendauga, Pa.; of the Warren Foundry and Machine works, Phillipsburg, N. J. Address, 123 North Second street.

Class of 1848.

*ELI BOOTH, Lawyer, Dayton, O.

A. B., A. M. Admitted to the bar and practised at Dayton, O. Died, 1860.

*JOSEPH BRADY, Teacher, Contreras, O.

A. B., A. M. Admitted to the bar, 1850, but practised for a short time only. Principal of Public Schools at Lexington, Ky.; New Castle, Ind.; Connersville, Ind. On account of failing health he was committed to Longview Asylum in 1864, where he died, May 24, 1867.

JAMES MANNING CORY, General Business, Fresno, Cal.

A. B., A. M. Member of the California Legislature. Engaged in Real Estate, Loan and Insurance business. Brother of Benjamin, '42, and Andrew J, '55.

*JOHN CROZIER, Minister, Remington, Ind.

A. B., A. M. B. D., New Albany Theol. Sem., 1851. Ordained by the Presbytery of Palestine, Ills., 1852. Pastor of Pres. churches at Palestine, Ills.,1851-52; Charleston,Ind.,1852-53; Iowa City, Ia., 1853-54; Palestine,Ills., 1854-55; Olney, Ills., 1857-66; Oxford, O., 1867-69; North Sangamon, Ills., 1869-80; Olney, Ills., 1880-83; Taylor's Falls, Minn., 1883-85; Tama and Toledo, Ia., 1885-88; Tolono, Ills., 1888-91. General Fiscal Agent for the Board of Home Missions for the Synods north of Ohio, 1855-57. Born, Manchester, O., Aug. 27, 1822. Died, Dec. 24, 1891.

*JOHN WILSON DRAKE, Minister, Bluffton, Ind.

A. B., A. M. B. D., New Albany Theol. Sem., 1851. Ordained, 1852. Pastor of Pres. churches at Marysville, O., 1852-65; Union City, Ind., 1865-72; Bluffton, Ind., 1872-75. Died, April 19, 1875.

SAMUEL SPAHR LAWS, Minister and Teacher, Kansas City, Mo.

A. B., A. M. B. D., Princeton Theol. Sem., 1851. L L. B., Columbia Law School, 1869. M. D., Bellevue Med. Coll., 1874. L L. D., Westminster Coll., 1869. Prof. of Physics in Westminster Coll., 1853-54. President of the same, 1854-61. President of Missouri State Univ., 1876-89. Visitor to West Point since 1881. Address, Centropolis Hotel.

*ISAIAH LITTLE, Editor, Glenwood, Ind.

A. B., A. M. Editor of the Fayette Co., Ind., "Gazette," 1849-51. Died, March 9, 1852.

JAMES R. MCARTHUR,

A. B., A. M. Cannot be traced.

ALGERNON SIDNEY STEVENS, Physician, King's Mills, O.

A. B., A. M. Was graduated from the Med. Coll. of Ohio. Acting Assistant Surgeon, U. S. A., 1861-65. Brother of Edward Bruce, '43.

Class of 1849.

JAMES B. COMBS, Physician, Washington, Iowa.

A. B., A. M. M. D., Ohio Med. Coll. Retired.

*THOMAS CHALMERS HEARNE, Teacher, Chillicothe, O.

A. B., A. M. Principal of Female Seminary, Chillicothe, O. Died, Feb. 27, 1865.

ROBERT MORRISON, Minister and Teacher, Fulton, Mo.

A. B., A. M. B. D., Princeton Theol. Sem., 1853. Principal of Academies at Poplar Grove, Tenn., 1850-52; Westminster, O., 1869-75. Financial Agent of Westminster Coll., 1879-81. Editor of "Presbyterian Herald," Louisville, Ky., 1854-60; of the "True Presbyterian," 1862-63. Pastor of Pres. churches at Penn Run, Pa., 1854-60; Waterford, O., 1868-77; Potosi, Md., 1877-80; Aurora Springs, Mo., 1880-91. A founder of the Phi Delta Theta Fraternity, 1848.

JAMES NESBIT SWAN, Minister, Calcutta, O.

A. B., A M. B. D., New Albany Theol. Sem., 1851. Ordained, 1852. Pastor of Pres. churches at Columbia City, Ind., 1852-60; Yellow Creek, O., 1860-74; New Hagerstown, O., 1875-80; Calcutta, O., 1881—.

*JOHN J. TIFFANY, Minister, Urbana, O.

A. B., A. M. Pres. minister. Died, 1859.

*CHARLES WATERMAN, Student of Law, Lebanon, O.

A. B. Died, 1851.

*JOHN MCMILLAN WILSON, Minister and Teacher, Benton, Ills.

A. B., A. M. Studied theology, Oxford, O., 1852. Principal of Academy, Morning Sun, O., 1856-60. Managing editor of the "Banner of the Covenant," 1860-61. Member of the Ohio National Guards, 1861-65. Pastor of Pres. church, College Corner, O., 1866-71. Loan Agent, Mt. Vernon, Ills., 1871-74. A founder of the Phi Delta Theta fraternity, 1848. Died, July 19, 1874.

Class of 1850.

ANDREW MEANS BROOKS, Teacher, Springfield, Ills.

A. B., A. M. Ph. D., Wooster Univ., 1878. Admitted to the bar, 1854. Superintendent of Public Schools, Springfield, Ills.

MIAMI UNIVERSITY. 53

*ROBERT THOMPSON DRAKE, Minister, New Castle, Ind.

A. B., A. M. B. D., Princeton Theol. Sem., 1854. Pastor of Pres. churches at Des Moines, Ia., 1855-60; Troy, O., 1860-66; Winchester. O., 1867-68; Newport, Ky., 1868-70; Dayton, O., 1870-72; New Castle, Ind., 1873. A founder of the Phi Delta Theta fraternity, 1848. Died, March 19, 1873.

*BENJAMIN DIVANIA FURROW, Farmer, Piqua, O.

A. B. Read law after graduation but abandoned it on account of ill-health. In the government survey in Kansas, 1854-67. Born, Piqua, O., 1823. Died, March 4, 1890.

*MATTHEW HUESTON, Lawyer, Hamilton, O.

A. B., A. M. Admitted to the bar. Deputy Treasurer of Butler county. Died, 1872.

ABNER S. LATHROP, Lawyer, Dallas, Tex.

A. B., A. M. Member of the Texas Legislature, 1876-77. Judge of the Northern district of Texas. Now Master in Chancery in the U. S. Circuit Court.
Address, 240 Main street.

JOHN WOLFE LINDLEY, Teacher and Farmer, Fredericktown, O.

A. B., A. M. Prof. in Academy, New Hagerstown, O., 1850-52. Principal of Academy, Poplar Grove, Tenn., 1852-53. Prof. in Richmond, (O.) Coll., 1853-55. Principal of Female Institutes, Charleston, Ind., 1855-61; Paducah, Ky., 1861-63. Now farmer and Justice of the Peace. A founder of the Phi Delta Theta fraternity, 1848.

JOHN MILLER TREMBLY, Physician, Woods, O.

A. B., A. M. Admitted to the bar, 1856, but never practised. Has practised medicine for 25 years.

Class of 1851.

ALLEN AUGUSTUS BARNETT, Physician, Jerseyville, Ills.

A. B., A. M. M. D., Louisville Med. Coll., 1853.
Address, 309 North Washington street.

*CHARLES W. H. CATHCART, Teacher, Urbana, O.

A. B., A. M. Died about 6 years ago.

GEORGE CRANE, Lawyer, Dubuque, Ia.

A. B., A. M. Admitted to the bar. Attorney for the Illinois Central R. R. Co., for many years. Postmaster at Dubuque, Ia., 1881-85; 1891—.

JOHN MCKNIGHT LAYMAN, Minister, Piqua, O.

A. B., A. M. B. D., Princeton Theol. Sem., 1853. Stated Supply of Pres. churches at Hicksville, O., 15 years; Union, O., 7 years; and Gilead, O., 2 years. Now retired.

54   MIAMI UNIVERSITY.

THOMAS NELSON HASKELL,   Minister,   Denver, Col.

A. B., A. M. Licensed and ordained by the Presbyterian church. Pastor of Pres. churches at Washington, D. C., 1854-58; Boston, Mass., 1858-66. Prof. of Logic, Literature, and Political Economy, Univ. of Wisconsin, 1866-73. Founded Colorado College, 1874. Author of "Volume of Sermons," "Soldier's Mission," "Life of Sir Henry Havelock," "Echoes of Inspired Ages," "Civil Ethics in the United States," "Lives and Wives of the Presidents," "Domestic Poems," 1889; "Young Konkaput, the King of the Utes, a Legend of Twin Lakes," 1889; a reply to Ridpath's eulogy of Jefferson Davis; frequent contributor to current reviews. Address, 1643 Sherman Avenue.

*JAMES A. LOWRIE,   Lawyer,   Denver, Col.

A., B., A. M. Admitted to the bar. Brother of Samuel T, '52. Died, about 1886.

*SAMUEL R. MATTHEWS,   Lawyer,   Cincinnati, O.

A. B., A. M. Admitted to the bar. Judge of the Court of Common Pleas of Hamilton Co., O., 1883-88. Died, Dec., 1891.

*WALTER B. PEASE,   U. S. Army Officer,   Dayton, O.

A. B., A. M. Died, about 1873.

ANDREW WATTS ROGERS,   Lawyer,   Warrensburg, Mo.

A. B., A. M. Admitted to the bar, 1853. Major, Lieutenant-Colonel, and Colonel of the 81st Ills. Vol. Inf., 1862-65. Prosecuting Attorney of Johnson Co., Mo., 1873-74. Special Judge of Circuit and Criminal Courts. Member of the General Assembly of Mo., 1883-84. President of the Board of Regents of State Normal School, Mo., 1890—. Member of the Deepwater Convention, Topeka, Kan., 1889. A founder of the Phi Delta Theta fraternity, 1848.

*ARDIVAN WALKER ROGERS,   Teacher,   Brighton, Ia.

A. B., A. M. Teacher of public school at Piqua, O., 1853 and 1855; St. Mary's. O., 1854. A founder of the Phi Delta Theta fraternity, 1848. Born, Piqua, O., Oct. 20, 1824. Died. Dec. 11, 1856.

*WILLIAM WRIGHT,   Minister,   Grand Rapids, O.

A. B., A. M. Studied theology, Oxford, O. Licensed by Springfield Presbytery, 1853. Ordained by Sidney Presbytery, April 18, 1854. Pastor of United Pres. churches at Quincy, Springhill and Bethel, O., 1854-58; Hopewell, Ills., 1859-63; Grand Rapids, Wood Co., O., 1868-73. Died, March 24, 1873.

Class of 1852.

*JOHN STEWART BAKER,   Lawyer,   Cincinnati, O.

A. B., A. M. L L. B., Cincinnati Law School, 1858. Abandoned the law after two years' practice on account of ill-health. Born, Cincinnati, O., April 19, 1834. Died, Aug. 24, 1878.

MIAMI UNIVERSITY.   55

JOHN KNOX BOUDE,   Physician,   Washington, D. C.

A. B., A. M. M. D., Univ. of Pa., 1857. Practised at Carthage, Ills., 1857-81. Assistant Surgeon, 118th Ills. Vol. Inf., 1862-65. U. S. Examining Surgeon for Pensions, 1866-81. Medical Examiner and Assistant Medical Referee, Bureau of Pensions, Washington, D. C.
Address, 905 R St., N. W.

*JAMES H. CHILDS,   Manufacturer,   Pittsburg, Pa.

A. B. Civil Engineer, Pittsburg & Connelsville R. R., 1853-54. Wholesale Dry Goods merchant, Pittsburg, Pa., 1857-59. Manufacturer of cotton goods, Pittsburg, Pa., 1859-62. First Lieutenant, Co. K., 12th Pa. Inf., U. S. A., April 25 to Oct. 18, 1861. Lieutenant-Colonel, 4th Pa. Cavalry, Oct. 18 to March 12, 1862. Colonel of same, March 12 to Sept. 17, 1862. Killed in the battle of Antietam, Sept. 17, 1862.

JOHN PURDY CRAIGHEAD,   Lawyer,   New York, N. Y.

A. B., A. M. Admitted to the bar, Baltimore, Md., 1860. Now engaged in newspaper advertising. Residence, 107 Ocean avenue, Jersey City, N. J.
Address, Tribune Building.

HARMAR DENNY,   Catholic Priest,   New York, N. Y.

A. B., A. M. Studied theology at London and at Rome, The Collegio Pio. Ordained, 1860. Assistant pastor in churches of Baltimore, Md.; Washington, D. C.; and New York City. Now in the College of S. Francis Xavier. Member of the Society of Jesus.
Address, 30 West 16th street.

BENJAMIN HARRISON,   Lawyer,   Washington, D. C.

A. B., A. M. L L. D., Miami Univ., 1888; Coll. of New Jersey, 1889. Admitted to the bar, 1854. Practised law at Indianapolis, Ind., 1854-89. Reporter of the Supreme Court of Indiana, 1860-62 and 1864-68. Was commissioned as Second Lieutenant of Ind. Vol., July, 1862. Raised Company A of the 70th Ind. Vol. Inf., and was commissioned Captain and later Colonel, 1862-65. Brevetted Brigadier-General, Feb., 1865. Republican candidate for Governor of Ind., 1876. Appointed a member of the Mississippi River Commission, 1879. U. S. Senator from Indiana, 1881-87. President of the U. S., 1889—. Author of Indiana Supreme Court reports, Vols. 15-17 and 23-29; "Digest of Indiana Reports," three vols.

*JAMES ANDERSON HUGHES, Student of Theology, Somerville, O.

A. B. Attended Pres. Theol. Sem. Died, 1854.

ANTHONY CANNON JUNKIN,   Minister,   Westminster, Cal.

A. B., A. M. Studied theology at Oxford, O. Licensed, April 7, 1854. Ordained, May 6, 1856. Labored as an evangelist, 1856-59. Pastor of Pres. churches at Greenville, Pa., 1859-67; R. R. Creek, Del., 1868-71; Dayton, O., 1873-78; Connersville, Ind., 1878-85; Missionary in Kansas, 1885-88; Westminster, Cal., 1888—.

*ISAAC STANLEY LANE,   · Lawyer,   Ogden, Ind.

A. B., A. M. Admitted to the bar and practised for several years at Memphis, Tenn. Died, April 16, 1859.

SAMUEL THOMPSON LOWRIE, Minister, Philadelphia, Pa.

A. B., A. M. D. D., Washington and Jefferson Coll., 1875. B. D., Western Theol. Sem., 1856. Matriculated in the Univ. of Heidelberg, Germany, 1856; Univ. of Berlin, 1863. Licensed by the Presbytery of Ohio, Jan. 1856. Ordained, 1858. Pastor of Pres. churches at Alexandria, Pa., 1858–63; Philadelphia, Pa., 1865–69; Abington, Pa., 1869–74; Ewing, N. J., 1879–85; Co-Pastor Wylie Memorial church, Philadelphia, Pa., 1891—. Prof. of New Testament Literature and Exegesis, Western Theol. Sem., Allegheny, 1874–78. Chaplain of the Pres. Hospital, Philadelphia, Pa., 1886–89. Principal translator of the Commentaries on Isaiah and Numbers in Lange—Schaff Bible work. Author of "An Explanation of the Epistles to the Hebrews," 1884. Translator of "Beyond the Sea," 1885, and "The Lord's Supper," 1888.
Address, 2104 Pine street.

DAVID MORROW, Minister, Oakland, Cal.

A. B., A. M. Studied theology at Oxford, O. Licensed by the Michigan Presbytery, May 11, 1854. Ordained by same, June 20, 1857. Pastor of United Pres. churches at Murray and Warren, Ind., 1857–63; Roseville, Cal., 1873–76. Home Missionary. Brother of Joseph A, '58.
Address, 1015 Twenty-first street.

WILLIAM HAZLETT PRESTLEY, Minister, Kankakee, Ills.

A. B., A. M. Studied theology at Oxford, O. Licensed by First Ohio Presbytery, 1854. Ordained by Big Spring Presbytery, 1855. Pastor of Pres. churches at Chillicothe, O., 1856–74; Tuscola, Ills., 1874–76; Decatur, Ills., 1876–89; Kankakee, Ills., 1890—.

LEWIS WILLIAMS ROSS, Lawyer, Council Bluffs, Ia.

A. B., A. M. Admitted to the bar. State Senator of Iowa, 1864–68. Trustee of Iowa State Univ., 1864–70; Regent of same, 1874–80. Chancellor of the Law Department of Iowa State Univ., 1880–87. Firm name, Ross & Ross, 203–204 Merriam Block.

MILTON SAYLER, Lawyer, New York, N. Y.

A. B., A. M. L L. B., Cincinnati Law School. Principal of the Preparatory Department, Miami Univ., 1852–53. Practised at Cincinnati, O., for a number of years. Member Ohio Legislature, 1862–63. U. S. Representative from Ohio, 1873–79; elected Speaker pro. tem, 1876. Author (with Swan) of Supplement to the Revised Statutes of Ohio. Brother of Nelson, '57, and J. Riner, '60.
Address, 316 West Twenty-third street.

DAVID SWING, Minister, Chicago, Ills.

A. B., A. M. Studied theology at Cincinnati, O., 1852–53. Principal of the Preparatory Department, Miami Univ., 1853–66. Pastor of Pres. church at Chicago, Ill., 1866–75. Organized the Central church of Chicago, 1876, and has since acted as its pastor.
Address, 66 Lake Shore Drive.

*JOSEPH WALKER, Minister, Zanesville, O.

A. B., A. M. Studied theology at Newburgh and Allegheny. Licensed by the Second Asso. Ref. Presbytery of Ohio, 1855. Prof. of Mathematics in Madison Coll., 1856–59; and the same in Muskingum Coll., 1859–61. Ordained, 1862. Pastor of United Pres. church at Cedar Rapids, Ia., 1861–62. Resumed the professorship of Mathematics in Muskingum Coll., 1862, retained it until his death. Born, Adams Co., Pa., March 24, 1827. Died, Dec. 17, 1869.

Class of 1853.

JOHN ALEXANDER ANDERSON,   Minister,   Manhattan, Kan.

A. B., A. M.   B. D., New Albany Theol. Sem., 1857. Pastor of Pres. church at Stockton, Cal., 1857-62. Chaplain of 3rd Cal. Vol. Inf., U. S. A., 1862-63. First Relief agent, 3rd Army Corps, U. S. Sanitary Commission, 1863-67. Pastor of Pres. church at Junction City, Kan., 1868-73. President of State Agricultural Coll., Manhattan, Kan., 1873-78. Member U. S. House of Representatives, 1879-91. U. S. Agent and Consul-General, Cairo, Egypt, 1891—. Son of President Rev. Wm. C. Anderson, D. D.

*GIBSON ATHERTON,   Lawyer,   Newark, O.

A. B., A. M. Admitted to the bar, 1855. Principal of Academy, Osceola, Mo., 1853-54. Prosecuting Attorney of Licking Co., O., 1857-64. Mayor of Newark, O., 3 years. Member of U. S. House of Representatives, 1879-83. Judge of the Supreme Court of Ohio, 1885-87. Died, Nov. 12, 1887.

JAMES HALL BROOKES,   Minister,   St. Louis, Mo.

A. B., A. M. D. D., Westminster Coll. B. D., Princeton Theol. Sem., 1854. Ordained by the Presbytery of Miami, April, 1854. Pastor of Pres. churches at Dayton, O., 1854-58; St. Louis, Mo., 1858—. Editor of the "Truth," St. Louis, Mo., 1874—. Author of "Till He Come," "Mystery of Suffering," "Did Jesus Rise?" "Marantha, or the Lord Cometh," "Is the Bible True?" "Is the Bible Inspired?" "Israel and the Church," "The Way Made Plain," "From Death Unto Life," etc. Address, 4429 Pine street.

WILLIAM MONTGOMERY BURGOYNE   Merchant,   Cincinnati, O.

A. B., A. M. At present connected with the National Insurance Co., Cincinnati, O. Address, 69 West Third street.

*CALEB DUNN CALDWELL,   Merchant,   Zanesville, O.

A. B., A. M. Auditor of Muskingum Co., 1855-71. Wounded by Quantrill's Guerillas, Lawrence, Kan., 1864. Died, Sept. 6, 1871.

*JAMES CARSON,   Lawyer,   Omaha, Neb.

A. B., A. M. Principal of Academy, Chillicothe, O., 1848-51. Admitted to the bar, 1855. Practised law at Des Moines, Ia., 1855-57; Omaha, Neb., 1857-59. Brother of William, '46. Died, Aug. 25, 1859.

ANDREW GOWDY CHAMBERS,   Minister,   Freehold, N. J.

A. B., A. M. Principal of Normal School, Miami Univ., 1853-56. Superintendent of Public Schools, Piqua, O., 1856-60. B. D., Princeton Theol. Sem., 1864. Pastor of Pres. church, New York, N. Y., 1864-65. Prof. of Mathematics and Astronomy, Mt. Auburn Female Seminary, 1865-66. Superintendent of Ohio Female Coll., 1866-68. Principal and Proprietor of Freehold Institute, 1868—.

JAMES HUTCHINSON CLARK,   Minister,   Mound Valley, Kan.

A. B., A. M. Attended Danville, Ky., Theol. Sem. Ordained, 1857. Pastor of Pres. churches at Carlisle, O.; Council Bluffs, Ia.; Warrensburg, Mo.; Emporia, Kan.; Santa Ana, Cal., and Mound Valley, Kan.

PIERSON CORY CONKLIN, Lawyer, Hamilton, O.

A. B., A. M. L L. B., Cincinnati Law School, 1855. City Solicitor of Hamilton, O., 1860-64.
Address, 27 B street.

THOMAS ARTEMAS FULLERTON, Minister, Georgetown, D. C.

A. B., A. M. D. D., Wooster Univ., 1872. Admitted to the bar and practised law, 1855-60. Chaplain 17th Ohio Vol. Inf., 1861-62. Attended Princeton Theol. Sem., 1860-64. Licensed and ordained, 1864. Pastor of Pres. churches at Walnut Hills, Cincinnati, O., 1864-66; Springfield, O., 1866-70; Erie, Pa., 1872-84; Georgetown, D. C., 1884—. Prof. of English Literature, Wooster Univ., 1870-72. Brother of George H., '58.
Address, 3121 P. street.

ROBERT CHRISTY GALBRAITH, Minister, Chillicothe, O.

A. B., A. M. B. D., Princeton Theol. Sem. D. D., Parsons Coll. Pastor Pres. churches at Lancaster, O.; Concord, O.; Chillicothe, O. Chaplain, Ohio Vol. Inf., U. S. A., 4 months. Chaplain, Ohio Reform Farm, Lancaster, O., 4 years. Author of "History of Presbytery of Chillicothe."

HENRY THOMAS HELM, Lawyer, Chicago, Ills.

A. B., A. M. Admitted to the bar, 1854. Has practised in Chicago, Ills., since 1854. Author of "American Roadster and Trotting Horse," and "Election and Rejection,"
Address, 189 La Salle street.

*SAMUEL HIBBEN, Minister, Peoria, Ills.

A. B., A. M. B. D., Danville Theol. Sem., 1858. Principal of Academy, Bardstown, Ky., 1853-55. Pastor of Pres. churches at Eckmansville, O., 1858-59; Peoria, Ills., 1859-62. Chaplain, 4th Ill. Cav., 1861-62. Born, Hillsboro, O., Jan. 31, 1834. Died, June 10, 1862.

*JAMES HOLMES, Minister, Allegheny, Pa.

A. B., A. M. Studied theology at Oxford, O. Licensed by Springfield Presbytery, April, 1854. Ordained by Monongahela Presbytery, May 3, 1855. Pastor of United Pres. church at Allegheny, Pa., 1855-57. Died, Jan. 14, 1857.

WILLIAM HARRISON HONNELL, Minister, St. John, Kan.

A. B., A. M. B. D., Danville Theol. Sem., 1856. Has been continuonsly engaged in Home Missionary work for the Presbyterian church in Kentucky, Ohio and Kansas. Captain and Chaplain, 1st Kentucky Vol. Cav., 1861-65. Author of adventures in the army, among the Indians, and in Home Mission life.

FRANKLIN M. HUNT, Farmer, Elston, Ind.

A. B., A. M. At present business manager of Woodlawn Sanitarium, Elston, Ind. Brother of John S., '53.
Address, Elston, care Lafayette, Ind.

*JOHN SEABURY HUNT, Accountant, Eaton, O.

A. B. Auditor of the Chicago and Great Eastern R. R. Co. Auditor and General Ticket Agent of the Evansville, Terre Haute and Chicago R. R. Co. Brother of Franklin M, '53. Died, Sept. 1, 1885.

MIAMI UNIVERSITY.	59

SAMUEL C. KERR,	Minister,	Lyndon, O.

A. B., A. M. B. D., New Albany Theol. Sem., 1856. Ordained by the Presbytery of Oxford, 1862. Licentiate, Sigourney, Ia., 1859-62; Amanda, O., 1860-61; Dunlapsville, Ind., 1861-62. Pastor of Pres. churches at Harrison, O., 1862-65; St. Mary's, O., 1865-68; Bloomville, O., 1868-72; Lyndon, O., 1872—. Author of "The Jewish Church in Its Relations to the Jewish Nation and the Gentiles," and "The Primary Ideas of Biblical Science."

JEREMIAH PROPHET ELIAS KUMLER,	Minister,	Pittsburg, Pa.

A. B., A. M. B. D., Lane Seminary, 1856. D. D., Marietta Coll. Ordained by the Dayton Presbytery, April, 1857. Pastor of Pres. churches at Greenville, O., 1856-60; Oxford, O., 1860-68; Evansville, Ind., 1868-71; Indianapolis, Ind., 1871-75; Cincinnati, O., 1875-84; Pittsburg, Pa., 1884—. Member and president of the Board of Trustees of the Western Female Seminary, Oxford, O.
Address, 413 Highland avenue.

*JACOB DERRICK LOWE,	Lawyer,	Dayton, O.

A. B., A. M. Admitted to the bar, 1855. Brother of William B, '55. Born, Dayton, O., Sept. 13, 1833. Died, March 12, 1859.

JOSEPH HENRY MARSHALL,	Minister,	Mediapolis, Ia.

A. B., A. M. B. D., Danville Theol. Sem. Ordained, 1858. Pastor and Home Missionary of Pres. churches at Mt. Sterling, Ills., 1855-57 and 1865-70; Woodhull, Ills., 1857-62; Doddsville, Ills., 1862-65; Kirkwood, Ills., 1870-74; Hamilton, Ills., 1874-79; Quincy, Ills., 1879-80; Knoxville, Ia., 1880-83; Burlington, Kan., 1883-86; Kingman, Kan., 1886-87; Wythe, Ills., 1887-90; Mediapolis, Ia., 1890—.

ALEXANDER CALDWELL MCCLURG,	Publisher,	Chicago, Ills.

A. B., A. M. Entered the U. S. Army as a private in the 88th Ills. Vol. Inf., 1862. Promoted to Captain and A. A. G. Mustered out as chief of staff of the 14th Army Corps and Brevet-Brigadier-General. Publisher and Bookseller, Chicago, Ills. Contributor to the "Atlantic Magazine." Author of "Memorial of Jefferson C. Davis."
Residence, 60 Lake Shore Drive.

JAMES WILSON MCDILL,	Lawyer,	Creston, Ia.

A. B., A. M. Teacher in academy, Koputh, Iowa, 1853-54. Admitted to the bar, Akron, O., 1856. Practised law, Afton, Ia., 1857-85. Elected County Judge of Union Co., Ia., 1858; County Superintendent of Schools, 1860. Appointed Secretary of the Senate Committe on D. of C., 1861; clerk in the Treasury Department, 1862-65. Elected Circuit Judge of Union Co., Ia., 1868; District Judge, 1870. Member of the U. S. House of Representatives, 1873-77. Commissioner of Railroads in Iowa, 1879-81 and 1883-86. U. S. Senator, 1881-83. Member of the Inter-state Commerce Commission, Washington, D. C., 1892—. Son of John, '29.

*ANDREW JAMES MCMILLAN,	Minister,	Ravenswood, W. Va.

A. B. Licensed and ordained a minister in the Pres. church. Pastor at Norwich, O., 1857-59; Shelby, O., 1866-70; Ravenswood, W. Va., 1870-79. Died, 1879.

*WILLIAM STEELE MCNAIR, Minister, Louisville, Ky.

A. B. B. D., Danville Theol. Sem., 1856. Died, Washington, D. C., May 3, 1856.

*JOSEPH G. MCNUTT, Lawyer, Richmond, Ind.

A. B. Admitted to the bar. Captain in U. S. Regular Army. Died, March 2, 1877.

*POLLARD MCCORMICK MORGAN, Catholic Priest, Pittsburg, Pa.

A. B., A. M. Attended Western Theol. Sem., 1855-58. Ordained a Roman Catholic Priest, 1860. Prof. of Rhetoric and Theology, St. Michael's Coll., England, 1861. Pastor of St. Andrew's, Manchester, Pa., 1861-70. Born, Pittsburg, Pa., 1834. Died, April 16, 1872.

WILLIAM MONTGOMERY MORRISON, Teacher, Fern Creek, Ky.

A. B., A. M. Has been constantly engaged in teaching since graduation.

*JOHN NOBLE, Minister, Wilkesville, O.

A. B., A. M., B. D., Lane Seminary, 1859. Ordained by Athens Presbytery, 1859. Pastor of Pres. churches at Newport, O., 1859-62; Washington Co., O., 1868-76; Wilkesville, O., 1877-79. Born, Cleves, O., May 10, 1822. Died, March 25, 1879.

GEORGE RANDOLPH PATTON, Physician, Lake City, Minn.

A. B., A. M. M. D., Miami Med. Coll., 1855; Ohio Med. Coll., 1858. Lecturer on Materia Medica and Therapeutics, Miami Med. Coll., 1857-58. Acting Assistant Surgeon, U. S. A., 1863-65. President of the Wabasha Co., (Minn.) Pension Board, 1884-91.
Adresses, from June to October, Lake City, Minn.; from November to May, 1113 Los Angeles street, Los Angeles, Cal.

JOHN HARRISON RODGERS, Physician, Springfield, O.

A. B., A. M. M. D., Univ. of Pa., 1856. Assistant Surgeon, 44th Ohio Vol. Inf., U. S. A., 1861-62. Surgeon, 104th Ohio Vol. Inf., U. S. A., 1862-65. U. S. Pension Examining Surgeon, 1865-85. Trustee Ohio Blind Asylum and the Ohio Soldiers' and Sailors' Orphans Home.
Address, 90 North Limestone street.

*JOSEPH C. ROSS, Physician, Lincoln, Ills.

A. B., A. M. M. D. Died, Oct. 1884.

JOHN WILLIAM STEEL, Lawyer, Wabasha, Minn.

A. B., A. M. Admitted to the bar, 1856. Private, Co. E, 15th Ohio Vol. Inf.; Co, K, 88th O. V. I.; Co. A, 60th O. V. I., 1862-65. Prosecuting Attorney of Van Wert Co., O., 1858-62. City attorney of Brainerd, Minn., 3 years.
Address, Corner Pierce and Second streets.

WILLIAM M. TREVOR, Officer of Corporation, Parkersburg, W. Va.

A. B., A. M. Deputy clerk in the courts of Hamilton Co., O., 1855-58 and 1860-74. Clerk of the Common Pleas Court, Hamilton Co., 1874-77. Now Treasurer of the Ohio River Railroad Co.

*HUGH STEWART USTICK, Minister, Hamilton, O.

A. B., A. M. B. D., New Albany Theol. Sem., 1856. Licensed by the Chillicothe Presbytery, 1855. Pastor of Pres. church at Hamilton, O., 1857. Born, Bloomingburg, O., Sept. 9, 1832. Died Oct. 31, 1857.

Class of 1854.

*WILLIAM TRIMBLE BEATTY, Presbyterian, Pittsburg, Pa.

A. B., A. M. B. D., Western Theol. Sem., 1860. D. D., Western Univ. of Pa., 1878. Licensed by the Zanesville Presbytery, April, 1859. Ordained, 1861. Pastor of Pres. churches at Greencastle, Penn., 1861-63; New Brunswick, N. J., 1863-67; Pittsburg, Pa., 1867-81. Born, Fairfield Co., O., June 1, 1834. Died, Minneapolis, Minn., April 10, 1882.

*ALEXANDER PERRY BELL, Minister, Antrim, O.

A. B., A. M. Studied theology at Allegheny, Pa. Licensed, 1858. Died, May 4, 1859.

CHARLES ELWOOD BROWN, Lawyer, Cincinnati, O.

A. B., A. M. Admitted to the bar, 1859. Practised law at Chillicothe, O., 1859-72. Commissioned Captain of the 63rd Ohio Vol. Inf., Sept. 2, 1861. Promoted to Major, March, 1863; to Lieutenant-Colonel, May, 1863; Colonel, June, 1865. Brevet-Brigadier-General, 1865. Seriously wounded in the battle of Atlanta, July 22, 1864, which resulted in the loss of his left leg. Provost Marshal, Cleveland, O., 1865. Postmaster of Chillicothe. Removed to Cincinnati, O., 1872. Pension Agent, 1872-77. Member U. S. House of Representatives, 1885-89. Father of Jacob N, '88. *Vide*, sketch and portrait, "Miami Journal," Vol. I, No. 6. Address, 27 Johnston Building. Residence, College Hill, O.

JOSIAH E. BROWN, Real Estate Broker, Pleasant Ridge, O.
A. B.

*GEORGE K. CLARK, Lawyer, Chicago, Ills.

A. B., A. M. Admitted to the bar, 1856. Practised law and was engaged in many business enterprises. Died, July 2, 1881.

DAVID R. COLMERY, Minister, Monrovia, Cal.

A. B., A. M. Teacher at Hannibal, Mo., 1854-55; Female Seminary, Springfield, O., 1855-56; Principal of Mt. Pleasant Academy, Kingston, O., 1856-57. Attended Western Theol. Sem., 1857-60. Licensed by the Columbus Presbytery, April 20, 1859. President Waveland Collegiate Institute, Waveland, Ind., 1861-62. Pastor of Pres. churches at Pleasant Ridge, O., 1862-64; Clifton, O., 1864-69; Yellow Springs, O., 1869-72; Thornton, Ind., 1872-75; Jersey, O., 1875-81; Columbus, O., 1881-86. Removed to Monrovia, Cal., on account of ill-health.

*THOMAS FOSTER CORTELYOU, Minister, Montgomery, O.

A. B., A. M. B. D., Danville Theol. Sem., 1857. Licensed by the Cincinnati Presbytery, 1856. Ordained, 1857. Pastor of Pres. churches at Williamsburg, O., 1857–61; Montgomery and Somerset, O., 1861–71; Montgomery, O., 1871–88. Born, Reading, O., Aug. 28, 1832. Died, Jan. 7, 1888.

STEPHEN CRANE, Lawyer, Hamilton, O.

A. B., A. M. Admitted to the bar. Law office, Beckett block.

*GEORGE FLETCHER DYCHE, Merchant, Chicago, Ills.

A. B. Died, Jan. 24, 1866.

DAVID FRANCIS,

A. B. Attended Western Theol. Sem., 1855. Can not be traced.

THEOPHILUS CANNON HIBBERT, Civil Engineer, Smyrna, Tenn.

A. B., A. M. Admitted to the bar, 1857 and practised law, 1857–61. Captain and Provost Marshal, Bates' Division, Army of Tenn., C. S. A., 1861–65. Engaged in civil engineering since 1865.

GEORGE A. HOWARD,

A. B. Can not be traced.

*JOHN HUSSEY, Minister and Teacher, Lafayette, Ind.

A. B., A. M. B. D., Lane Seminary. 1859. Ph. D., Hanover Coll., 1871. Ordained by Hamilton Presbytery, June 17, 1859. Pastor of Pres. church, Lockland, O., 1859–67. Served in the U. S. Christian Commission, 1864. Captured and imprisoned at Libby Prison. Teacher in Female Coll., Glendale, O., 1867–73. Member of the Fish Commission and of the Geological Survey of Ohio, Kentucky and Indiana, 1873–74. Prof. in Purdue Univ., Lafayette, Ind., 1874–79. Stricken with paralysis, 1879, and never rallied. Born, Hillsboro, O., Aug. 19, 1831. Died, Dec. 26, 1888.

DAVID JOHNSTON, Middle Point, Van Wert Co., O.

A. B., A. M.

WILLIAM JOHNSTON, Physician, Blue Ash, Hamilton Co., O.

A. B., A. M. M. D., Ohio Med. Coll., 1858.

HENRY L. KESSLING,

A. B. Cannot be traced.

JOHN THOMAS KILLEN, Minister, Devil's Lake, N. Dak.

A. B., A. M. Principal of the Normal Department, Miami Univ., 1856–60. Pastor of Pres. churches at Constantine, Mich.; Green Bay, Wis., Morris, Ills.; Baraboo, Wis. Removed to Devil's Lake, on account of ill-health.

MIAMI UNIVERSITY.   63

FREDERICK MALTBY,   Farmer,   Pine Bend, Minn.

A. B., A. M.

DAVID WADDLE MCCLUNG,   U. S. Collector,   Cincinnati, O.

A. B., A. M. Superintendent of Schools, Hamilton, O., 1855-56. Editor Hamilton "Intelligencer," 1857-58. Appointed Probate Judge of Butler Co., 1859. Captain U. S. Vol., 1861-65. Assistant Postmaster, Cincinnati, O., 1879-81. Surveyor of the Port, Cincinnati, O., 1881-85. Collector of Internal Revenue, 1889—. Trustee of Miami, 1866-75 and 1887—. Delivered annual address before the Alumni Association of Miami, 1889. *Vide*, Sketch and Portrait, "Miami Journal," Vol. II, No. 8.

*ROBERT MCMILLAN,   Minister,   Cincinnati, O.

A. B., A. M. Studied theology, Philadelphia, Pa. Pastor, of Pres. churches at Newcastle, Pa., and Cincinnati, O. Chaplain, 9th Division, 3rd Army Corps, U. S. A., 1864. Died, May 24, 1876.

*MINOR MILLIKIN,   Journalist,   Hamilton, O.

A. B., A. M. L L. B., Harvard Law School, 1856. Editor and Proprietor of the Hamilton "Intelligencer." Colonel of the 1st Ohio Vol. Cav., 1861-62. Killed in the battle of Stone River, Dec. 31, 1862.

*WILLIAM OWENS,   Lawyer,   Pittsburg, Pa.

A. B., A. M. Admitted to the bar, 1857. Born, Wales, G. B., July 4, 1831. Died, Dec. 25, 1875.

ELISHA PAINE POTTER,   Merchant,   Steubenville, O.

A. B., A. M. First-Lieutenant, 97th Ohio Vol. Inf., U. S. A., 1862-65.

EDWARD PATRICK SHIELDS,   Minister,   Bristol, Pa.

A. B. A. M. D. D., Miami Univ., 1887. B. D., Princeton Theol. Sem. 1858. Pastor of Pres. churches at Pittsgrove, N. J., 1858-70; Cape May City, N. J., 1871-84; Bristol, Pa., 1884—. Stated clerk of the West Jersey Presbytery, 1872-84. Superintendent of Public Instruction, Cape May Co., N. J., 1881-84.

*JONATHAN STEWART,   Minister,   Tranquillity, O.

A. B., A. M. Studied theology, Oxford, O. Licensed by Springfield Presbytery, April 2, 1856. Ordained by La Claire Presbytery, Sept. 22, 1858. Pastor of United Pres. churches at Andrew and LaMotte, Iowa, 1858-65; Unity, O., 1867-71; Tranquillity, O., 1871-78. Born, Xenia, O., Sept. 2, 1827. Died, March 2, 1878.

HENRY STODDARD,   Real Estate Broker,   Santa Barbara, Cal.

A. B., A. M. First Lieutenant and Quartermaster, 131st Ohio National Guards, 1861-65. Postmaster of Santa Barbara, Cal., 1877-82; and County, Recorder, 1882-84. Engaged in Real Estate and Insurance.

THOMAS WILLIAMS, Lawyer, Philadelphia, Pa.

A. B., A. M. Admitted to the bar, 1858. First Lieutenant, 5th U. S. A. Artillery, 1861–62; Brevet-Captain of same, 1862–65;, Brevet-Major, March 13, 1865. Brother of Alexander R, '57. Address, 128 South Nineteenth street.

HENRY MARTYN WOODRUFF, Merchant, Pewee Valley, Ky.

A. B., A. M. Principal of Academy, Owensboro, Ky., 1855–62. Editor and proprietor of the "Monitor," Owensboro, Ky., 1862–64. State Inspector of Tobacco, Ky., 1864–67. Postmaster, Pewee Valley, Ky., 1870–89.

Class of 1855.

*ISAAC ANDERSON, Farmer, Ross, O.

A. B. Died, Oct. 12, 1862.

JOHN LONG ATEN, Minister, Madison, Ind.

A. B., A. M. Studied theology, Oxford, O. Ordained by the Lake Presbytery, Feb. 7, 1860. Pastor of United Pres. churches at Union City and Wayne, Erie Co., Pa., 1860–63; College Corner, O., 1863–75; Cleveland, O., 1876–79; Madison, Ind., 1883—. Served in the U. S. Christian Commission, 1865. Brother of Aaron M, '59. Address, 806 W. Second street.

LAZARUS NOBLE BONHAM, Agriculturist, Oxford, O.

A. B., A. M. Principal of Bonham Female Seminary, St. Louis, Mo., 1859–72. Agricultural Editor, "Cincinnati Commercial Gazette, 1880–91. Secretary of the Ohio State Board of Agriculture since 1885. Trustee of Miami Univ., 1872–88. Brother of John C, '47.
Address, Oxford, O., or Columbus, O.

NATHAN McGAW BROWN, Horticulturist, Stuttgart, Ark.

A. B., A. M. M. D., Jefferson Med. Coll., 1858. Practised medicine for several years.

JAMES EDWARD BRUCE, Minister, Center White Creek, N. Y.

A. B., A. M. M. D., Eclectic Med. Coll., Cincinnati, O., 1852. Studied theology, Cambridge Univ., England. Ordained, 1855. Pastor of Universalist churches at Taunton, Mass.; Middletown, Conn.; Melrose, Mass.; Eastport, Me.; King's Lynn, England; Center White Creek, Washington Co., N. Y.

*ANDREW JACKSON CORY, Physician, San Jose, Cal.

A. B., A. M. M. D., Ohio Med. Coll., 1860. Physician to County Hospital, San Jose, Cal., 1861–70. Coroner, 8 years. Brother of Benjamin, '42, and James M, '48. Born, Oxford, O., Dec. 25, 1832. Died, March 3, 1892.

WILLIAM CRAIGHEAD, Lawyer, Dayton, O.

A. B., A. M. Admitted to the bar, 1861. City Solicitor of Dayton, O., 1892—. Brother of John P, '52. Law firm, Craighead & Craighead, Firemen's Insurance Building.
Address, 449 West Second street.

BENTON JAY HALL, Lawyer, Chicago, Ills.

A. B., A. M. Admitted to the bar, 1857. Practised law at Burlington, Ia., until 1888. Member Iowa House of Representatives, 1872–74. Member of the State Senate, 1882–84. Member of U. S. House of Representatives, 1885–87. U. S. Commissioner of Patents, 1887–88.
Address, 25 and 26 Honore Building.

*WILLIAM HAYS, Physician, Covington, Ky.

A. B., A. M. M. D., Cincinnati Med. Coll., 1857. First Lieutenant, 2nd Ky. Cav., C. S. A., 1862–64. Died, Feb. 8, 1869.

ISAAC MENOR HUGHES, Minister, Richmond, Ind.

A. B., A. M. D. D., Hanover Coll., 1883. Licensed by the Presbytery of Oxford, Oct. 1858. Ordained by same, 1860. Prof. of Greek, Westminster Coll., 1855–58. Principal Seven Mile Academy, 1858–60. Pastor of Pres. churches at Venice, O., 1860–70; Richmond, Ind., 1870—.
Address, 323 North Ninth street.

THOMAS EDGAR HUGHES, Minister, La Grange, Ind.

A. B., A. M. Attended McCormick Theol. Sem. Ordained, 1858. Pastor of Pres. churches at Springdale, O.; 1858–66; Constantine, Mich., 1867–70; La Grange, Ind., 1870—.

*WILLIAM BOMBERGER LOWE, Ranchman, Junction City, Kan.

A. B. Captain, 11th Ohio Vol. Inf., U. S. A., 1861–64. Wounded at the battle of the Wilderness, May 5, 1864. Brother of Jacob D., '53. Died, Sept. 1889.

JOHN BROWN MACDILL, Physician, Camp Grove, Ills.

A. B., A. M. M. D., Ohio Med. Coll., 1859. Assistant Surgeon, 1st Ohio Vol. Inf. and 63rd Ohio Vol. Inf., 1861–65.

*JAMES TORBET MANNING, Merchant, Oakley, O.

A. B. A. M., Farmer's Coll. Private, Co. H, 137 Ohio National Guards, 1862. Engaged in the wholesale grocery business, Cincinnati, O., for many years. Died, Jan. 15, 1891.

OMAR NEWMAN, Broker, Kansas City, Mo.

A. B., A. M. Attended Harvard Law School. Admitted to the bar, 1857. Real Estate and Loan Broker.
Office, Sheidley Building.

66   MIAMI UNIVERSITY.

WILLIAM HARVEY REID,   Minister,   Howard, Kan.

A. B. Studied theology at Oxford, O., and Philadelphia, Pa. Licensed by the Reformed Presbytery of Philadelphia, May 20, 1860. Ordained by the Northern Presbytery, 1861. Pastor of Ref. Pres. church at West Barnet, Vt., 1862–67. Pastor of United Pres. church, Ontario, Canada, 1880–83. Pastor of Pres. church, Malvern, Kan., 1886–88. Home Missionary.

HENRY M. SHOCKLEY,   Minister,   Speareville, Kan.

A. B., A. M. Pastor of Pres. churches at Connersville, Ind.; Sedalia, Mo.; Hutchinson, Kan.; Larned, Kan.; Speareville, Kan. Principal of schools, New Castle, Ind., 6 years.

RANSFORD SMITH,   Lawyer,   Ogden City, Utah.

A. B., A. M. Admitted to the bar, 1856. Principal Grammar school, Hamilton, O., 1855–56. Mayor of Hamilton, O., 1859–61. Captain, Co. B, 35 Ohio Vol. Inf., 1861–63. Practised law at Cincinnati, O., 1865–80. Removed to Ogden City, Utah, 1880.

LAWRENCE MONFORT STEVENS,   Minister,   Kissimmee, Fla.

A. B., A. M. Attended Western Theol. Sem., 1857–60. Licensed by the Presbytery of Miami, Dec. 27, 1858. Ordained by Presbytery of Chicago, March 6, 1861. Pastor of Pres. churches at Marengo, Ills., 1860–67; Brookville, Ind., 1867–68; Laporte, Ind., 1869–71; Delphi, Ind., 1871–73; Cedar Grove, Pa., 1873–74; Sturgis, Mich., 1875–77; Constantine, Mich., 1877–79; Prattsburg, N. Y., 1879–87; New Berlin, N. Y., 1888–91; Kissimmee, Fla., 1891—.

ALEXANDER TELFORD,   Minister,   Hastings, Minn.

A. B., A. M. Attended Princeton Theol. Sem., 1855–58. Pastor of Pres. churches at Spring Hills, O., 1858–73; New Castle, Ind., 1873–75; Hastings, Minn., 1875–78. Elected Pastor Emeritus of latter church, 1878.

GATES PHILLIPS THRUSTON,   Lawyer,   Nashville, Tenn.

A. B., A. M. LL.B., Cincinnati Law School, 1859. Captain, 1st Ohio Vol. Inf. U. S. A., 1861–63. Lieutenant Colonel and Assistant Adjutant General, 20th Army Corps, U. S. A., 1863–65. Brevetted Brigadier-General, 1865, for special acts of gallantry at Shiloh, Stone River and Chickamauga. Retired from law. President of State Insurance Co. Author of "Antiquities of Tennessee and Adjacent States." Brother of Dickinson P., '58.
Address, 318 N. High street.

*THOMAS BAYLESS WARD,   Lawyer,   Lafayette, Ind.

A. B., A. M. Admitted to the bar, 1857. Mayor of Lafayette, Ind., 1861–65. City Attorney of same, 1869–75. Judge of the Superior Court of Tippecanoe Co., 1875–80. Member U. S. House of Representatives, 1883–87. Born, Marysville, O., April 27, 1835. Died, Dec., 1891.

Class of 1856.

ALBERT SEATON BERRY, Lawyer, Newport, Ky.

A. B., A. M. L.L. B., Cincinnati Law School, 1860. Captain, 5th Ky. Inf.,
C. S. A., 1861-65. State Senator of Kentucky, 1880-88. Mayor of Newport, 1874-80 and 1888—.

*****JAMES COOPER,** Lawyer, Zanesville, O.

A. B., A. M. Admitted to the bar. Died, 1863.

ULYSSES THOMPSON CURRAN, Lawyer, Sandusky, O.

A. B., A. M. L.L. B., Cincinnati Law School, 1872. Assistant Superintendent of Schools, Ripley, O., 1856-59. Principal Academy, Hartford, Ky., 1859-61. Superintendent Public Schools, Glendale, O., 1862-65. Conducted a Private Classical School, Cincinnati, O., 1865-72. Superintendent Public Schools, Sandusky, O., 1873-80. Has been engaged in practice of law since 1880.

JOSEPH SCOTT FULLERTON, Lawyer, St. Louis, Mo.

A. B., A. M. Admitted to the bar. Secretary of Commission on Fremont Claims, 1861-62. Private in Halleck's Guards, Aug., 1862—Oct. 4, 1862. Lieutenant, Co. E, 2nd Mo. Inf., Oct. 14, 1862—March 13, 1863. Assistant Adjutant, with the rank of Major, Army of Ky., March 13, 1863—Nov. 10, 1863. Lieutenant Colonel, 4th Army Corps, Nov. 10, 1863—April 22, 1864. Transferred to the Army of the Tennessee. Assigned by President Johnson to duty with Gen. O. O. Howard, May 19, 1865. Promoted to Colonel for brave and meritorious service, April 5, 1866. Promoted to Brigadier-General, April 9, 1866. Postmaster of St. Louis, Mo., 1867-69.

JOHN J. GLENN, Lawyer, Monmouth, Ills.

A. B., A. M. Admitted to the bar, 1858. Circuit Judge, 1877—.

JOHN HANNA, Lawyer,

A. B., A. M. Cannot be traced.

*****JOHN HUGHES HARRIS,** Minister, Glendale, Cal.

A. B., A. M. Attended Western Theol. Sem., 1856. Licensed by the Presbytery of Wooster, April 21, 1857. Ordained by same, April, 1858. Pastor of Pres. churches at McArthur, O., 1858-60; New Richmond, O., 1860-61; Liberty, Ind., 1861-63. District Secretary of the American and Foreign Christian Union, Aurora, Ills., 1863-68. Stated Supply at Taylorville, Chatham, and Auburn, Ills., 1870-73; Whiteland, Ind., 1873-78; Monteno, Ills., 1879-80; Los Angeles, Cal., 1884. Born, Middlebury, O., May 22, 1832. Died, Nov. 26, 1886.

LUTELLUS HUSSEY, Physician, Lockland, O.

A. B., A. M. M. D., Ohio Med. Coll. Captain, 83rd Ohio Vol. Inf., 1862-65. Brother of John, '54.

JOHN CALVIN HUTCHISON, Minister and Teacher, Cherokee, Ia.

A. B., A. M. Ph. D., Wooster Univ., 1879. Prof. of Natural Science, Monmouth Coll., Monmouth, Ills., 1858-91. Ordained a minister in the United Pres. church, June 6, 1862. Vice-President of Monmouth Coll., 1870-91. Prof. of Chemistry and Physics, Buena Vista Coll., Storm Lake, Ia., 1891—. Manager of the Cherokee Electric Light Co., Cherokee, Ia., 1891—. Electrician, Storm Lake Electric Light Co., Storm Lake, Ia., 1891—. Author of "Life of Rev. D. A. Wallace, D. D.", and "History of Monmouth Coll."

*HENRY J. LATHROP, Lawyer, Murfreesboro, Ark.

A. B., A. M. Admitted to the bar, 1858. Practised law at Chicago, Ills., 1858-60. Removed to Osceola, Ark., 1860. Colonel of the 15th Ark. regiment, 1861-65. Removed to Murfreesboro, Ark., 1866. Born, Oxford, O., Dec., 1836. Died, Feb., 1872.

JOHN NEWTON MCCLUNG, Minister, Oswego, Kan.

A. B., A. M. First Lieutenant, Co. D, 74th Ohio Vol. Inf., 1861-62. Pastor of Pres. churches at Russellville and Decatur, O., 1873-76; Winchester and Decatur, O., 1876-78; Paola, Kan., 1878-81; Wellington, Kan., 1881-85; Junction City, Kan., 1886-91; Independence, Kan., 1891.

JAMES ALEXANDER PORTER MCGAW, Minister, Toledo, O.

A. B., A. M. D. D., Monmouth Coll., 1871. Studied theology at Oxford, O., 1856-57. Licensed, April, 1857. Ordained, 1858. Pastor of United Pres. church at South Henderson, Ills., 1858-67. Vice-President of Monmouth Coll., and Prof. of English Literature, 1867-68. Pastor of Pres. churches at Urbana, O., 1869-80; Rock Island, Ills., 1880-81; Toledo, O., 1881—.
Address, 1828 Adams street.

WILLIAM JASPER MCSURELY, Minister, Hillsboro, O.

A. B., A. M. D. D., Wooster Univ., 1881. Studied theology at Oxford, O. Licensed by Presbytery of Chillicothe, April 14, 1858. Ordained by the First Ohio Presbytery, May 5, 1859. Pastor of United Pres. churches at Oxford, O., 1858-66; Kirkwood, Ills., 1867-68. Pastor of Pres. church at Hillsboro, O., 1869—. Member of the Board of Trustees of Miami Univ., 1887—. Delivered annual address before the Alumni, 1885. *Vide*, "Miami Journal," Vol. II, No. 8.
Address, 32 East Walnut street.

BENJAMIN F. MILLER, Lawyer, Toledo, O.

A. B., A. M. L L. B., Cincinnati Law School. Private, Co. F, 3rd Ohio Vol. Inf., April 17, 1861—Aug. 18, 1861. Lieutenant, Co. C., 35th Ohio, 1861-64. Captain, Co. A., 35th Ohio. Editor of a monthly literary magazine, 1880-81.

*JOHN MINICH MILLER, Lawyer, Alpha, O.

A. B., A. M. Admitted to the bar, 1859. Member Ohio House of Representatives, 1862-63. Born, Feb. 12, 1829. Died, Jan. 9, 1863.

THOMAS LATTA PENDERY, Farmer, Morrow, O.
A. B., A. M.

*JOHN W. PINKERTON, Minister, Iola, Kan.
A. B., A. M. Studied theology at Oxford, O. Licensed by the First Ohio Presbytery, April 9, 1857. Ordained, Aug. 3, 1858. Pastor of United Pres. churches at Smithville, Ills., 1858–62; Lake Presbytery, 1862–66. Joined the Pres. church, 1866. Died, Feb. 12, 1875.

WHITELAW REID, Editor, New York, N. Y.
A. B., A. M. LL. D., Miami Univ., 1890. Editor, Xenia, O., "News," 1858–60. Legislative correspondent at Columbus, O., for the Cincinnati "Times," Cleveland "Herald," and Cincinnati "Gazette," 1860–61. Editor Cincinnati "Gazette," 1861. War and Washington correspondent for the Cincinnati "Gazette," 1861–68. Editorial writer, New York "Tribune 1868; Managing Editor, 1869–72; Editor, 1872–89 and 1892—. Chief proprietor since 1872. Minister of the U. S. to France, 1889–92. Volunteer Aide, Staff of Major-General Thomas A. Morris during the first West Virginia campaign; Staff of Major-General W. S. Rosecrans during the second West Virginia campaign; Staff of General Thomas J. Wood. Librarian, House of Representatives, Washington, D. C., 1863–66. Regent of Univ. of New York, 1878—. Author of "After the War," "A Southern Tour," "Ohio in the War," "Schools of Journalism," "The Scholar in Politics," "Some Newspaper Tendencies," etc. *Vide*, "Miami Journal," Vol. I, No. 3.

THOMAS HENRY ROGERS, Teacher, Monmouth, Ills.
A. B., A. M. Prof. of Mathematics, Monmouth, Coll., Monmouth, Ills., 1864—.

WILLIAM C. SMITH, Commercial Traveller, Springfield, O.
A. B.
Address, 71 West Washington street.

DAVID JACKSON STRAIN, Minister, Virginia, Ills.
A. B., A. M. Ordained, 1866. Principal North Sangamon Academy, Ills., 1856–66. Pastor Pres. churches at Virginia, Ills., 1866–80; North Sangamon, Ills., 1880–84; Virginia, Ills., 1884—.

*JAMES TAYLOR, Banker, Newport, Ky.
A. B., A. M. LL. B., Cincinnati Law School, 1858. Never practised law. Assistant Principal of Newport (Ky.) High School, 1858–60. Died, Feb. 2, 1875.

WILLIAM TAYLOR, Farmer and Banker, Bourneville, O.
A. B., A. M. Taught school at Chillicothe, O., 1857–67. Has since been engaged in farming and banking.

JACOB A. ZELLER, Teacher, Lafayette, Ind.
A. B., A. M. Admitted to the bar, 1859. Principal of Public Schools, Oxford, O.; Evansville, Ind.; Richmond, Ind.; Lafayette, Ind. Private, U. S. A., Vol. Inf., 1864.

Class of 1857.

*JOHN WILSON BAIRD,   Teacher,   Chester, S. Car.

A. B., A. M. Graduated Erskine Coll., S. Car., 1855. Taught in Portersville, Tenn., and Chester, S. Car. Volunteer in C. S. A., 1861-62. Killed in Virginia, 1862.

THOMAS COWAN BELL,   Teacher,   Dallas, Ore.

A. B., A. M. Captain, Major and Lieutenant-Colonel 74th Ohio Vol. Inf., U. S. A., 1861-63. Has been constantly engaged in teaching since graduation, except two years in U. S. A. President of Philomath Coll., 1885-86. Principal of La Creole Academy, Dallas, Ore., 1887—. A founder of the Sigma Chi fraternity.

JOHN SHAW BILLINGS,   Physician,   Washington, D. C.

A. B., A. M. M. D., Ohio Med. Coll., 1860. L L. D., Edinburgh Univ., 1884. Same, Harvard Univ., 1886. D. C. L., Oxon., 1889. M. D., Univ. of Munich, 1889. Acting Assistant Surgeon, U. S. A., in charge of hospitals, Washington, D. C., and Philadelphia, Pa., 1861-63; with 5th corps, Army of Potomac, 1863; at David's and Bedlow's Islands, 1864. Inspector of the Army of the Potomac, 1864-65. Appointed surgeon, with the rank of Major, 1876. Now Curator Army Medical Museum and Library, Washington, D. C. President of the first Congress of American Physicians and Surgeons. Member Statistical Society of London; National Academy of Sciences, American Medical Association. Lecturer on Municipal Hygiene and Medical Adviser, Johns Hopkins' Univ., Baltimore, Md. Author of "Principles of Ventilation," 1884; Index Catalogue of Library of Surgeon-General's o.fice, Vols. 1-13, 1879-91.

JACOB NEWTON BROWN,   Physician,   San Jose, Cal.

A. B., A. M. M. D., Ohio Med. Coll., 1860. Prof. of Anatomy, Univ. of Cal., 1864-65.
Address, 29 East Santa Clara street. P. O. Box, 444.

JAMES PARKS CALDWELL,   Lawyer,   Mississippi City, Miss.

A. B. Teacher in Mississippi, 1858-59. Principal Palmetta Academy, Panola, Miss., 1860-64. First Lieutenant of Artillery, C. S. A., 1864-65. Admitted to the bar, 1866. Practised law, Los Angeles, Cal., 1867-75; Mississippi City, Miss., 1875—. A founder of the Sigma Chi fraternity.

DANIEL WILLIAM COOPER,   Minister,   McComb, O.

A. B. Attended Western Theol. Sem., 1857-59. Licensed by Richland Presbytery, 1858. Ordained by same, 1859. Pastor of Pres. churches at Olivesburg and Bloomington, O., 1859-65; Ottowa, Ills., 1865-72; West Point, Ind., 1872-78; N. Baltimore and Harrison, O., 1878-82; McComb, O., 1882—. A founder of the Sigma Chi fraternity.

JOHN COOPER,   Teacher and Merchant,   New York, N. Y.

B. S. A. M. Principal of Academy, Dublin, Ind., 1858-70. Superintendent of Public Schools, Richmond, Ind., 1870-78; Evansville, Ind., 1878-83; Leavenworth, Kan., 1883-87. Member Indiana State Board of Education, 5 years. Merchant, New York, N. Y., 1888—.
Address, 146 West Forty-Third street.

JAMES M. DEARMOND, Farmer, Texas.

B. S. Exact location not known.

ARCHIBALD STEWART DUNLAP, Physician, Chattanooga, Tenn.

A. B., A. M. M. D., Univ. of Mich., 1867. Assistant Surgeon, National Military Home, Dayton, O., 1870-86.

JAMES S. FERGUSON, Physician, Camden, O.

A. B., A. M. M. D., Ohio Med. Coll., 1861. Assistant Surgeon, U. S. A., 1861-65. Appointed member of the Eaton Board of Pension Examiners, Sept., 1890.

*ROBERT JOHN MIRABEAU GOODWIN, Lawyer, Brookville, Ind.

A. B., A. M. Prof. in College, Brookville, Ind., 1857-59. Admitted to the bar, 1861. Lieutenant and Captain, 37th Ind. Vol. Inf., 1861-63. Promoted to Assistant Provost-Marshal of the Army of the Cumberland. Practised law at Brookville, Ind., 1866-84. Died, July 2, 1884.

WILLIAM CLARK HUTCHISON, Merchant, Xenia, O.

B. S. Dealer in Carpets and Dry Goods, Xenia, O., 1863—. Brother of John C, '56.

*ISAAC M. JORDAN, Lawyer, Cincinnati, O.

A. B., A. M. Admitted to the bar, May, 1858. Practised law at Dayton, O., 1858-60; Cincinnati, O., 1860—90. Presidential Elector on Democratic ticket, 1872. Member U. S. House of Representatives, 1883-85. Declined a unanimous renomination. Declined First Assistant Secretaryship of the Interior, tendered by President Cleveland. A founder of the Sigma Chi fraternity. Born, Union Co., Pa., May 5, 1835. Killed by falling down an elevator shaft, Dec. 12, 1890.

DENNIS NELSON KELLEY, Manufacturer, Columbus, O.

B. S. Lieutenant, 93rd Ohio Vol. Inf., 1862-65. Manufacturer of Steam Heating Apparatus, Gas Fixtures, Plumbing, etc. Firm name, Kelley & Co., 22 and 24 West Broad street. Residence, 634 East Rich street.

HENRY MITCHELL MACCRACKEN, Minister, New York, N. Y.

A. B. D. D., Wittenberg Coll. LL. D., Miami Univ., 1887. Attended Princeton Theol. Sem., 1862. Pastor of Pres. churches at Columbus, O., 1863-67; Toledo, O., 1868-81. Chancellor and Prof. of Philosophy, Western Univ. of Pa., 1881-84. Vice-Chancellor and Prof. of Philosophy, Univ. of the City of New York, 1884-91. Chancellor of same, 1891—. Delivered address at inauguration of Rev. W. O. Thompson, D. D., as President of Miami Univ., 1891. Author of numerous addresses and pamphlets.
Address, 84 Irving Place.

SAMUEL MCKEE, Lawyer, Louisville, Ky.

A. B., A. M. Admitted to the bar. Captain, Co. D., 14th Ky. Vol. Inf., 1861-63. Entered Volunteer Cavalry Service. Captured, March, 1863, and was confined in Libby Prison until May, 1864. Member of U. S. House of Representatives, 1865-69. U. S. Pension Agent, Louisville, Ky., 1869-71. Address, 216 Fifth street.

WILLIAM H. MCKINNEY, Dayton, O.

A. B. A. M.

GEORGE BACHELER PECK, Minister, Boston, Mass.

A. B., A. M. M. D., Harvard Univ., 1863. Graduated at Theol. Sem., Auburn, N. Y., 1868. Acting Assistant Surgeon, Army of Va., U. S. A., 1863-64. Ministerial labors have been almost wholly as an evangelist in the Pres. church. Pastor of Pres. churches at Beverly, N. J., and Bond Hill, O., for a few years. Author of "Steps and Studies, an Inquiry concerning the gift of the Holy Spirit," 1884; Second edition of the same, 1890; "Throne Life, or the Highest Christian Life," 1888; "The Gate and The Cross, or Pilgrim's Progress in Romans," 1889. Address, 38 Humphreys street, Dorchester district.

JAMES B. PORTER, Physician, Oxford, O.

A. B., A. M. M. D., Miami Med. Coll., 1866. Served in U. S. Vol. Army, 1861-65.

BEN PRATT RUNKLE, Soldier and Minister, Alpine, N. J.

A. B. Admitted to the bar, 1859. Practised law at Cincinnati, O., 1859-61. Commissioned Lieutenant-Colonel, 13th Ohio Vol. Inf., May 15, 1862; Colonel, 45th Ohio Vol. Inf., Aug. 19, 1862. Brevet Major-General, U. S. Vols. Editor of Urbana, O., "Union," 1873-75. Attended Theol. Sem., Gambier, O., 1879-80. Rector of parishes at Galena, O.; Midland, Mich.; Minneapolis, Minn.; Greencastle, Ind., 1880-85. Contributor to and manager of "Belford's Magazine," 1888—. Trustee of Miami Univ., 1863-72. A founder of the Sigma Chi fraternity. Author of several books.

NELSON SAYLER, Lawyer, Cincinnati, O.

A. B., A. M. L L. B., Cincinnati Law School, 1859. Prof. of Chemistry, Natural Philosophy. Geology and Latin, Mt. Auburn Female Coll., Cincinnati, O., 1861-66. Practised law, Cincinnati, O., 1866—. Trustee of Miami Univ., 1875—. Brother of Milton, '52; and J. Riner, '60. *Vide*, Portrait and Sketch, "Miami Journal," Vol. II, No. 8. Law office, 58 West Third street. Residence, Home City.

JOHN ROBERT SMITH, Coal Merchant, Du Quoin, Ills.

A. B., A. M. Admitted to the bar, 1858. Practised law, Paris, Ky., 1858-68. At present connected with the Jupiter Coal Mining Co., Du Quoin, Ills.

DAVID STEELE, Minister and Teacher, Philadelphia, Pa.

A. B. D. D., Rutger's Coll. Prof. of Hebrew, Greek and Pastoral Theology, Ref. Pres. Theol. Sem., 1863-75; of Doctrinal Theology in the same, 1875—. Served in the Christian Commission, U. S. A., 1862. Delegate to the Council of Pres. Alliance, 1880 and 1884. Author of article on "The Reformed Presbyterian Church-General Synod" in Schaff-Herzog Encyclopedia; "The Times in Which We Live and the Ministry They Require;" "The Two Witnesses;" "The Apologetics of History." Address, 2102 Spring Garden street.

BENJAMIN F. THOMAS, Lawyer, Hamilton, O.

A. B., A. M. Admitted to the bar. School Examiner of Butler Co., O., 1863-68. Probate Judge of Butler Co., 1876-82.

JOSEPH LYLE THORNTON, Manufacturer, Middletown, O.

A. B., A. M. M. D., Ohio Med. Coll., 1862. Principal Hughes High School, Cincinnati, O., 1860-73. President of the Ohio Valley Paper Co., Middletown, O.

*JOEL TUTTLE, Keosauqua, Ia.

A. B. Private Co. F, 2nd Iowa Vol. Inf., 1861-62. Died of typhoid fever, St. Louis, Mo., May 13, 1862.

JAMES WELSH, Minister, Salem, Ia.

A. B., A. M. Studied theology at Xenia, O. Licensed by First Ohio Presbytery, April 6, 1859. Ordained by same, Dec. 4, 1860. Pastor of United Pres. churches at College Corner, O., 1860-62; Springdale, O., 1863. Pastor of Pres. churches at Camden and New Paris, O., 1864-68; St, Francisville, Mo., 1868-70; West Point, Ia., 1870-76; Bonaparte, Ia., 1876-86; Troy, Ia., 1886-91. Principal of Whittier Coll., Salem, Ia., 1891—.

ALEXANDER REYNOLDS WILLIAMS, Merchant, Washington, D. C.

A. B., A. M. Dealer in Builder's Supplies. Brother of Thomas, '54. Address, 615 Seventh street, N. W.

WELLINGTON WRIGHT, Minister, Nortonville, Kan.

A. B., A. M. Studied theology at Oxford, O. Licensed by First Ohio Presbytery, April, 1858. Ordained by Michigan Presbytery, Oct. 19, 1859. Pastor of United Pres. churches at Lafayette, Ind., 1859-63; Brighton, Ia., 1865-69; Greenwood, Mo., 1877-83; Winchester, Kan., 1883-88.

Class of 1858.

*WILLIAM STAVELY BRATTON, Minister, Grand Cote, Ills.

A. B. Attended Western Theol. Sem., 1858-60. Licensed by Ohio Presbytery, 1859. Ordained by Western Presbytery of Ref. Pres. church, Dec. 15, 1859. Pastor of United Pres. church, Grand Cote, Ills., 1859-73. Born, York district, S. Car., July 21, 1822. Died, Jan. 11, 1873.

ROBERT F. BROOKS, Physician, Carthage, Mo.

A. B., A. M. M. D. Brother of John K, '64, and Peter H, '68.

NOAH CARTWRIGHT, Farmer and Fruit Grower, Fern Creek, Ky.

A. B., A. M. President Masonic Sem., Columbus, Ky., 1859-61. Captain, Major and Lieutenant-Colonel, 15th Ky. Vol. Inf., 1861-63. Wounded at the battle of Perryville, Ky., Oct. 8, 1862.

JOHN REILEY CHAMBERLIN,   Journalist,   Cincinnati, O.

A. B., A. M. Private, Second Sergeant and Sergeant-Major, 81st Ohio Vol. Inf., 1861-62. Commissioned Second Lieutenant, Feb., 1863. Discharged on account of granulation of eyes, 1864. Journalist, Cincinnati, O., 1867—. Author of article, "Cincinnati" in Appleton's Cyclopedia; "A Century of Cincinnati," etc. Office, Kankakee Building.
Address, 11 Prospect street, Mt. Auburn.

WILLIAM WILDER CHESHIRE,   Examiner,   Washington, D. C.

B. S. Private, Co. E, 151st Ind. Vol. Inf., 1865. Clerk of the Circuit Court, Lake Co., Ind., 1867-75. County Superintendent of Schools, Lake Co., Ind., 1878-82. Examiner in Pension office, Washington, D. C., 1882-85 and 1889—.
Address, 105 Eleventh street, S. E.

JAMES GIBSON CHESTNUT,   Lawyer,   Oakland, Cal.

A. B. Teacher at Cincinnati, O.; Virginia City, Mo., and Nevada City, Nevada; 25 years. Assayer and Metallurgist in Virginia City, Mo., 1863-70. Admitted to the bar, 1889.
Address, Vernon Heights.

CHRISTIAN A. COLER,   Farmer,   Farmersville, O.

A. B. First Lieutenant, Co. F, 131st Ohio Vol. Inf., 1861-63. Captain, 12th Ohio National Guards, 1863-65. Member Ohio Legislature, 1874-75.

ALEXANDER M. CRAWFORD,

A. B.

*ISAAC J. CUSHMAN,   Minister,   Murdock, O.

A. B., A. M. Studied theology at Oxford, O. Principal Salem Academy, 1858-60. Ordained, Nov. 30, 1860. Pastor of Pres. church at Murdock, O., 1860-81. Born, Monongahela Co., W. Va., Sept., 19, 1830. Died, Aug. 26, 1881.

JAMES STODDARD DEWEY,   Lawyer,   Detroit, Mich.

A. B., A. M. Admitted to the bar, 1863. Judge of Circuit Court, 1867-73. Compiler of Statutes of Michigan, 1871.
Address, 66 Joy street.

ADOLPHUS SPRING DUDLEY,   Minister,   Morrow, O.

A. B., A. M. Was graduated at Lane Sem., 1861. Ordained by Dayton Pres., Dec., 1861. Chaplain, 146th Ohio Vol. Inf., 1864. Pastor of Pres. churches at Morrow, O., 1860-65; Logansport, Ind., 1865-69; Granville, O., 1869-75; Cincinnati, O., 1875-79; Emporia, Kan., 1879-81. Prof. of Philosophy, Granville Female Coll., 1882. Pastor at Morrow, O., 1883—.

PINCKNEY M. FERGUSON,   Farmer,   Alquina, Ind.
A. B.

MIAMI UNIVERSITY. 75

AARON MILLER FLORY, Lawyer, Emporia, Kan.

A. B., A. M. Admitted to the bar, 1860. Assistant in Seminary, Logansport, Ind., 1858-59. Lieutenant-Colonel, 46th Ind. Vol. Inf., 1861-65. Wounded at Mansfield, La., May 16, 1864. Attorney for Lyon Co., Kan., 1889-91.

*JAMES BONNER FOSTER, Minister, Cincinnati, O.

A. B. Studied theology at Monmouth Coll., Licensed by First Ohio Presbytery, April 6, 1859. Ordained by same, Jan. 3, 1861. Pastor of United Pres. churches at Dayton, O., 1861-63; Young America, Ills., 1863-67. Pastor of Pres. church at Cincinnati, O., 1867-73. Born, Morning Sun, O., July 6, 1837. Died, Due West, S. Car., Feb. 27, 1873.

GEORGE HUMPHREY FULLERTON, Minister, Springfield, O.

A. B. D. D., Wabash Coll., 1883. Graduated at Princeton Theol. Sem., 1861. Chaplain, 1st Ohio Vol. Inf., 1861-62. Ordained by the Presbytery of Columbus, May 4, 1863. Pastor of Pres. churches at Lancaster, O., 1862-64; Sandusky, O., 1864-67; Cincinnati, O., 1867-74; Springfield, O., 1874-79; Walnut Hills, Cincinnati, O., 1879-86; Springfield, O., 1886—. Brother of Thomas A., '53; Hugh S., '62, and Erskine B., '63. Address, 314 Limestone street.

*JOHN MILLIGAN GRAHAM, Minister, Oxford, O.

A. B. Studied theology at Monmouth Coll., and licensed a minister in the United Presbyterian church. Born, March 31, 1839. Died, June 17, 1863.

EDWARD ALEXANDER GUY, Evangelist, Cincinnati, O.

A. B., A. M. Attended Princeton Theol. Sem., 1858-60. Has labored as an evangelist in New York, N. Y.; Cambridge, Mass.; Cincinnati, O.; London, England. Author of "Textual Corrections of the New Covenant;" Translation of "St. Matthew." Address, 10 Hopkins street.

*SAMUEL TELFORD HANNA, Broker, Fort Wayne, Ind.

A. B. Confident Clerk of the Vice-President of the Pittsburg, Fort Wayne & Chicago R. R., 1859-66. President of the Plymouth & Kansas R. R., 1880. Real Estate Broker and Insurance Agent, 1866-87. Died, Nov. 9, 1887.

ROBERT NEWMAN JOHN, Minister, Dublin, Ind.

B. S. Ph. B. Corporal, Co. K, 83rd Ohio Vol. Inf., 1862-63. Wounded at Arkansas Post, Jan. 11, 1863. Ordained a Universalist minister, 1874. Prof. of Mathematics, Wesbrook Seminary, Maine, 1870-73. Acting President of Smithson Coll., 1875-78. Pastor of Universalist churches at Mt. Carmel, Ind., 2 years; Fairfield, Ind., 4 years. Superintendent of Universalist churches in Indiana, 1882-91.

76   MIAMI UNIVERSITY.

*ABNER FRANCIS JONES,   Minister,   Columbus, O.

A. B. Attended Lane Seminary, 1858-61. Ordained by Miami Congregational Conference, 1861. Pastor of Pres. churches at New Albany, Ind., and Columbus, O. Served in the three months' service, U. S. A., 1864. Died on board a boat near Washington, D. C., on his return home, Aug. 1864.

*WILLIAM LEWIS LOCKWOOD, Manufacturer, Usquepaugh, R. I.

A. B. Admitted to the bar, 1860. Recruited Co. H, 48th N. Y. Vol. Inf., 1861. First Lieutenant and Captain of the same, 1861-63. Wounded at Fort Wagner, July 18, 1863. Appointed A. A. G., 2nd Division, 10th Army Corps, Jan., 1864. Resigned and entered the manufacturing business, Usquepaugh, R. I., 1864. Died, Aug. 17, 1865.

*GEORGE MUNNS LYTLE,   Oxford, O.

A. B. Travelled through the Central American states after graduation. Died, Aug. 4, 1861.

*CHARLES BEATTY MAGILL,   Minister,   Birmingham, Ia.

A. B. Attended Western Theol. Sem., 1858-61. Licensed by Presbytery of Washington, April, 1860. Ordained by Presbytery of Fairfield, May 13, 1864. Pastor of Pres. church at Birmingham, Ia., 1864. Served in the U. S. Christian Commission. Born, Wellsville, O., Oct. 3, 1840. Died, Aug. 27, 1864.

JOHN MCCLENAHAN,

A. B., A. M. Last address known, Cambridge City, Ind.

ARMOUR JAMES MCFARLAND,   Minister,   St. John, N. B.

A. B., A. M. Ordained by Ref. Pres. church, 1862. Pastor of Ref. Pres. churches at Jefferson Co., Pa., 1862-82; St. John, New Brunswick, 1882—. Brother of James, '59.
Address, 25 Peel Street.

ROBERT MOORE,   Civil Engineer,   St. Louis, Mo.

A. B., A. M. Assistant U. S. Engineer, Camp Nelson, Ky., 1863. Chief Engineer and Contractor in building Belleville and Carondelet R. R. Sewer Commissioner of St. Louis, Mo., 1877-81. Now Chief Engineer of the St. Louis Merchants' Bridge Terminal Railway. Member American Association of Civil Engineers. Member Institution of Civil Engineers, England.
Address, 61 Vandwenter Place.

JOSEPH ARMSTRONG MORROW,   Minister,   Kansas City, Mo.

A. B. Studied theology at Monmouth and Allegheny. Licensed by Monmouth Presbytery, April 26, 1860. Ordained by Chicago Presbytery, Oct. 16, 1862. Spent 7 years as missionary in the Northwest. Pastor of United Pres. churches at New Jefferson and New Market, O., 1870-85; Greenwood and Kingsville, Mo., 1886-89; Kansas City, Mo., 1889—. Brother of David, '52.
Address, 1603 Penn street.

*TUDOR HOMER PARKER, Lawyer, Covington, Ky.

A. B. Admitted to the bar. Died, June 21, 1861.

JAMES BARNES PATERSON, New York, N. Y.

A. B. Attended Western Theol. Sem., 1858-59. Licensed by Pres. of Miami, Dec. 1858. Ordained by Presbytery of Steubenville, 1860. Pastor of Pres. churches at Steubenville, O., 1860-65; Elizabeth, N. J., 1865-76. Suspended from the ministry, 1876.

JAMES RAMSEY PATTERSON, Merchant, Glendale, O.

A. B. Was engaged in business in Cincinnati, O. Special correspondent, Cincinnati "Commercial Gazette." Now retired.

GARNET ADRIAN POLLOCK, Minister, Mendota, Ills.

A. B., A. M. Was graduated from Western Theol. Sem., 1860. Licensed by Presbytery of Sidney, Sept., 1861. Ordained by Presbytery of Wabash, June, 1867. Prof. of Mathematics, Augusta Coll., Ky., 1860-61. President Okaw Seminary, Shelbyville, Ills., 1862-67. Pastor of Pres. churches at Tower Hill and Prairie Bird, Ill., 1866-69; Effingham, Ills., 1869-77; Mendota, Ills., 1877—.

OLIVER WYATT ROOT, Lawyer, Newport, Ky.

A. B., A. M. Admitted to the bar. Was City Attorney for Newport, Ky., and County Attorney for Campbell Co., Ky.

*FRANKLIN HOWARD SCOBEY, Editor, Woods, O.

A. B. Private, 5th Ohio Cav., U. S. A., 1861. In Provost General's office, Dayton, O., 1863. Editor of "Telegraph," Hamilton, O., 1867-79. Stock raiser in Kansas, 1879-82. Farmer, Woods, O., 1882-88. A founder of the Sigma Chi fraternity. Died, July 22, 1888.

*WILLIAM VALENTINE SMELTZER, Lawyer, New Orleans, La.

A. B. Admitted to the bar, 1861. Practised law at New Orleans, La., 1861-66. Mysteriously disappeared in 1866 and has never been heard from. Supposed to have been murdered.

JOHN BUCK SMITH, Minister, Crockett, Tex.

A. B., A. M. Was graduated from Western Theol. Sem, 1861. Licensed by the Presbytery of Allegheny, April, 1860. Ordained by Presbytery of Oxford, 1867. Chaplain, 19th Ohio Vol. Inf., U. S. A., 1862-65. Pastor of Pres. churches at Spring and Clyde, O., 1867-69; Kentland, Ind., 1869-73; Williamsburg and Batavia, O., 1873-77. President of Farmer's Coll., 1877-79. Pastor at Monticello, Ind., 1879-87. President Mary Allen Sem., Crockett, Tex., 1887—.

NATHANIEL J. THOMPSON, Farmer, Denver, Col.

A. B., A. M. Principal in Public Schools, 1858-71. Retired to a farm on account of ill health. In Paymaster's department, U. S. A., Fortress Monroe, 1863.
Address, 2229 Clarkson street.

*DICKINSON PHILLIPS THRUSTON, Dayton, O.

A. B. Studied theology but was never an active minister. Adjutant and Captain, 93rd Ohio Vol. Inf., 1862–63. Aid-de-camp on staff of General R. C. Schenck, 1863. Discharged on account of ill health. Brother of Gates P, '55. Died, Jan. 31, 1872.

JOSEPH BENNETT TITUS, Lawyer, Sullivan, Ills.

A. B., A. M. L L. B., Cincinnati Law School, 1860.

DAVID MEIKLEHAM URE, Minister, Allegheny, Pa.

A. B., A. M. D. D., Wooster Univ., 1883. Studied theology at Allegheny. Licensed by Presbytery of Monongahela, April 8, 1861. Ordained by Presbytery of Argyle, Oct. 8, 1862. Pastor of United Pres. churches at Argyle, N. Y., 1862–72; Monmouth, Ills., 1872–74. General Agent of Monmouth Coll., 1874–76. General Agent and Treasurer of same, 1876–86. Member of the United Pres. Board of Education, Monmouth, Ills., 1874–88. Superintendent of Finance of Allegheny Theol. Sem., 1888—. Brother of Walter, '59.
Address, 25 Esplanade street.

EDGAR MELVILLE WARD, Artist, New York, N. Y.

A. B., A. M. Prof. of the National Academy of Design, New York City. National Academician.
Address, 51 West Tenth street.

HERBERT HENRY WEAKLEY, Journalist, Dayton, O.

A. B., A. M. Admitted to the bar, 1860. Practised law at Dayton, O., 1860–64. Land Commissioner of a Land Grant R. R. and identified with railroad interests, St. Paul, Minn., 1864–72. Removed to Troy, O., where he was engaged in banking business for a number of years. Removed to Dayton, O., and became the principal owner of the "Evening Herald." President of the Board of Trade when first organized in Dayton and continued as such for three years. A Director in various stock companies.
Address, 337 West Second street.

EDWARD PEET WILLIAMS, Merchant, Fort Wayne, Ind.

A. B., A. M. Admitted to the bar, 1861. First Lieutenant, 100th Ind. Vol. Inf., 1862–63. Captain of same, 1863–64. Engaged in wholesale drug business, Fort Wayne, Ind., and Dallas, Tex.; 1865–88. Largely interested with Meyer Bros. Drug Co., St. Louis and Kansas City, Mo., and Dallas, Tex. Retired since 1879. Resides in New York City.

MARK WILLIAMS, Minister, Oberlin, O.

A. B., A. M. Was graduated at Lane Seminary, 1861. Ordained, March, 1865. Pastor of Pres. churches in Illinois, 1865–66. Missionary at Kalgan, North China, 1867–92.

Class of 1859.

*AARON MONFORT ATEN, Lawyer, Cincinnati, O.

A. B. Studied theology at Monmouth, Ills., 1859–60. Private, 50th Ohio Vol. Inf., 1861. Promoted to a staff position in Quarter-master's department, where he served until the close of the war. Admitted to the bar, 1866. Was Pension Agent at Cincinnati, O. Brother of John L., '55. Died, Aug. 13, 1878.

*JOEL ALLAN BATTLE,   Student of Law,   Lavergne, Tenn.

A. B. Studied law at Cincinnati Law School, 1859-61. Adjutant, 20th
Tenn. Inf., C. S. A., 1861-62. Killed at the battle of Shiloh, April 7, 1862.

*DAVID RILEY CALDWELL,   Physician,   Montrose, Mo.

A. B. M. D., Univ. of Michigan, 1865. Served three months in U. S. A.,
1863. Died, April 10, 1883.

*OLIVER S. CANBY,   Manufacturer,   Albion, Ills.

A. B. Died about 1872.

*DANIEL CARGILL COOPER,   Minister,   McComb, O.

A. B. Was graduated from the Ref. Pres. Theol. Sem. Licensed, April,
1862. Pastor of Ref. Pres. church at Elgin, Ill., 1863-68. Pastor of Pres.
churches at Venango, Pa., 1868-69; Centreville, Pa., 1869-74; Leipsic and
McComb, O., 1874-82. Brother of James H, '61. Died, Feb. 9, 1882.

JOHN S. CRAIG,

A. B., A. M. Last known address, Columbia, Tenn.

SAMUEL WATTS DAVIES,   Merchant,   Dayton, O.

A. B., A. M. Captain, First Ohio Vol. Inf., 1861-64. Aid-de-camp to Gen-
eral A. D. McCook. Member Board of Education, Dayton, O., 1873-82.
Member of Tax Commission, 1892—. Brother of J. Pierce, '63.
Address, 211 West Third street.

*JAMES HARMON DILLS,   Tobacconist,   New York, N. Y.

B. S., 1857. A. B. Admitted to the bar and practised law, Cincinnati, O.,
1858-61. Removed to New York, 1866, and became a wholesale merchant
in tobacco. Born, Piqua, O., Oct. 23, 1838. Died on board the steamer
"Bothnia" on his return from Europe, Sept. 1, 1882.

DANIEL HENRY EVANS,   Minister,   Youngstown, O.

A. B., A. M. D. D., Wooster Univ., 1886. Attended Western Theol. Sem.,
1859-60. Licensed by Presbytery of Pittsburg, 1861. Ordained by Presbytery of Monro, 1863. Teacher in Sewickly Academy, Pa., 1860. Pastor
of Pres. churches at Blissfield and Palmyra, Mich., 1862-66; Grand Haven,
Mich., 1866-69; Minersville, Pa., 1869-70; Youngstown, O., 1870—.

HUGH PARKS JACKSON,   Minister,   Greenfield, O.

A. B., A. M. Studied theology at Xenia and Allegheny. Licensed by
Presbytery of Xenia, March 28, 1865. Ordained by Presbytery of Lake,
Dec. 19, 1865. Sergeant in Militia, Cincinnati, O., 1862. Pastor of United
Pres. churches at Waterford, Pa., 1865-69; Hanover, Ind., 1876-89;
Greenfield, O., 1889—; Superintendent of Schools, Cedarville, O., 1871-75.
Author of "History of the Waterford and Carmel Congregations," and
"The Jackson Genealogy."

JOSHUA R. KYLE, Minister, Amsterdam, N. Y.

A. B. Studied theology at Xenia, O. Licensed by Presbytery of Xenia, March, 1862. Ordained by Presbytery of St. Louis, Oct. 12, 1864. Pastor of United Pres. churches at Fall River, Mass., 1867-75; Pittsburg, Pa., 1876-79. Joined the Ref. Dutch church, Dec., 1880, and has since been pastor at Amsterdam, N. Y. Address, 61 Arch street.

*MARTIN MAY, Student of Law, Eaton, O.

B. S. Studied law, but died in 1860, before he was admitted to the bar.

*DUNCAN MCDONALD, Lawyer, Urbana, O.

A. B. Admitted to the bar, 1871. Chief Clerk in the subsistance department of the U. S. Army at Kelley's Ferry, Atlanta, Ga., Marietta, Ga., and Eastport, Miss. Prosecuting Attorney for Morris Co., Kan., 1872-73. Prosecuting Attorney for Champaign Co., O., 1879-82. Born, West Liberty, O., Nov. 24, 1841. Died, Dec. 23, 1882.

JAMES SMITH MCDONALD, Minister, San Rafael, Cal.

A. B., A. M. Attended Princeton Theol. Sem. Ordained, 1862. Pastor of Pres. churches at Arcata, Cal., 1862-64; Sacramento, Cal., 1864-69; South Salem, O., 1869-70; San Diego, Cal., 1870-72; Eureka, Cal., 1872-75; San Rafael, 1875-84. Synodical Missionary of the Synod of the Pacific, San Rafael, Cal., 1884—.

JOSEPH MCFARLAND, Farmer, Stanton, Pa.

A. B. Studied theology. Licensed by the Ref. Pres. church, 1867. Preached for six months. Brother of Armour J, '58.

*SAMUEL MCKINLEY, Mt. Leigh, O.

B. S. Died, 1861.

*HENRY JOHNSON MCLANDBURGH, Chillicothe, O.

B. S. Captain, 17th Ohio Vol. Inf., U. S. A., 1861-62. Killed in the battle of Fredericksburgh, Va., Dec. 14, 1862.

*SAMUEL HARVEY MCMILLAN, Teacher, Xenia, O.

A. B. Taught in South Carolina, 1859-61. Private in 110th Ohio Vol. Inf., U. S. A., 1861-65. Died, April 15, 1869..

*JOSEPH MILLIKIN, Minister, Hamilton, O.

A. B., A. M. Ph. D., Ohio State Univ., 1881. Attended Princeton Theol. Sem. Prof. of Greek, Miami Univ., 1870-71. Prof. of Modern Languages and Literature, Ohio State Univ., Columbus, O., 1873-81. Resigned on account of ill-health. Brother of Minor, '54. Died in the fall of 1882.

JOSIAH MORROW, Lawyer, Lebanon, O.

A. B., A. M. Admitted to the bar. Author of "History of Warren County, Ohio," 1882.

*JAMES MURDOCH ORR, Minister, East Greenwich, N. Y.

A. B. Studied theology at Allegheny. Licensed by First Presbytery of Ohio, April 4, 1862. Ordained by Presbytery of Argyle, March 10, 1864. Pastor of United Pres. church at East Greenwich, Washington Co., N. Y., 1864-65. Born, Fairhaven, O., March 31, 1838. Died, April 18, 1865.

JACOB J. PUGSLEY, Lawyer, Hillsboro, O.

A. B., A. M. Admitted to the bar. Member Ohio House of Representatives, 64th and 65th General Assemblies. Member Ohio State Senate, 2 years. Member U. S. House of Representatives, 1887-91.

JOHN ABERCROMBIE REYNOLDS, Minister, Putnam, N. Y.

A. B. D. D., Monmouth Coll. Studied theology at Monmouth Coll. Licensed by First Presbytery of Ohio, June, 1861. Ordained by Presbytery of Monmouth, June 17, 1863. Pastor of United Pres. churches at Cedar Creek, Ills., 1863-72; Rock Island, Ills., 1872-85; Putnam, N. Y., 1885—.

ISAAC COE SICKELS, Farmer, Schell City, Mo.

A. B.

*GEORGE WILLIAM SIMPSON, Physician, Morning Sun, O.

A. B. M. D., Cincinnati Med. Coll., 1867. Born, Morning Sun, O., Nov. 21, 1839. Died, June 21, 1870.

JAMES McLAIN SMITH, Editor and Farmer, Dayton, O.

A. B., A. M. Admitted to the bar, 1861, but never took an active part in practice. Editor and Proprietor "Daily and Weekly Ledger," 1867-68. Member Ohio House of Representatives, 1871-72. Editor and Proprietor "Daily and Weekly Democrat," 1874-77. Now a farmer and stock raiser. Member Board of Trustees of Miami Univ., 1872—.

JOSEPH HOVER STEVENSON, Minister, Mt. Carmel, Ills.

A. B. D. D., Miami Univ., 1889. Was graduated from Western Theol. Sem., 1864. Licensed by Presbytery of Sidney, April, 1863. Ordained by Presbytery of Redstone, Oct., 1864. Principal of Greenfield Academy, 1859-61. Pastor of Pres. churches at Brownsville and Little Redstone, Pa., 1864-68; Birmingham, Pa., 1868-70; Groveport, O., 1870-73; Fairview, W. Va., 1873-75; Tyrone and Scottdale, Pa., 1875-83; Nashville, Ills., 1883-87; Mt. Carmel, Ills., 1888—.

SAMUEL RUTHERFORD STORMONT, Minister, Princeton, Ind.

A. B. Studied theology at Philadelphia, Pa. Ordained, 1871. Pastor of Ref. Pres. churches at Fayetteville, Tenn., 1871-78; Linden, Nova Scotia, 1880-87. Now retired.

PAUL FITZHUGH THORNTON, Lawyer, Austin, Tex.

B. S. Studied law, Univ. of Louisville, Ky., 1860–61. Admitted to the bar, 1866. Captain in C. S. A., 1861–65. County Judge of Vernon Co., Mo., 1876–82.
Address, 1909 August street, Austin, Tex. From June to September, Nevada, Mo.

WALTER URE, Physician, Allegheny City, Pa.

A. B., A. M. M. D., College of Physicians and Surgeons, New York City, 1866. Assistant Surgeon, U. S. Vols., 1864–65. Brother of David M, '58.
Address, 176 Federal street.

WILLIAM ALLEN WALLACE, Broker, Denver, Col.

A. B. Has been employed in teaching and farming. At present Real Estate Broker. Brother of James A, '61.
Address, 429 East Bayard street.

*JAMES C. WYATT, Minister, New York, N. Y.

A. B. Attended Ref. Pres. Theol. Sem., Philadelphia, Pa. Ordained, 1862. Chaplain in U. S. Army. Brother of Richard C, '59. Died in hospital at Memphis, Tenn., July 10, 1863.

RICHARD CALVIN WYATT, Minister, Norwich, O.

A. B. Studied theology at Monmouth Coll. Licensed by Presbytery of Monmouth, April 19, 1871. Ordained by Presbytery of Des Moines, Sept. 20, 1872. Pastor of United Pres. churches at Clifton, O., and Norwich, O. Brother of James C, '59.

ALEXANDER HAMILTON YOUNG, Minister, Newton, N. J.

A. B., A. M. Attended Lane Seminary, 1860–63. Ordained by Presbytery of Chillicothe, Nov. 8, 1864. Pastor of Pres. churches at South Salem, O., 1864–69; Oxford, O., 1869–72; Greenville, N. J., 1872–81; Newton, N. J., 1883—. Trustee of Miami Univ., 1869–72.

Class of 1860.

*JOHN JEFFERSON ABERNETHY, Minister, Terre Haute, Ind.

A. B. Attended Princeton Theol. Sem., 1860–63. Licensed by the Presbytery of Louisville, Aug. 8, 1866. Principal of White Water Academy, Md., 1863–64. Stated supply of the Pres. church at Pennsylvania Run, Ky., 1864–69; Big Bend, Ky., 1867. Teacher at Bell Grove and Edenwood, Ky., 1868–71. Pastor-elect at Ridgewood, Ky., 1869–72. Brother of Allen, '65, and Henri M., '65. Born, Dunlapsville, Ind., Sept. 7, 1836. Died, Oct. 12, 1873.

MIAMI UNIVERSITY. 83

*HENRY NEWTON ANKENEY, Teacher, Panola, Miss.

A. B. Private tutor near Panola, Miss. Died, Dec. 8, 1860.

MAYNARD C. ATKINSON,

B. S.

EDGAR ALLEN BALDWIN, Farmer, Bird City, Kan.

B. S. Dealer in Real Estate and Farmer.

JOHN BARRETT, Minister, Lyndon, O.

A. B., A. M. Attended Western Theol. Sem., 1860-62. Licensed by the Presbytery of Chillicothe, Sept., 1862. Ordained by same, Sept., 1863. Pastor of Pres. church at Lyndon, O., since 1863.

*DAVID C. BECKETT, Hamilton, O.

A. B. Brother of William, '44. Died, 1864.

SAMUEL MONTGOMERY CAMBERN, Lawyer, Elsinore, Cal.

A. B. Admitted to the bar. Assistant Adjutant General and Captain of Volunteers, U. S. A., 1861-65.
Address, Elsinore, San Diego Co.

WILLIAM COLEMAN, Minister and Teacher, Deepwater, Mo.

A. B. Western Theol. Sem., 1860-62. Licensed by Presbytery of Chillicothe, O., April, 1862. Ordained by same, 1862. Pastor of Presbyterian churches at West Union and Manchester, O., 1862-67; Pleasant Hill, Mo., 1872-75; Columbus, Kan., 1876-81; Garnett, Kan., 1881-87; Deepwater, Mo., 1887—. Principal of Public schools at West Union and Manchester, O.; and Pleasant Hill, Mo.

GEORGE T. CRISSMAN, Minister, Longmont, Col.

A. B., A. M. D. D., Miami Univ., 1889. Attended Western Theol. Sem., 1860-62. Licensed by Presbytery of Chillicothe, April, 1862. Ordained by Presbytery of Rock River, April, 1864. Pastor of Presbyterian churches at Morrison, Ills., 1863-78; Kearney, Neb., 1878-82. State Superintendent of Missions for Neb., 1883-86. Pastor of Pres. church, Hastings, Neb., 1886-90. President of Longmont Coll., 1890—.

ELIJAH FRANCIS DEWEY, Lawyer, Big Rapids, Mich.

A. B., A. M. Admitted to the bar. Circuit Court Commissioner, 1870-71 Local Editor, "Detroit Free Press," 1861-62; "Chicago Times," 1862-63.

*JAMES R. FINNEY, Minister, Coultersville, Ills.

A. B. Studied theology at Xenia, O. Licensed by Presbytery of Xenia, June 26, 1866. Ordained by Presbytery of Kansas, June 20, 1867. Pastor of United Pres. church at Prosperity, Ills., 1868-73. Principal Coultersville Academy. Died, July 18, 1873.

84   MIAMI UNIVERSITY.

ANDREW LINTON HARRIS,   Lawyer,   Columbus, O.

B. S. Admitted to the bar, 1863. Captain, Co. C, 20th Ohio Vol. Inf., 1861-63. Promoted to Major of same, Jan. 12, 1863, and to Colonel, May 3, 1863. Brevetted Brigadier-General, March 13, 1865. Member of Ohio State Senate, 1866-67. Member Ohio House of Representatives, 1886-89. Lieutenant-Governor of Ohio, 1891—. Brother of Joseph, '60. Father of Walter C, '91.
Permanent address, Eaton, O.

JOSEPH HARRIS,   Farmer,   Darrtown, O.

B. S. Private, Corporal and First Sergeant, Co. C, 75th Ohio Vol. Inf., U. S. A., 1862-65. Brother of Andrew L, '60.

JOHN CALVIN LEWIS,   Superintendent,   Chicago, Ills.

A. B. Second Lieutenant, First Lieutenant, and Captain, 41st Ills. Vol. Inf., 1861-63. Wounded at the battle of Shiloh, April 6, 1862. Captain's commission received for meritorious service at Fort Donelson. Now Superintendent of Manufactory.
Address, 4138 Ellis avenue.

ABRAHAM BROWER LOWES,   Minister,   Washington, Pa.

A. B., A. M. Attended Western Theol. Sem., 1860-63. Licensed by Presbytery of Cincinnati, Sept. 6, 1865. Ordained by the Presbytery of Fort Wayne, June 6, 1867. First Lieutenant and Captain, 18th Ind. Vol. Inf., 1861-64. Pastor of Pres. churches at Decatur, Ind., 1867-68; Tidioute, Pa., 1869-70; Mason, O., 1871-74; Belle Vernon, Pa., 1874-82; Cool Spring and Fredonia, Pa., 1884-86. Teacher at Canonsburg, Pa., 1882-84. Evangelist for Presbytery of Washington, 1886-91; Parkersburg, W. Va., 1892—.

*BENJAMIN MCLEAN MCCARTY,   Lawyer,   Brookville, Ind.

A. B. Private, 13th Ind. Vol. Inf., 1861-64. Clerk in Revenue Collector's office, 1868. Died, Feb. 18, 1872.

*HENRY FOSTER MORROW,   Teacher,   Fosters, O.

A. B. Engaged in teaching for a few years, then entered the employ of the Little Miami R. R. Co. Died, Nov. 19, 1867.

ASA MULFORD,   Farmer,   Greenville, Ills.

B. S. Private, U. S. A. Volunteers, 1861-64.

EZRA FITCH PABODY,   Druggist,   Minneapolis, Minn.

A. B. Hospital Steward in the 3rd Minnesota Vol. Inf., 1861-65.
Address, 28 Thirteenth street.

ABRAM M. PENCE,   Lawyer,   Chicago, Ills.

A. B., A. M. L L. B., Cincinnati Law School, 1862.
Address, 550 North State street.

CORNELIUS CLARK PLATTER, Farmer, Red Oak, Ia.

A. B. Captain, Co. D., 81st Ohio Vol. Inf., 1861-63. Assistant Adjutant-General, 15th Army Corps, 1864. Member Iowa House of Representatives, 1873-74 and 1883-84. Farmer and Stock Raiser.

GEORGE WASHINGTON POTTER, Physician, Sterling, Kan.

B. S. M. D., Cincinnati Physio-Medical Coll., 1873. Volunteer in U. S. Army.

JOHN RINER SAYLER, Lawyer, Cincinnati, O.

A. B., A. M. LL. B., Cincinnati Law School, 1863. LL. D., Heidelberg, Germany, 1865. Appointed Judge of Superior Court, Cincinnati, O., 1890. Elected to same position, 1891, for a term of five years. Author of "Sayler's American Form Book;" "Sayler's Revised Statutes of Ohio," 1875. Brother of Milton, '52; and Nelson, '57. Address, Grand Hotel.

FRANK ASBURY SPENCER, Minister, Columbus, O.

A. B., A. M. Private, Co. B, 141st Ohio Vol. Inf., 1864. Ordained, 1865. Missionary in India, 1865-70; Italy, 1872-74. Pastor at Westerville, O., 1870-72; Harmar, O., 1874-76. Now General Book Agent. Address, 628 Franklin avenue.

EDWARD LIVINGSTON TAYLOR, Lawyer, Columbus, O.

A. B., A. M. Admitted to the bar, 1862. Private in volunteer company, 1861. Captain, 95th Ohio Vol. Inf., 1862-63. Trustee of Miami Univ., 1881—. *Vide*, Sketch and Portrait, "Miami Journal," Vol. II., No. 8.

WALTER SCOTT THOMAS, Lawyer, Troy, O.

A. B., A. M. LL. B., Harvard Law School, 1862. Ensign in U. S. Navy, 1863-65. United States Commissioner, since 1865. Prosecuting Attorney for Miami Co., O., 1870-75. Editor of "Miami Union," 1883—. Trustee of Miami Univ., 1872-81.

DAVID WILLIAM TODD, Lawyer, Urbana, O.

A. B., A. M. Admitted to the bar. Private, 2nd Ohio Vol. Inf., U. S. A. Quartermaster, 86th Ohio Vol. Inf., 1861-62. Lieutenant Colonel, 134 Ohio Vol. Inf., 1862-63. Prosecuting Attorney for Champaign Co., O., 1864-67. Probate Judge, 1878—.

*CHARLES D. WARREN, U. S. Civil Service, Washington, D. C.

A. B., A. M. Private tutor, 1860-61. Teacher in Public Schools, McDonough and Fulton Cos., Ills., 1861-62. M. D., Georgetown Coll., 1864. Clerk, U. S. War Department, 1866-70. Principal Clerk, U. S. Bureau of Education, 1870-72. Chief Clerk of same, 1872-81. Statistician, 1881. Member American Association for the Advancement of Science; Anthropological Society, and American Public Health Association. Died, Sept. 9, 1889.

JOHN ANDREWS WEBB,   Merchant,   Austin, Tex.

A. B. Dealer in agricultural implements and State agent for the Moline Plow Co.

BURWELL GOODE WILKERSON,   Lawyer,   Sedalia, Mo.

A. B., A. M. Admitted to the bar, 1862. County Attorney for Pettis Co., Mo., 1868-72. City Attorney for Sedalia, Mo., 1869-71. Also engaged in farming.
Address, 322 West Seventh street.

*SPENCER H. WILSON,   Tranquillity, O.

B. S. Killed in the late war, 1862.

JOHN WOODS,   Minister,   St. Paul, Minn.

A. B., A. M. D. D., Miami Univ., 1889. Studied theology at Western Theol. Sem., and Princeton Theol. Sem., 1860-62. Ordained by Presbytery of Oxford, Sept. 25, 1861. Chaplain, 3rd Ohio Vol. Inf., U. S. A., 1864. Pastor of Pres. churches at Urbana, O., 1865-68; Bloomingburg, O., 1868-72; Chicago, Ills., 1872-73; Fort Wayne, Ind., 1873-75; Chico, Cal., 1875-76; Cedar Falls, 1877-78; White Bear Lake, Minn., 1879-81; Wilmot and Diamond Lake, Minn., 1883-84; Chicago, Ills., 1884-86; St. Paul, Minn., 1886—.
Address, Merriam Park.

CYRUS MANSFIELD WRIGHT,   Dentist,   Cincinnati, O.

B. S. D. D. S., 1864. Teacher of Physiology and Pathology, Ohio Coll. of Dental Surgery. President American Dental Society of Europe, 1876. President Mississippi Dental Society, 1883-84; President Ohio Dental Society, 1888. Author of "Practical Hints about the Teeth," translated into German.
Address, 277 West Seventh.

JOHN LEE YARYAN,   Lawyer,   Richmond, Ind.

A. B., A. M.

Class of 1861.

STEPHEN COOPER AYRES,   Oculist,   Cincinnati, O.

A. B., A. M. M. D., Ohio Med. Coll., 1864. Assistant Surgeon, U. S. Volunteers, 1861-64. Lecturer on Ophthalmology, Cincinnati Hospital, 1870-82. Associate editor of "American Journal of Ophthalmology."
Address, 64 West Seventh street.

*SAMUEL Z. BRACKENRIDGE,   Harrison, O.

B. S. Born, Sept. 21, 1840. Died, Jan. 17, 1890.

MIAMI UNIVERSITY. 87

*ROBERT STEWART BROWN,   Farmer,   Bainbridge, O.

A. B. Served in first three month's call, U. S. A., 1861. Orderly Sergeant, Co. H., 89th Ohio Vol. Inf., 1861-62. Was captured at Chickamauga and kept a prisoner of war at Libby, Wilmington and Andersonville prisons until April, 1865. His health was so impaired from long confinement in prisons that he was an invalid until his death, which was caused by blood poison arising from a wound, Dec. 24, 1872.

*EDWARD NICHOLAS CLOPPER,   Teacher,   Houston, Tex.

A. B., A. M. First Lieutenant, 83rd Ohio Vol. Inf., 1861-65. Teacher in public school at Newport, Ky., 1865-68; Cumminsville, O., 1868-70; Camp Washington, O., 1870-80. Superintendent of Public Schools, Houston, Tex., 1880-81. Born, Dec., 1840. Died, Oct. 2, 1881.

JAMES H. COOPER,   Minister,   Red Oak, O.

A. B., A. M. Studied theology at Philadelphia, Pa. Ordained by the Presbytery of Chicago, Sept. 12, 1866. Served in the Sanitary and Christian Commissions, U. S. A., 1863-65. Pastor of Ref. Pres. churches at Mt. Vernon, Ia., 1866-67; Morning Sun, O., 1867-70. Pastor of United Pres. churches at Morning Sun, O., 1870-74; Topeka, Kan., 1874-76. Pastor of Pres. churches at Mt. Vernon, Iowa, 1876-82; Hanging Rock, O., 1890-91; Red Oak, O., 1891—. Field Agent for Coe Coll., 18 months. Missionary in Florida and Tennessee, 3 years. Brother of Daniel C, '59.

ISAAC EDWIN CRAIG,   Lawyer,   Troy, O.

B. S. L L. B., Cleveland Law Coll., 1862. Author of "Radiation, a Function of Gravity."

*EBENEZER CURRIE,   Minister,   Alexandria, Egypt.

A. B. Studied theology at Xenia. Licensed by the Presbytery of Xenia, June 24, 1862. Ordained by the same, Oct. 8, 1863. Sailed as a Missionary to Egypt, March 4, 1865. Born, Greene Co., O., Feb. 10, 1834. Died, Oct. 18, 1869.

*AUGUSTUS SAMUEL DAMERON,   Physician,   Dayton, Ky.

A. B., A. M. M. D., Ohio Med. Coll. Practised in Newport and Dayton, Ky. Died, April 2, 1890.

*OZRO JENNISON DODDS,   Lawyer,   Cincinnati, O.

A. B. Organized Co. B., 20th Ohio Vol. Inf., known as the University Rifles, and captain of same, 1861. Captain, 81st Ohio Vol. Inf., U. S. A., 1861-63. Lieutenant-Colonel of First Alabama Cavalry, U. S. Vols., 1863-64. Member Ohio House of Representatives, 1870-71. Member U. S. House of Representatives, 1872-74. Trustee of Miami Univ., 1875-82. Orator at the Reunion of the Army of Tennessee, 1881. Died, Columbus, O., April 18, 1882.

*NATHAN PALMER DUNN,   Logansport, Ind.

A. B. Editor of "Miami Monthly," 1860-61. Captain, 29th Ind. Vol. Inf., 1861-63. Killed at the Battle of Chickamauga, Sept. 19, 1863.

88 MIAMI UNIVERSITY.

*FRANK DAVENPORT EVANS, Minister, Eaton, O.

A. B. First Lieutenant, 20th Ohio Vol. Inf., 1861-62. Major of same, 1862-64. Studied law, but never practised. Entered the ministry of the Universalist church and preached at Boston, Ind.; Mt. Gilead, O.; and Eaton, O. Died, Oct. 2, 1879.

WILLIAM H. EVANS, Physician, Sanford, Fla.

B. S. M. D., Univ. of Michigan, 1865.

JAMES ALEXANDER HAIR, Broker, Chicago, Ills.

A. B. Private, Co. B, 20th Ohio Vol. Inf., 1861. Lieutenant, 133rd Ind. Vol. Inf., 1863. Real Estate broker. Address, 4823 Lake avenue.

*JOHN MILTON HIATT, Physician, Peoria, Ills.

A. B., A. M. M. D., Rush Med. Coll., 1864. Contract Surgeon in U. S. A. Officers Hospital, Lookout Mountain and Indianapolis, Ind., 1864-65. Died, Crawfordsville, Ind., March 20, 1869.

JOHN E. HILL, Riverside, Cal.

A. B.

WILLIAM ROPER HOLLINGSWORTH, Editor, Sigourney, Ia.

A. B., A. M. Private, Co. B, 20th Ohio Vol. Inf., 1861. Editor and proprietor, "Review," Sigourney, Ia.

*HORACE H. JUSTICE, Cincinnati, O.

B. S. Died, 1862.

DAVID C. KYLE, Civil Engineer, Washington, Ia.

A. B. Private in 10th Ohio Battery, U. S. A. County Surveyor of Washington Co., Iowa, for many years. Employed mostly in railroad work.

*JOHN MARSHALL, Teacher, Morning Sun, O.

A. B. Prof. in Academy, Morning Sun, O., 1862-73. Born, Preble Co., O., March 19, 1838. Died, May 9, 1873.

THOMAS BRAINARD MARSHALL, Book-keeper, Sidney, O.

A. B. Private and First Sergeant, Co. K, 83rd Ohio Vol. Inf., 1862-65.

AUSTIN MORRIS, Lawyer, Chicago, Ills.

A. B., A. M.

JOHN WORRELL MORRIS, Lawyer, Troy, O.

A. B., A. M. Admitted to the bar, 1863. Mayor of Troy, 1868-71. Member Ohio State Senate, 1871-75. Postmaster of Troy, O., 1885-90.

*JOHN RILEY ORR, Cedarville, O.

A. B. Died, Jan. 31, 1866.

*WILLIAM L. PORTER, Army Officer, Gallatin, Tenn.

A. B. Private, Co. B, 20th Ohio Vol. Inf., 1861. Enlisted Co. B., 24th Ohio Vol. Inf., 1861. Promoted to First Lieutenant, Co., D, 56th Ohio Vol. Inf., Nov. 10, 1862, and ordered to report to General Rosecrans, on whose staff he served until General Thomas assumed command. Captain and Assistant Adjutant General, U. S. Vols., 1864-65. Brevetted Major for meritorious service, 1865. Appointed Second Lieutenant, 5th Regular U. S. Cavalry, Aug. 1867, and stationed at Gallatin, Tenn. Wounded in the leg by the explosion of an anvil while firing a salute, Feb. 22, 1868. Died, about two months afterward. Son of Joseph, '35.

WILBERFORCE REYNOLDS, Clerk, Oquawka, Ills.

A. B. Deputy County Clerk of Henderson Co., Ills.

WILLIAM S. SLOAN, Solicitor, Denver, Col.

A. B. Private, Co. B, 20th Ohio Vol. Inf., 1861. Private, Co. D, 47th Ohio Vol. Inf., 1862-65. Solicitor and Manager of the Advertising department of the "Rocky Mountain News," Denver, Colo.

*WILLIAM SMITH, Teacher, Newport, R. I.

A. B. Superintendent of Public Schools, Dayton, O., 1866-76. Principal of Private school, Newport, R. I., 1876-78. Born, Glasgow, Scotland, May 15, 1835. Died, June 20, 1878.

HENRY VAN MATRE, Lawyer, Cincinnati, O.

A. B., A. M. L L. B., Cincinnati Law school, 1866. Private, Co. A., 137th Ohio Vol. Inf., 1861. Clerk in Provost Marshal's office, 1862-63. Address, 22½ East Fourth street.

JOHN C. WAKEFIELD, Druggist, Lane, Kan.

A. B. Private, 20th Ohio Vol. Inf., 1861. Private, 4th Ohio Vol. Inf., 1862-65.

*JAMES ARNON WALLACE, Civil Engineer, Pawnee City, Neb.

A. B., A. M. County Surveyor for a number of years. Was also engaged in farming and in the furniture business. Brother of William A., '59. Died, Feb., 1889.

JAMES A. WHITESIDE, Agent, San Francisco, Cal.

B. S. Private, 20th Ohio Vol. Inf., 1861. Private, 86th Ohio Vol. Inf., 1862-64. Also served in U. S. Navy. Coast agent for the Harter Medicine Co.
Address, 105 Taylor street.

*JOSEPH H. WILEY, Fair Haven, O.

B. S. Private, Co. H, 93rd. Ohio Vol. Inf., 1862. Promoted to First Sergeant of same, Aug. 20, 1862. Killed in the battle of Stone River, Dec. 31, 1862.

MEADE CREIGHTON WILLIAMS, Minister, St. Louis, Mo.

A. B., A. M. D. D., Wooster Univ., 1882. Attended Princeton Theol. Sem., 1861-64. Member of Christian Commission, U. S. A., 1863. Pastor of Pres. churches at Sterling, Ills., 1865-73; Sandusky, O., 1873-77; Williamsport, Md., 1877-80; Princeton, Ills., 1880-92. Member Board of Directors of McCormick Theol. Sem., Chicago, Ills.; Collegiate Institute, Genessee, Ills.; Knox College, Galesburg, Ills. Editor of "The Mid Continent," 1892—.

JAMES AVERY WORDEN, Minister, Philadelphia, Pa.

A. B., A. M. D. D. Lafayette Coll. Attended Princeton Theol. Sem. Ordained by the Presbytery of Mohawk, Feb. 14, 1867. Second Lieutenant, Ohio Vols., U. S. A., 1861-63. Pastor of Pres. churches at Oswego, N. Y., 1866-72; Steubenville, O., 1872-78. Superintendent of Sabbath-School work in the Presbyterian Board of Publication, 1878-80. Secretary of Sabbath School work, 1880—.
Address, 1334 Chestnut street.

IRVIN BUCHANAN WRIGHT, Lawyer, Brookland, D. C.

A. B., A. M. Admitted to the bar, 1868. Private, Co. B, 20th Ohio Vol. Inf., 1861. Private, Second Lieutenant, and First Lieutenant, 11th U. S. Inf., 1861-63. Brevetted Captain of same at the Battle of Gettysburg, July 2, 1863. Aid-de-camp on staff of Gen. M. R. Patrick. Provost Marshal, Army of Potomac, 1864-65. Resigned, Nov. 1, 1866. Member Ohio House of Representatives, 1879-80.

Class of 1862.

ROBERT WILSON ANDREWS, Honolulu, Sandwich Islands.

B. S. Principal of the Kauai Industrial School, Malumala, 1890-91. Civil and Mechanical Engineer, Ewa Plantation Company.

J. EDWARD BAKER, Physician, Hartwell, O.

A. B. M. D.

ROBERT JOSEPH BROWN, Farmer, Morning Sun, O.

B. S. Corporal, Co. A, 156th Ohio Vol. Inf., 1864.

*JOHN A. COLESCOTT, Teacher, Brookville, Ind.

A. B., A. M. Teacher in public schools, 1862-72. U. S. Postal Service, 1872-82. Died about Christmas, 1891.

QUINCY CORWIN, Lawyer, Dayton, O.

A. B., A. M. LL. B., Cincinnati Law School, 1864. Private, Co. B, 20th Ohio Vol. Inf., 1861. Trustee of Miami Univ., 1887—. *Vide*, Sketch and Portrait, "Miami Journal," Vol. II., No. 8.
Address, Beckel Hotel.

MIAMI UNIVERSITY.

JAMES DAVIS, Farmer, Fosters, O.

A. B. Studied theology at Monmouth Coll., but on account of ill-health, — — was never ordained.

*JOHN EDWARDS, Lawyer, Maryville, Mo.

A. B., A. M. Admitted to the bar. Superintendent of Public Schools, Hillsboro, O., 1862-64; Hamilton, O., 1864-67. District Attorney for Nodaway Co., Mo., 1876-78. Died, Sept. 13, 1888.

HUGH STUART FULLERTON, Physician, Hillsboro, O.

A. B., A. M. M. D., Ohio Med. Coll., 1866. First Lieutenant, 1st Ohio Vol. Heavy Artillery, 1863-64. Assistant Physician, Central Ohio Insane Asylum, 1866-68. Author of "Ben Foraker's Breeches." Brother of Thomas A, '53; George H, '58 and Erskine B, '63.

THOMAS D. GARVIN, Minister, Pasadena, Cal.

A. B., A. M. Ordained a minister in the Christian church, 1872. President of Franklin Coll., 7 years. Brother of James H, '65.

GEORGE VERNON HALLIDAY, Manufacturer, Cincinnati, O.

A. B., A. M. President and Treasurer of the Cincinnati Safe and Lock Company.
Address, 41 Elm street.

JOHN THOMAS HARBINE, Manufacturer, Xenia, O.

B. S. Private, Co. D, 60th Regiment, Ohio National Guards, 1863.

JOHN MORELAND HENDERSON, Lawyer, Cleveland, O.

A. B. Attended Cleveland Law School. Admitted to the bar, 1864.
Address, 219 Superior street.

WILLIAM SLOCUM LUDLOW, Broker, Cincinnati, O.

A. B. L L. B., Cincinnati Law School, 1867, but never practised law. Real Estate Broker.
Address, 77 Garfield Place.

ISAAC BENNETT MORRIS, Lawyer, Richmond, Ind.

A. B. Admitted to the bar, Aug. 13, 1863. Author of "American Economy," and "The Battle of the Standards."

GEORGE VALENTINE NAUERTH, Lawyer, Chicago, Ills.

A. B., A. M. Student at Heidelberg, Germany, 1862-63; Ecole de Droit, Univ. of Paris, 1863-64. L L. B., Cincinnati Law School, 1865. Prosecuting attorney of Montgomery Co., O., 1868-70. Manufacturer of office and library furniture, Cincinnati, O., 1882-88. Manufacturer, Chicago, Ills., 1888—.
Address, 340 Dearborn street.

JAMES W. OWENS, Lawyer, Newark, O.

B. S. A. M. Attended law school, Ann Arbor, Mich., 1864-65. Admitted to the bar, 1865. Private, Co. B, 20th Ohio Vol. Inf., 1861. First Lieutenant, Co. A, 86th Ohio Vol. Inf., 1862-63. Captain Co. K, 86th Ohio Vol. Inf., 1863-64. Prosecuting Attorney of Licking Co., O., 1867-71. Member Ohio State Senate, 1875-79. President pro tem. of the same, 1877. Member U. S. House of Representatives, 1889—. Trustee of Miami Univ., 1878—. *Vide*, Portrait and Sketch, "Miami Journal," Vol. II, No. 8.

HIRAM DAVID PECK, Lawyer, Cincinnati, O.

A. B., A. M. L L. B. Harvard Law School, 1865. L L. D., Univ. of Cincinnati, 1892. Private, Co. A, 86th Ohio Vol. Inf. Assistant City Solicitor for Cincinnati, 1876-77. Judge of the Superior Court of Cincinnati, 1883-89. Director of Univ. of Cincinnati, 1878-84. Author of "Guide for Township Officers," seven editions. "Municipal Laws of Ohio," four editions. Address, 32 McGregor Avenue.

MORRIS PECK, Accountant, Cincinnati, O.

A. B., A. M. Private, Co. A, 86th Ohio Vol. Inf. 1862.
Address, United Bank Building. Residence, Red Bank.

*WILLIAM JAMES RONALD, Jeweler, Grand View, Ia.

B. S. Died, Feb. 20, 1882.

JOHN S. SCHENCK, Lawyer, Maryville, Mo.

A. B., A. M. Admitted to the bar, 1865. Private, 86th Ohio Vol. Inf., 1862.

Class of 1863.

*ROBERT NOBLE BISHOP, Lawyer, Paris, Ills.

A. B., A. M. Admitted to the bar, 1863. School Commissioner of Edgar Co., Ill., 1863-65. Member Illinois House of Representatives, 1870-71. Died, April 2, 1881.

CALVIN STEWART BRICE, . Lawyer, Lima, O.

A. B., A. M. Studied law at Ann Arbor, Mich, 1865-66. Admitted to the bar, 1866. Private, Co. B, 20th Ohio Vol. Inf., 1861. Private, Co. A, 86th Ohio Vol. Inf., 1862. Recruited Co. E, 180th Ohio Vol. Inf., and served as Captain of same, 1864-65. Retired from the practice of law, 1880, and devoted his attention to railroad interests. Completed the Lake Erie & Western R. R., 1871. Stockholder in New York, Chicago & St. Louis R. R.; Lake Erie & Western R. R.; Chicago & Atlantic R. R.; Ohio Central R. R.; Richmond & West Point Terminal R. R.; East Tennesee, Virginia & Georgia R. R.; Memphis & Georgia R. R.; Mobile & Birmingham R. R.; The National Telegraph Company; The Southern Trust Company; The Croton Aqueduct; The Chase National Bank; The Lima First National Bank, and various other enterprises. Chairman National Democratic Executive Committee, 1888. U. S. Senator from Ohio, 1891—. Trustee of Miami Univ., 1881—. President of the Alumni Association of Miami Univ. Delivered Alumni address at the Inauguration of President Warfield, 1889. Donor of $15,500 for the erection of Brice Hall, $500 for Alumni and Former Student Catalogue, $5,000 partial endowment of President's chair and various other sums. *Vide*, Sketch and Portrait, "Miami Journal," Vol. I, No. 5. and Vol. II, No. 8. New York address, 693 Fifth avenue.

JOHN GOLDEN BRONSON, Broker, Chicago, Ills.

A. B., A. M. Grain, Commission, Real Estate and Mining Broker. Now retired.
Address, 235 Michigan avenue.

CALVIN WHITFIELD COURTWRIGHT, Minister, Chicago, Ills.

A. B., A. M. Was graduated from Princeton Theol. Sem., 1868. Pastor of Pres. churches at Senecaville, O., 1867-69; Bristol and Deerfield, O., 1870-73; Cross Roads, O., 1871-75; Hayesville, O., 1885-87; Maywood, Ills., 1888-89.
Address, 4033 Vincennes avenue.

JOSEPH PIERCE DAVIES, Manufacturer, Dayton, O.

A. B., A. M. Manufacturer of Lard Oil, Tallow Oil, and Laundry Soap. Brother of Samuel W, '59.
Address, First and Ludlow streets.

FERMAN DICKASON DAVIS, Teacher, Graham, Mo.

A. B., A. M.

JAMES HENRY ELLIOTT, Minister, Washington, Ia.

A. B. Studied theology at Xenia, O. Licensed by the First Presbytery of Ohio, July 11, 1866. Ordained by Presbytery of Nebraska, Sept. 17, 1868. Corporal, Co. H, 156th Ohio Vol. Inf., 1864. Pastor of United Pres. churches at Pawnee City, Neb., 1868-69; Sycamore and Hopkinsville, O., 1870-80; Crawfordsville, Ia., 1881-88; Washington, Ia., 1888—.

CHARLES HENRY FISK, Lawyer, Covington, Ky.

A. B., A. M. L L. B., Cincinnati Law School, 1864. Captain, Co. A, First Regiment and Division of Squirrel Hunters, recruited at Miami Univ., 1862. Delivered address before Alumni Association, 1891.
Address, Fifth and Madison streets.

ERSKINE BOIES FULLERTON, Physician, Columbus, O.

A. B., A. M. M. D., Sterling Med. Coll., 1866. Private and First Lieutenant 86th Ohio Vol. Inf., 1862-63 and 1863-64. Prof. of Materia Medica and Therapeutics, Sterling Med. Coll., 1874—. Brother of Thomas A. '53, George H, '58, and Hugh S, '62.
Address. 131 East State street.

*WILLIAM ANDREW GRAHAM, Oxford, O.

A. B. Born, Feb. 3, 1841. Died, Nov. 7, 1863.

WILLIAM ANDREW HUTCHISON, Minister, Franklin, O.

A. B., A. M. Studied theology at Xenia, O. Licensed by Presbytery of Sidney, April 12, 1865. Ordained by same, April 18, 1866. Pastor of United Pres. church at Milroy, Ind.; 1867-69. Pastor of Pres. churches at Lockland, O.; Knightstown, Ind.; Evansville, Ind., and Franklin, O.

JAMES W. MCGREGOR, Minister, Minneapolis, Minn.

A. B., A. M. Entered the ministry of the Methodist Episcopal church. On account of failing health, retired from the ministry, 1876. Lived at Oxford, O., 1876-90. *Vide*, Sketch and Portrait, "Miami Journal," Vol. II, No. 8.
Address, Palatka, Fla., during the winter months.

CLAUDIUS NEWELL MITCHELL, Manufacturer, Dayton, O.

A. B., A. M. First Sergeant, 86th Ohio Vol. Inf., U. S. A., 1863-64. President of the Dayton Leather and Collar Company.
Address, 112 East First street.

GEORGE CAMPBELL OGDEN, Physician, Cincinnati, O.

A. B. M. D., Ohio Med. Coll., 1866.
Address, Price Hill.

ALEXANDER H. ROWAN, Lawyer, Shawneetown, Ills.

A. B. Admitted to the bar, 1865. Private, Co. A, 86th Ohio Vol. Inf., U. S. A., 1862.

VIRGIL G. SHEELEY, Minister, Bridgeville, Pa.

A. B., A. M. Was graduated from the Western Theol. Sem., 1866. Licensed by Presbytery of Saltsburg, April 12, 1865. Ordained by the Presbytery of Dubuque, June, 1867. Private, Co. A, 86th Ohio Vol. Inf., U. S. A., 1862. Pastor of Pres. churches at Waverly, Ia., 1866-69; Red Oak, Ia., 1869-70; Dalton, O., 1871-86; Bridgeville, Pa., 1886–.

HENRY CLAY THORNTON, Lawyer, Logansport, Ind.

B. S. A. M. LL. B., Univ. of Michigan, 1866.

JAMES THOMAS WHITTAKER, Physician, Cincinnati, O.

A. B., A. M. M. D., Univ. of Penn., 1866; Ohio Med. Coll., 1867. LL. D., Miami Univ., 1891. Assistant Surgeon, U. S. Navy, 1863-65. Prof. of Physiology, Ohio Med. Coll., 1869-79; of Theory and Practice, 1879—. President Cincinnati Academy of Medicine, 1887. Lecturer on Clinical Medicine, Good Samaritan Hospital. Fellow, College of Physicians, Philadelphia, Pa. Recorder, Association of American Physicians. Author of "Lectures on Physiology, 1879. Contributor to Pepper's System of Medicine," and "Wood's Handbook of Medicine."

WILLIAM HUFFMAN WINTERS, Lawyer, New York, N. Y.

A. B., A. M. LL. B., Harvard Law School, 1868.
Address, Post-office Building.

Class of 1864.

MYRON BANNING, Merchant, Cincinnati, O.

B. S. Coal merchant.

JOHN K. BROOKS, Physician, Avilla, Mo.

A. B., A. M. M. D. Brother of Robert F, '58, and Peter H, '68.

JOSEPH WHITE CONNAWAY, Lawyer, Liberty, Ind.

B. S. Admitted to the bar, 1867. Superintendent of Public Schools, Liberty, Ind., 1865-66. Member Indiana House of Representatives, 1878-80. — —

ANDERSON NELSON ELLIS, Physician, Cincinnati, O.

B. S. A. M. M. D., Bershire Med. Coll., 1867; Ohio Med. Coll., 1868. Student at Univ. of Heidelberg, 1878; Univ. of Vienna, 1879. Second Lieutenant, 60th Ohio Vol. Inf., 1861. Commissioned Second Lieutenant, 49th Ohio Vol. Inf., March 18, 1862. Commissioned Captain and Aid-de-Camp, U. S. Vols., May 1, 1862. Resigned, Aug. 24, 1863. Acting Assistant Surgeon, U. S. Regular Army, Department of Missouri, 1872-75. Captain and Assistant Surgeon, 1st Regular Ohio National Guard, 1883-88. Clinical Assistant, London Central Throat and Ear Hospital, 1879. Assistant Physician, Longview Asylum, 1881. Prof of Laryngology, Cincinnati College of Medicine and Surgery, 1882-90. Secretary Butler County Medical Society, 1883-86. Author of "Influence of the Trade Winds on the Health of the World," and "The Land of the Aztec." Office, Northwest corner of Sixth and Walnut streets. Address, 213 Findlay street.

JOHN RUSH EVANS, Physician, Troy, O.

A. B., A. M. M. D., Bellevue Med. Coll. Assistant Surgeon, Soldiers' Home, Dayton, O., 1869-70. Prof. of Chemistry, Toledo Med. Coll., 1882-84. Brother of Henry O, '67.

NELSON WILEY EVANS, Lawyer, Portsmouth, O.

A. B., A. M. LL. B., Cincinnati Law School, 1866. First Lieutenant, Co. G, 129th Ohio Vol. Inf., 1863. First Lieutenant, Adjutant, and Captain, Co. K, 173rd Ohio Vol. Inf., 1864-65. Register in bankruptcy, 11th District of Ohio, 1870-78. City Solicitor of Portsmouth, O., 1871-75. Trustee of Miami Univ., 1888-90. *Vide*, Portrait and Sketch, "Miami Journal," Vol. II., No. 8.

*MAHLON F. GEYER, Piqua, O.

A. B. Died in Camp Ethan Allen, Washington, D. C., July 12, 1864.

*HORACE EDMANDS GREER, Manufacturer, Dayton, O.

B. S. Captain of Volunteers and Aid-de-Camp on staff of General Thomas J. Wood, 1862-63. Resigned on account of ill-health. Manufacturer of stoves, ranges, etc. Died, May 22, 1873.

*MELANCTHON HUGHES, Minister, Sante Fe, New Mex.

A. B. Was graduated from Princeton Theol. Sem., 1867. Pastor of Pres. churches at Bellevue, Neb.; Atlanta, Ia.; Sante Fe, New Mexico. Died, Nov. 18, 1873.

MILES JOHNSTON, Lawyer, Cincinnati, O.

A. B., A. M. Admitted to the bar, 1867. Volunteer, U. S. A. Office, 271 Main street. Residence address, Branch Hill, O.

MIAMI UNIVERSITY.

SAMUEL FURMAN HUNT, Lawyer, Cincinnati, O.

A. B., A. M. L L. B., Cincinnati Law School, 1867. L L. D., Univ., of Cincinnati, 1890. Travelled through Sicily, Greece, Arabia, Egypt and the Holy Land, 1867-68, contributing descriptive letters to the "Cincinnati Enquirer" and "Herald and Presbyter." Member Ohio State Senate. 1869-73. President pro tem of same and acting Lieutenant-Governor, 1870-71. Declined nomination for Congress, 1871. Candidate for Lieutenant-Governor, 1871. Member Ohio Constitutional Convention, 1873. Judge Advocate General of Ohio, rank Brigadier-General, 1878-79. Declined nomination for Circuit Judge, 1887. Appointed Judge of Superior Court, Cincinnati, O., 1890. Elected to the same position, 1891, for a term of five years. Trustee of Miami Univ., 1872—. Director of the Univ. of Cincinnati, 1874-90. President of same, 1880-90. Delivered annual address before Alumni Association of Miami Univ., 1888. Centennial Orator, Findlay, O., 1876. Orator at Dedication of Soldier's Monument, Findlay, O.; the dedication of the Garfield statue, Cincinnati, O., banquet to General Grant, Cincinnati, O.; Centennial of the adoption of the Ordinance of 1787; and numerous Delta Kappa Epsilon conventions. Has delivered annual addresses before literary societies in twelve colleges. Author of Campaigns of Anthony Wayne and Arthur St. Clair," "Conscience in Public Life," "Duty of Educated Men to the Republic," etc. Office, Fifth and Main streets. *Vide*, "Miami Journal," Vol. II, No. 9. Residence, Glendale, O.

JOHN PRESSLY LOGAN, Physician, Ottawa, Kan.

A. B., A. M. M. D., Ohio Med. Coll., 1867.
Address. 721 East Fourth street.

FRANKLIN ELLIS MILLER, Minister, Paterson, N. J.

A. B., A. M. Studied theology at Princeton Theol. Sem., 1865-68. Major, 66th U. S. Colored Infantry, 1865-66. Pastor of Pres. churches at Asbury, N. J., 1868-71; Easton, Pa., 1871-87; Paterson, N. J., 1887—.

WILLIAM MILTON MIXER, Manufacturer, New York, N. Y.

B. S. Manufacturer of refrigerating and ice-making machines.
Address, 133 West Twenty-fifth street.

DAVID MURDOCK, Minister, Howard Lake, Minn.

A. B. General Missionary.

AMBROSE E. NOWLIN, Farmer, Lawrenceburg, Ind.

B. S. Supervisor of Census, District of Southern Indiana, 1890. Father of Okey B., '92.

SAMUEL M. RAMSEY, Minister, Cedarville, O.

A. B. Attended Reformed Pres. Theol. Sem., Philadelphia, Pa., 1865-68. Ordained, 1869. Pastor of Reformed Pres. churches at Chicago, Ills., 1869-73; Duanesburgh, N. Y., 1873-87. Evangelist, 1887—.

EDWARD LEONIDAS ROWE, Lawyer, Dayton, O.

A. B., A. M. Admitted to the bar, May, 1866. President of the Dayton Bar Association. Firm name, Gunckel & Rowe, 6 North Main street. Address, 134 West Fifth street.

ROBERT CUMMING SCHENCK, Manufacturer, Dayton, O.

B. S. Private, 146th Ohio National Guards. President of the Dayton Malleable Iron Co. Director in Dayton National Bank, Columbia Insurance Co., and various other companies.
Address, 305 West Second street.

BRADFORD SHINKLE, Merchant, Cincinnati, O.

B. S. Wholesale Grocer, Second street. Vice-President, Fifth National Bank, Cincinnati, O.
Residence address, 165 East Second street, Covington, Ky.

DAVID B. SMITH,

A. B., A. M. Reported dead.

PALMER W. SMITH, Lawyer, Oxford, O.

A. B., A. M. LL. B., Univ. of !Mich., 1870. Private, Co. A, 167th Ohio Vol. Inf., 1864-65. Solicitor Oxford Loan and Building Association for 12 years. Trustee of Miami Univ., 1884—. *Vide*, Portrait and Sketch, "Miami Journal," Vol. II., No. 8.

DAVID STANTON TAPPAN, Minister, Portsmouth, O.

A. B., A. M. D. D., Lenox Coll., 1887. Was graduated from Western Theol. Sem., 1867. Licensed by Presbytery of Allegheny, April, 1866. Ordained by Presbytery of Des Moines, April, 1868. Principal, Salt Lake Academy, Penn., 1865; Collensburg Academy, 1866; Mt. Pleasant Female Seminary, 1876. Pastor of Pres. churches at Chariton, Ia., 1867-71; Mt. Pleasant, Ia., 1871-90; Portsmouth, O., 1890—. Trustee of Parsons Coll., Ia., 1887-90.
Address, 59 West Sixth street.

JAMES SAMUEL TODD, Minister, Arcata, Cal.

A. B., A. M. Was graduated from Princeton Theol. Sem., 1867. Pastor of Pres. churches at Arcata, Cal., 1868-77; Healdsburg, Cal., 1877-80; Arcata, Cal., 1880—.

THOMAS J. WOODRUFF, Farmer, Oxford, O.

A. B.

Class of 1865.

*ALLEN ABERNETHY, Farmer, Dunlapsville, Ind.

B. S. Brother of John J, '60, and Henri M, '65. Died, Dec. 26, 1891.

*HENRI MERLE ABERNETHY, Teacher, Dunlapsville, Ind.

B. S. Engaged in teaching and farming at Darlington and Dunlapsville, Ind. Brother of John J., '60, and Allen, '65. Died, May 3, 1876.

*ABSALOM GAINES ARMSTRONG,   Clerk,   McAfee, Ky.
A. B. Died, March, 1866.

*WILLIAM H. AUSTIN,   Student of Medicine,   Springboro, O.
B. S., 1863. A. B. Studied medicine at Ann Arbor, Mich., and Cincinnati, O. Born, Jan. 17, 1840. Died, Dec., 1868.

*JOHN W. BROADBENT,   Physician,   Ogden, Ind.
B. S. M. D., Ohio Med. Coll. Died, 1875.

*ROBERT FOXCROFT BROADBENT,   Lawyer,   Ogden, Ind.
B. S. Admitted to the bar, June 11, 1867. Died, March 17, 1875.

*SAMUEL E. CRAWFORD,   Lawyer,   Cincinnati, O.
A. B., A. M. Admitted to the bar and practised in Cincinnati, O., Died, 1870.

JOHN JAMES DAVIS,   Lawyer,   Des Moines, Ia.
A. B., A. M. Second Lieutenant, U. S. A., 1862. L L. B., Univ. of Mich., 1866. Practised law in Savannah, Mo., 1867-71; Des Moines, Ia., 1871—. City Attorney of Savannah, Mo., 1868-69. Deputy U. S. Internal Revenue Collector, Sixth District of Mo., 1869-70. Address, 1169 Twenty-second street.

WILLIAM THOMAS DOUGAN,   Physician,   Niles, Mich.
A. B., A. M. M. D., Rush Med. Coll., 1867. Examining Surgeon for Pensions, 1869-76.

AMHERST FRANKLIN,   Lawyer,   Ottawa, Kan.
A. B., A. M. Admitted to the bar, 1866.

JAMES HANEN GARVIN,   Minister,   Sherman Heights, Tenn.
A. B., A. M. Prof. of Mathematics and Natural Sciences, Franklin Coll., 1865-68. Editor of "Journal," Wilmington, O., 1868-70. Pastor of Church of Christ, Mt. Vernon, O., 1873-74. Engaged in mission work, 1875-77. Pastor of Protestant Episcopal churches at Medina, O., 1878-84; Elyria, O., 1884-88; Sherman Heights, Tenn., 1890—. Brother of Thomas D, '62.

HEBER GILL,   Minister and Teacher,   Desplaines, Ills.
A. B., A. M. Private, Co. A, 167th Ohio Vol. Inf., 1864. Acting Prof. of Mathematics, Hanover Coll., Ind., 1869. Principal of South Salem Academy, 1870-73. Prof. of Latin and Greek, Lenox Coll., Ia.; 1879-86. Principal of Paw-Paw Academy, 1887-88. Pastor of Pres. church, Desplaines, Ills.

GEORGE HAGEMAN,   Minister,   Washington, Kan.
A. B., A. M. Attended Lane Seminary, 1874-77. Pastor of Pres. church at Washington, Kan., 1877—. Brother of Simon A, '65.

SIMON AUGUSTUS HAGEMAN, Physician, Cincinnati, O.

A. B., A. M. M. D., Pulte Med. Coll., 1881. Physician to the Widows' and Old Men's Home. Brother of George, '65.
Address, 524 McMillan street.

WILLIAM HENDERSON HILLIS, Minister, Lyons, Kan.

A. B. Western Theol. Sem., 1865–68. Licensed by Presbytery of Allegheny, April, 1867. Ordained by Presbytery of Carlisle, June, 1869. Pastor of Pres. churches at Gettysburg, Pa., 1869–72; Warrensburg, Mo., 1873–77; Rockville, Ind., 1877–80; Greenville, Ills., 1880–83; Carlinville, Ills., 1883–88; Lyons, Kan., 1889—.

HENRY C. JOHNSON, Minister, Newark, O.

A. B., A. M. Studied Theology at Western Theol. Sem. and Northwestern Theol. Sem. Ordained a minister in the Protestant Episcopal church, 1886. Rector of St James church, Wooster, O., 1886–87. Trinity Church, Newark, O., 1889—.
Address, 85 N. Fourth street.

JAMES ROBINSON JONES, Lawyer, Warsaw, Mo.

B. S. Admitted to the bar, Feb., 1868.

D. RICE KEMPER, Manufacturer, Cincinnati, O.

B. S.

*ISAAC WASHBURN MCAFEE, Teacher, Alton, Ky.

A. B. Teacher in Public schools at Alton, Ky. Born, Missouri, March 15, 1838. Died, Oct. 14, 1890.

GEORGE WILLIAM MACCRACKEN, Lawyer, Urbana, O.

A. B., A. M. Private, U. S. A., 1862. Admitted to the bar, 1868. Assistant U. S. District Attorney. Attorney for the Western Union Telegraph Co. Brother of Henry M, '57.

CLARK BATES MONTGOMERY, Lawyer, Cincinnati, O.

B. S. A. M. L L. B., Cincinnati Law School. U. S. Collector of Internal Revenue, First District, 1881–85. Trustee of Miami Univ., 1887—. *Vide*, Portrait and Sketch, "Miami Journal," Vol. II, No. 8.

BENJAMIN SHEEKS, Lawyer, Tacoma, Wash.

A. B., A. M. Member 1st and 2nd Sessions of Wyoming Legislature.

S. C. SHEPPARD,

B. S. Can not be traced.

HENRY C. TAYLOR, Lawyer, Columbus, O.

A. B., A. M. Private, Co. A, 86th Ohio Vol. Inf., 1862. L L. B., Harvard Law School, 1867. Member of the 67th General Assembly of Ohio.
Address, 1400 East Broad street.

100   MIAMI UNIVERSITY.

Class of 1866.

CARLISLE BARRERE,   Lawyer,   Columbus, O.
A. B., A. M. Admitted to the bar, 1868. Not in active practice.
Address 571 East Town street.

D. L. BIGHAM,   Redwood Falls, Minn.
B. S.

CHRISTOPHER BISHIR,   Nurseryman,   Hutchinson, Kan.
B. S. Taught school for six years after graduation and has since been engaged in the nursery business, farming and fruit growing.
Address, 201 West Sixth street.

OLIVER BROADBENT,   Physician,   Anderson, Ind.
B. S. M. D., Ohio Med. Coll. Brother of John W, '65.

*JOHN CARNEY,   Lawyer and Teacher,   Vernon, Ind.
B. S. Admitted to the bar, 1867. County Superintendent of Public Schools of Jennings Co., Ind., 1868-80. Deputy County Auditor 10 years. Auditor, 1880. Born, Vernon, Ind., March 21, 1844. Died, Nov. 13, 1880.

ROBERT CHRISTIE,   Minister,   St. Paul, Minn.
A. B., A. M. D. D., Hanover Coll. Studied theology at Danville Theol. Sem. and Princeton Theol. Sem. Was graduated from the latter, 1871. Ordained by the Presbytery of Louisville, May 8, 1872. Pastor of Pres. churches at Shelbyville, Ky.; Lexington, Ky.; Louisville, Ky.; and St Paul, Minn. Preached the Baccalaureate Sermon to the class of 1891. Prof.—elect of Systematic Theology, Western Theol. Sem., Allegheny, Pa. Vice Moderator Gen. Assembly 1892.

R. D. CRAIGHEAD,
B. S. Can not be traced.

WM. DURHAM,
B. S. Can not be traced.

RICHARD THOMAS DURRELL,   Lawyer,   Cincinnati, O.
A. B., A. M. LL. B., Cincinnati Law School, 1868.
Address, 332 Richmond street.

*ROBERT GILCHRIST,   Minister,   Delphos, O.
A. B., A. M. Ordained, April, 1871. Pastor of Pres. church at Delphos, O., 1871. Died, Dec. 5, 1871.

WILLIAM HAMILTON,   Horticulturist,   Benton Harbor, Mich
A. B., A. M. B. D., Yale Theol. Sem. Private, 167th Ohio Vol. Inf., 1864.

HENRY L. HAYNES, Lawyer, South McAllister, Indian Terr.

A. B. Admitted to the bar, 1870.

*CRAFT C. HOLBROOK, Lawyer, Vanceburg, Ky.

A. B. Practised law at Oxford, O., until 1870; Vanceburg, Ky., 1870-74. Died, 1874.

EDWARD HENRY KLEINSCHMIDT, Lawyer, Cincinnati, O.

A. B., A. M. Private, Co. A, 86th Ohio Vol. Inf., U. S. A., 1862-64. Admitted to the bar, 1868.
Law office, Debolt Building. corner of Main and Court streets.

JAMES M. NAYLOR, Teacher, Wichita, Kan.

A. B., A. M. Principal of Maple Grove Academy, Vincennes, Ind., 1866-68; Boys' department, Vincennes Univ., Ind., 1868-69; Waveland Collegiate Inst., Waveland, Ind., 1869-75; Principal of Butler Academy, Butler, Mo., 1879-86; Lewis Academy, Wichita, Kan., 1886—. Son of Arthur R, '41.

*JOHN ALLEN NUTTER, Civil Engineer, Richmond, Ind.

A. B., City Engineer of Leavenworth, Kan., 1867—69. Travelled and studied abroad, 1874-76. Born, Union Co., Ind., Sept. 11, 1841. Died, Nov. 17, 1876.

SAMUEL P. SCOTT, Lawyer, Hillsboro, O.

A. B., A. M. Admitted to the bar and has since practised at Hillsboro, O. Author of "Through Spain," 1886.

ALFRED MAYHEW SHUEY, Manufacturer, Minneapolis, Minn.

B. S. Musician, 167th Ohio Vol. Inf., 1864. Manufacturer of Agricultural Implements, 1866-73. Musical Critic, "Pioneer Press." Secretary of the Century Piano Comany.
Address, Century Building.

*OTIS CYRUS SMITH, Lawyer, London, O.

A. B. Admitted to the bar, 1868. Born, London, O., Sept. 29, 1845. Died, June 24, 1873.

MOSES DUNCAN ALEXANDER STEEN, Minister, Woodbridge, Cal.

A. B., A. M. D. D., San Joaquin Valley Coll., 1888. Ph. D. Wooster Univ., 1889. Was graduated from McCormick Theol. Sem.,1869. Ordained by the Presbytery of New Albany, Sept 8, 1870. Pastor of Pres. churches at Vevay, Ind., 1870-72; Solon, O., 1872-73; Conneautville, Pa., 1873-74; Waterford, Pa., 1874-75; Ludlow, Ky., 1875-81; Pleasant Ridge, O., 1881-82; Gunnison and Black Hawk, Col., 1883-85; Snohomish, Wash., 1885-86; Woodbridge, Cal., 1886—. Author of "Scriptural Sanctification"; "How to be saved"; etc.

SAMUEL YOUNG WASSON, Farmer, Hamilton, O.

A. B., A. M. Farmer near Middletown, O., for many years. Member of Ohio State House of Representatives, 1878-79. Retired. Address, 244 North Seventh street.

CHARLES SEELY WOOD, Minister, Urbana, O.

A. B., A. M. Was graduated from Princeton Theol. Sem., 1870. Ordained 1870. Pastor of Presbyterian churches at Winneconne, Wis., 1869; Stevens Point, Wis., 1870-73; Richwood, O., 1875. On account of ill-health, retired from active work, 1876.

Class of 1867.

WILLIAM THOMAS ASHFORD, Merchant, Atlanta, Ga.

B. S. Wholesale Dry Goods Merchant. Address, 258 Peachtree street.

SAMUEL THORTON BENNETT, Farmer, Plymouth, Kan.

B. S. Sergeant Co. G, 33rd Ohio Vol. Inf., 1862-65. Director in Plymouth National Bank.

GEORGE SPENCER BISHOP, Banker, Mankato, Kan.

A. B., A. M. Private, 167th Ohio Vol. Inf., U. S. A., 1864. Principal North Sangamon Academy, Ills., 1870-71. County Surveyor, 1871-76. Member Kansas State Legislature, 1872-80. President of National Bank. Son of Robert H, Jr., '31. Brother of Sylvester J, '72.

LUCIUS W. BISHOP, Physician, Batavia, O.

B. S. M. D., Ohio Med. Coll., 1870. Intern Good Samaritan Hospital for several years.

DAVID CLARK, Minister, Galena, Ills.

A. B., A. M. Private, 15th Penn. Cavalry, 1862-65. Studied theology at Northwestern and Danville Theol. Seminaries, 1867-68. Licensed by Presbytery of Sidney, Oct., 1868. Ordained, April, 1870. Pastor of Pres. churches at Hermon and Blue Grass, Ia., 1870-72; Lebanon, O., 1872-76; Austin, Ills., 1876-83; Dallas, Tex., 1883-86; Sandwich, Ills., 1886-87; Galena, Ills., 1887—.

ALSTON ELLIS, Teacher, Fort Collins, Col.

B. S. 1865 A. B., A. M. Ph. D., Univ. of Wooster, 1879; Ohio State Univ. '87. L L. D., Ohio State Univ., 1890. Principal of Public Schools at Covington, Ky., 1867-68; Newport, Ky., 1868-71; Hamilton, O., 1871-79; Sandusky, O., 1879-87; Hamilton, O., 1887-92. President of Colorado Agricultural Coll., Fort Collins, Col., 1892. President of Ohio Superintendents' Association and Ohio Teachers' Association for several years. Member Ohio Board of School Examiners, 1875-79, and 1887-92. Member Board Trustees of Ohio State Univ., 1878-83. Life Member Victoria Institute and the Philosophical Society of Great Britain. Orator Phi Delta Theta Convention, Indianapolis, Ind., 1880. Annual address before the Literary Societies of Miami Univ., 1888. Author of "History of the Ungraded Schools of Ohio," and numerous published educational reports, addresses, etc.

HENRY ORBISON EVANS, Civil Engineer, Riverside, Cal.

A. B., A. M. Civil Engineer of H. W. J. & S. R. R., 1868–70; M. C. & L. — —
M. R. R., 1870–71; B. W. & C. R. R.; 1872–73; Toledo Water Works, 1874;
C. R. I. & P. R. R., 1874. County Surveyor of Miami Co., O., 1875–81, and
1885–89. Assistant Engineer Arrowhead Reservoir Co., Riverside, Cal.
Brother of J. Rush, '64.
Permanent Address, Troy, Ohio.

HENRY HARRISON FARR, Merchant, Eaton, O.

A. B., A. M. Insurance and Real Estate Agent and Retail Grocer. Secretary of Preble County Agricultural Association, 1880—. Treasurer of Eaton Building Association, 1880—.

ROBERT M. L. HUSTON, Farmer, Oxford, O.

A. B. Private Co. A, 167th Ohio Vol. Inf., U. S. A., 1864.

JAMES ZACHARIE MOORE, Lawyer, Spokane, Wash.

A. B., A. M. L L. B., Harvard Law School, 1868. Register in Bankruptcy. Member of Constitutional convention which framed the constitution of the State of Washington. Now Judge of the Superior Court of Washington,
Address, 2209 Fourth street.

JAMES ELLWOOD MOREY, Lawyer, Hamilton, O.

B. S. A. M. Private Co. H, 93rd Ohio Vol. Inf., U. S. A., 1862–65. Trustee of Miami Univ., 1887—. *Vide*, Sketch and Portrait, "Miami Journal," Vol II, No. 8.

*ROBERT OLIVER STRONG, Lawyer, Cincinnati, O.

A. B. L L. B., Cincinnati Law School. Member of the 60th General Assembly of Ohio. Prosecuting Attorney of Hamilton Co., O., 1873–75. City Solicitor of Cincinnati, O., 1875–76. Died, Jan. 7, 1876.

H. M. SARGENT, Wakefield, O.

B. S.

MICHAEL WEAVER, Lawyer, Emporia, Kan.

B. S. Admitted to the bar, 1869. Police Judge of the City of Emporia, Kan. Assistant Grand Recorder of A. O. U. W. of Kansas.
Address, 806 Cottonwood street.

*JOHN NICHOL WYMAN, Lawyer, Topeka, Kan.

A. B. L L. B., Univ. of Mich., 1869. Died, June 28, 1879.

Class of 1868.

ALBERT ANKENEY, Farmer and Stock Raiser, Alpha, O.

A. B., A. M. Brother of Horace, '72.

JAMES SCOTT BAKER, Merchant, Battle Creek, Mich.

B. S. Private, 146th Ohio Vol. Inf., U. S. A., four months. Furniture Dealer.
Address, 10 North Jefferson street.

JAMES CLINTON BOATMAN,

B. S. Can not be traced.

PETER HILL BROOKS, Physician, Lima, O.

A. B., A. M. M. D., Miami Med. Coll., 1872. Secretary of Pension Examining Board of Surgeons, 1885-89. Brother of Robert F, '58, and John K, '64.

BENJAMIN HEYWARD BROWN, Farmer, Oxford, O.

B. S. Nurseryman and Fruit Grower.

JAMES LYMAN BROWN, Lawyer, Oklahoma City, Oklahoma Terr.

A. B. L L. B., Univ. of Mich., 1869. Private, U. S. A., 1861-65. District Judge, 1878-84. Territorial Senator, 1890—. Attorney for Choctaw Coal Co., Ardmore Mining Co., A. S. & T. R. R. Co. Compiler of Annotated Code of Oklahoma.

MATTHEW NELSON BROWN, Farmer, Thompsonville, Kan.

B. S.

AHIJAH RAYBURN BYRKETT, Lawyer, Troy, O.

A. B., A. M. Admitted to the bar, 1869. Private, 11th Ohio National Guards, 1861-64. Attorney for C. C. C. & St. L. R. R. Co.

*JULIUS LEWIS CORBIN, Cincinnati, O.

B. S. Died about 1887.

JAMES CALVIN ELLIOTT, Lawyer, Greenville, O.

B. S. Admitted to the bar, May 10, 1870. Private, Co. A, 156th Ohio Vol. Inf., 1864. Official Stenographer for Darke County Court, 1879-86. Prosecuting Attorney for Darke County, 1886-92.

CLINTON W. GERARD, Lawyer, Cincinnati, O.

A. B., A. M. L L. B., Cincinnati Law School, 1870. Sergeant, 83rd Ohio Vol. Inf., 1862-65. Assistant Prosecuting Attorney and Prosecuting Attorney for Hamilton Co., O. Also Assistant City Solicitor. Author of "History of 83rd Ohio Vol."
Residence address, 215 Woodburn avenue, Walnut Hills.

JOSEPH MATTHEWS HIBBEN, Merchant, Hillsboro, O.

A. B., A. M. Dry Goods Merchant.

LOUIS D. HOLMES, Lawyer, Omaha, Neb.
B. S.

JOHN BOYD JOHNSTON, Minister, Malta, Ills.

A. B., A. M. Studied theology at Lane and Union Theol. Seminaries. Ordained by Presbytery of Chillicothe, Dec. 30, 1873. Pastor of Pres. churches at McArthur and Hamden, O., 1873–75. Joined the Congregational church and has held the following pastorates: Edgewood, Ill., 1875–77; Hillsboro, Ills., 1877–80; Roberts and Thawville, Ills., 1880–84; Cincinnati, O., 1884–87; St. Louis, Mo., 1887–90. Malta, Ills., 1890—.

BRUCE PAUL JONES, Lawyer, London, O.

A. B., A. M. Editor of "Weekly Times," Ottawa, Kan. Judge of Police Court and City Attorney of Ottawa, Kan. Mayor of London, O. At present Prosecuting Attorney of Madison Co.

JOHN MILTON LOCKHART, Physician, Eckmansville, O.

A. B., A. M. M. D., Ohio Med. Coll., 1872.

ROBERT LEWIS LYONS, Lawyer, Chicago, Ills.

A. B., A. M. Private, 167th Ohio Vol. Inf., 1864. L L. B., Univ. of Mich., 1874.
Address, 172 La Salle street.

*ALVAN LEANDER MCLAIN, Lawyer, Springfield, O.

A. B., A. M. L L. B., Cincinnati Law School, 1869. Brother of James L, '68. Died, Urbana, O., May 15, 1871.

JAMES LAFOUSE MCLAIN, Physician, Findlay, O.

A. B., A. M. M. D., Univ., of Pennsylvania, 1871. Assistant Physician to Central Ohio Insane Asylum, Dayton. O., 1872–74. Brother of Alvan L, '68.
Address, 851 Maple avenue.

JESSE TAYLOR MCCLAVE, Farmer, Buckley P. O., Ills.

B. S. Private, Co. G, 89th Ohio Vol. Inf., 1861–65.

SAMUEL ISAAC MCCLELLAND, Merchant, Peoria, Ills.

A. B., A. M. Superintendent of Schools at Monroe, O., for many years. Wholesale Merchant. Vice-President of the Peoria Manufacturing Co. Brother of Thomas J, '68.
Address, 516 Perry street.

DANIEL ADDISON MCMILLAN, Teacher, Mexico, Mo.

A. B. Superintendent of Public Schools at Boonville, Mo., and Mexico, Mo.

THOMAS JEFFERSON MCCLELLAND, Minister, Richmond, Ind.

A. B., A. M. Was graduated from the Western Theol. Sem., 1872. Licensed by Presbytery of Pittsburgh, Dec. 20, 1871. Ordained by Presbytery of Marion, Nov. 13, 1872. Pastor of Pres. churches at Chesterville, O., 1872–80; Pleasant Run and Camden, O., 1880–81; New Paris, Ebenezer, and Fletcher, O., 1881–88; Knightstown, Ind., 1888–90; Richmond, Ind., 1890—. Brother of Samuel I, '68. Address, 311 North Eighth street.

AARON HARLAN MORRIS, Minister, Greencastle, Ind.

A. B., A. M. Private, Co. K, 86th Ohio Vol. Inf., and Co. I, 167th Ohio Vol. Inf., 1863–64. Ordained a minister in the Christian church (Disciples). Principal High School, Connersville, Ind., 1868–69. Principal of Academy and Pastor of Christian Church, Ladoga, Ind., 1869–72. Pastor of Christian churches at Waveland, Ind., 1872–75; Noblesville, Ind., 1875–80. County Superintendent of Public Schools, Hamilton Co., Ind., 1881–85. Superintendent of Indiana Soldier's and Sailor's Orphans' Home, Knightstown, Ind., 1885–90. Pastor of Christian church, Greencastle, Ind., 1890—. Author of "The Ex-Superintendent," "The Jewish Sabbath."

FREDERIC JULIUS PICARD, Civil Engineer, Columbus, O.

B. S. Chief Engineer, Columbus & Maysville R. R. Assistant Engineer, Columbus & Hocking Valley R. R. Receiver, Columbus & Eastern R. R. General Manager, Columbus & Eastern R. R. Vice-President and General Manager, Columbus, Shawnee & Hocking Valley R. R. Colonel, 13th Ohio National Guards, 1880. Address, 66 Jefferson avenue.

GEORGE FITZWATER ROBINSON, Merchant, Washington C. H., O.

B. S. Private, Co. M, 2nd Regiment Ohio Cavalry, 1862–65. Lumber Merchant.

*GEORGE ADAM SIDELL, Denver, Col.

B. S. Died, Dec. 10, 1883.

*JOHN QUINCY SPENCER, Murdoch, O.

B. S. Died, Oct. 17, 1868.

SAMUEL GRAVES STEWART, Physician, Topeka, Kan.

B. S. M. D., Starling Med. Coll., 1873. Sergeant, Co. D, 74th Ohio Vol. Inf., 1861–65. Now Prof. of Principles and Practice of Medicine, Kansas Med. Coll. Associate editor "Kansas Medical Journal." Trustee of Kansas Med. Coll. Address, 511 West Eighth street.

JONATHAN BYAL VAIL, Physician, Lima, O.

B. S. A. M. M. D., Med. Coll. of Ohio, 1871. Employed in the Commissary of Subsistence Department, Army of the Cumberland, U. S. A., 1864–65. Member Board of Education, Lima, O., 9 years. President and Treasurer of same. Member Allen County Medical Society; Ohio State Medical Society; American Medical Association. President of the Northwestern Ohio Med. Association. U. S. Pension Examiner, 1881–85.

MIAMI UNIVERSITY.   107

FAYE WALKER,   Minister,   Oxford, O.
A. B., A. M.   D. D., Centre Coll., 1886. Studied theology at Danville
Theol. Sem. and McCormick Theol. Sem. Ordained, May, 1870. Pastor
of Pres. churches at Dwight, Ills., 1870–71; Taylorville, Ills., 1872–75;
Indianapolis, Ind., 1875–77; College Hill, O., 1877–83; Collinsville, O.,
1883—. President of Oxford College, 1883—. Director Danville Theol.
Sem., 1879–83. Editor "Presbyterian Standard," 1875–77.

HORACE SUMNER WHITTAKER,   Merchant,   Cincinnati, O.
B. S.   Grain Commission Merchant.
Office, 34 Chamber of Commerce Building.

Class of 1869.

JAMES BELCH,   West Chester, O.
B. S.

FRANK STUART BROOKS,   Coal Merchant,   Columbus, O.
A. B., A. M.   Secretary of the American Coal Co.
Address, 253 East State street.

EUGENE HALLECK BUNDY,   Lawyer,   New Castle, Ind.
A. B., A. M.   Admitted to the bar, 1870. Member of Indiana State Senate, 1880–84. Nominee of Republican party for Lieutenant-Governor of Indiana, 1884. At present Judge of the Circuit Court.

CHARLES LEONARD CLARKE,   Switzerland, Fla.
B. S.

BENJAMIN FRANKLIN DAVIS,   Lawyer,   Cincinnati, O.
A. B. Private, Co. A, 56th Ohio Vol. Inf., and Co. M, 2nd Ohio Cavalry, 1863–65. Principal High School, Hamilton, O., 1871–73. Principal Public Schools, College Corner, O., 1877–78. Principal of High School, Hamilton, O., 1878–82. Superintendent of Schools, Eaton, O., 1882–84. Has since practised law in Cincinnati, O.
Address, 489 Central avenue.

CHARLES WRIGHT EARNIST,   Lawyer,   Cincinnati, O.
A. B., A. M.   L L. B., Cincinnati Law School, 1871.
Office, 43 Wiggins Block.

WILLIAM F. ELTZROTH,   Lawyer,   Lebanon, O.
A. B., A. M.   Admitted to the bar, 1873. Member Ohio State Senate, 1886–87.

WILLIAM EDGAR EVANS,   Lawyer,   Chillicothe, O.
A. B., A. M.   Admitted to the bar, 1871. Prosecuting Attorney for Ross Co., O., 1875–76. Judge of the Court of Common Pleas, 1886—.

JAMES KING GIBSON, Minister, South Charleston, O.

A. B., A. M. Private, Co. C, 149th Ohio Vol. Inf., three months' service. Attended Lane Theol. Sem., 1869-72. Ordained by Presbytery of Portsmouth, June 13, 1872. Pastor of Pres. churches at Jackson, O., 1872-79; Troy, O., 1880-85; Hardin, O., 1886-90; South Charleston, O., 1890—. Son of James R, '39.

HERDMAN EMELIEUS GRAND-GIRARD, Grand Rapids, Mich.

A. B., A. M. Druggist.
Address, 128 Monroe street.

WALTER DECAMP HANCOCK, Physician, Millville, O.

A. B.. A. M. M. D., Miami Med. Coll., 1872. Student at the General Hospital, Vienna, Austria, one year. Resident Physician, Cincinnati Hospital for several years.

JOHN MILTON JAMISON, Farmer, Roxabell, O.

B. S. Engaged in farming and stock raising.

*WILLIAM LEE, Physician, Dallas, Tex.

A. B., A. M. M. D. Brother of Harvey, '70. Died, Oct. 27, 1888.

ADDISON STORRS LEWIS, Civil Engineer, Clifton, O.

B. S. C. E., Lafayette Coll., 1870. Civil Engineer, B. & O. R. R., and P. R. R., 1871-75. Also Civil Engineer, N. Y., W. S. & C. R. R. Assisted in the Massachusetts State Survey. At present engaged in farming.

THOMAS C. MAGOFFIN, Merchant, Palestine, Ark.

B. S. County Treasurer of Rice Co., Kan., 1871-74. Lumber merchant.

ROBERT MITCHELL MARSHALL, Lawyer, Keokuk, Ia.

A. B. Admitted to the bar, 1871. Prosecuting attorney for Lee Co., Ia., 1884-87. Son of Samuel T, '40.
Address, 12 North Fifth street.

*LEONIDAS HAMLINE MCCLUNG, Lawyer, Bethany, O.

B. S. Admitted to the bar, 1871. Died, Dec. 7, 1871.

WILLIAM BRADFORD MEANS, Broker, Boone, Ia.

A. B. Admitted to the bar, 1870. Editor of "Republican," Boone, Ia., 1871-86. At present postmaster of Boone. Real Estate Broker and Loan Agent.

*BURTON A. MECUM, Physician, Reading, O.

B. S. M. D., Miami Med. Coll., 1873. Born, Cincinnati, O., March 3, 1844. Died, March 13, 1887. *Vide*, Sketch in "Miami Journal," by Hon. Sam F. Hunt, Vol. I., No. 6.

JAMES WILBERFORCE MOORE, Agent, Hamilton, O.

A. B., A. M. Insurance Agent.

JOHN RANDOLPH MOORE, Lawyer, Georgetown, O.

A. B., A. M. Admitted to the bar, 1871. Prosecuting attorney of Brown Co., O., 1879-83.

JEREMIAH M. OLDFATHER, Minister, Hanover, Ind.

A. B., A. M. D. D., Miami Univ., 1891. Attended Lane Seminary, 1869-72. Ordained by Cincinnati Presbytery, May, 1872. Sergeant-Major, 93rd Ohio Vol. Inf., 1862-65. Missionary of the Pres. church at Oroomiah and Fabreez, Persia, 1872-90. Presbyterial Missionary for the Presbytery of New Albany, 1890—.

JOSEPH CAMPBELL OLIVER, Broker, Los Angeles, Cal.

A. B., A. M. First Lieutenant, Co. I, 89th Ohio Vol. Inf., U. S. A., 1861-65. Real Estate Broker.
Address, 227 West First street.

JAMES C. QUINN, Banker, Chillicothe, O.

B. S.

KIRBY SMITH, Lawyer, Hillsboro, O.

A. B., A. M. Admitted to the bar, 1873.

WILLIAM HENRY TOLBERT, Crawfordsville, Ind.

A. B. Studied theology at Princeton Theol. Sem., 1869.

NEHEMIAH WADE, Farmer, Ross, O.

A. B., A. M. Brother of Matthew, '70.

WILLIAM FILETUS WILKINS, Physician, Kansas City, Mo.

B. S. A. M. M. D., Kansas City Univ. Assistant Brigade Surgeon, 1862-65. Practised at Ottawa, Kan., 1875-88; Kansas City, Mo., 1888—. President and Prof. of Anatomy, Kansas Med. Inst., Ottawa, Kan. Address, 1907 Holmes street.

JACOB P. WINSTEAD, Lawyer, Circleville, O.

B. S. L L. B., Univ. of Michigan, 1873. Prosecuting Attorney for Pickaway Co., O., 1880-85. Judge of Probate Court, 1891—.

MIAMI UNIVERSITY.

Class of 1870.

JOSIAH RENICK BELL, Lyons, Kan.

A. B.

ALEXANDER BUCKINGHAM, Lawyer, Chicago, Ills.

A. B. A. M. L L B., Cincinnati Law School, 1874. Brother of Holly R, '73 Address, 164 Madison street.

NELSON CARR, Teacher, Oakland, Cal.

A. B. Principal of Public Schools at Placeville, Cal., El Monte, Cal., Savannah, Cal., San Antonio, Cal., Silver City, Nevada, Reno, Nevada. Address, 1303 Jefferson street.

JOHN ICHABOD COVINGTON, Insurance, New York, N. Y.

A. B. A.M. Secretary Globe Insurance Co., 1870–76. Superintendent Insurance Adjustment Co., 1876–83. Manager Equitable Accident Insurance Co., Cincinnati, Ohio, 1883–86; Manager Insurance Department, American Cotton Oil Co., New York, 1885–92. Editor "Miami Student;" Editor "Beta Theta Pi." Editor and Proprietor "Business Observer", Insurance Editor "Cincinnati Price Current." Inventor. A frequent contributor to newspapers and magazines. Delivered the annual address before the Society of Alumni, Miami University, 1892. Son of Samuel F., a student of Miami in 1838.
Address, 45–47–49 Cedar street.

JAMES PATTON COWAN, Minister, Indianapolis, Ind.

A. B., A. M. D. D., Muskingum Coll. Studied theology at Xenia, O. Licensed by the Indiana Presbytery, Sept. 5, 1872. Ordained by Des Moines Presbytery, June 14, 1874. Pastor of United Pres. churches at Des Moines Ia., 1874–78; Indianapolis, Ind., 1880—.
Address, 313 N. East street.

JOHN BABB ELAM, Lawyer, Indianapolis, Ind.

A. B., A. M. L L. B., Univ. of Mich., 1872. Private 110th Ohio Vol. Inf., 1864–65. Prosecuting Attorney, Marion Co., Ind., 1878–82.
Address, 300 Park avenue.

EDWARD NICHOLAS EVANS, Lawyer, Emporia, Kan.

A. B., A. M. Deputy U. S. Internal Revenue Collector, Sixth Tenn. district, 1873–76, and 1882. U. S. Storekeeper, Sixth Tenn. district, 1880–81. Lawyer at Emporia, Kan., 1882—. City attorney for Emporia, Kan.

JOHN WALKER FEIGHAN, Lawyer, Spokane, Wash.

B. S. LL. B., Cincinnati Law School, 1872. Private and Second Lieutenant, 83rd Ind. Vol. Inf., 1862–65. City Attorney for Owensboro, Ky., 1874 and 1883–84. Republican Presidential Elector, 1876. Editor "Republican", Rockport, Ind., 1872. Prosecuting attorney for Lyon Co., Kan., 1882–88. Judge Advocate General, Kansas National Guards, 1884–88. City Attorney for Spokane, Wash., 1889. Member and Speaker Washington House of Representatives, 1889–90.
Address, 1803 Second avenue.

MIAMI UNIVERSITY.   111

ELAM FISHER,   Lawyer,   Eaton, O.

A. B., A. M. L L. B., Univ. of Mich., 1872. Attorney for C. H. & D. R. R. Member Ohio House of Representatives, 1891—. Trustee of Miami Univ., 1887—.

*HARVEY LEE,   Lawyer,   Austin, Tex.

A. B. Admitted to the bar, 1872. Brother of William, '69. Died, March 28, 1875.

JAMES MILLIKIN MCFARLAND,   Land Owner,   Alma, Kan.

A. B., A. M. State Statistician, Department of Agriculture, 1882-89. Assistant Secretary, Kansas State Board of Agriculture, 1882-86. Large owner of land, which he leases for farming and pasture.

EBEN S. MCKITRICK,   Minister,   Allegheny, Pa.

A. B., A. M. D. D., Monmouth Coll., and Muskingum Coll., 1889. Studied theology at Allegheny, Pa. Licensed by Muskingum Presbytery, May 12, 1874. Ordained by Allegheny Presbytery, June 15, 1875. Pastor of United Pres. church at Allegheny, Pa., 1875—. Moderator of the United Pres. General Assembly, 1889.
Address, 34 Beech street.

JOSEPH J. MCMAKEN,   Lawyer,   Hamilton, O.

A. B., A. M. Seaman, U. S. Navy, 1864. Admitted to the bar, April, 1874. U. S. Commissioner, Southern District of Ohio. Member Ohio House of Representatives, 1890-91. Member Ohio Senate, 1892—.

PHILIP NORTH MOORE,   Geologist,   St. Louis, Mo.

A. B., A. M. M. E., Columbia School of Mines, 1872. Assistant, Missouri Geological Survey, 1872-73; Kentucky Geological Survey, 1873-77. Metallurgist and Mining Engineer, Leadville, Col., 1878-82. Managing Director and Treasurer, State Creek Iron Co., Olympia, Ky., 1882-89. President Baker Hill Iron Co., Alabama, 1889—.
Address, 55 Laclede Building.

JOHN MCCURDY ROBINSON,   Minister,   Virden, Ills.

A. B., A. M. Was graduated from Western Theol. Sem., 1873. Licensed by Presbytery of Cairo, April 30, 1871. Ordained by Presbytery of Erie, May 28, 1873. Pastor of Presbyterian churches at Sheakleyville, Pa., 1873-78; Shawneetown, Ills., 1878-88; Virden, Ills., 1888—.

JOHN BOYD ROBY,   Santa Monica, Cal.

A. B.

DAVID CHAMBERLAIN SCOTT,   Farmer,   Seven Mile, O.

B. S. Farmer and stock-raiser.

WILLIAM VINCENT SHAFFER,   Physician,   Middletown, O.

A. B., A. M. M. D., Miami Med. Coll., 1880. Was engaged in mercantile pursuits, 1870-77.

EDWARD SCOFIELD SCOTT, Minister, Logansport, Ind.

A. B., A. M. Was graduated from Princeton Theol. Sem., 1872. First Lieutenant and Adjutant, 89th Ohio Vol. Inf., 1861-64. Wounded at Peach Tree Creek, Ga., July 20, 1864. Prisoner at Libby Prison and escaped by tunneling, Feb. 9, 1864. Pastor of Pres.churches at Delphos, O., 1872-82; Logansport, Ind., 1882—.

HOMER SHEELEY, Minister, Toronto, O.

A. B., A. M. Studied theology at Danville and Union Theological Seminaries. Ordained, June 10, 1874. Private, 81st Ohio Vol. Inf., 1865. Pastor of Pres. churches at Perryville, Loudonville and Clearfork, O., 1874-75; Lake Prairie, Ind., 1877-80; Pleasant Run, O., 1880-84; Williamsburg, O., 1884-85; Two Ridges and Cross Roads, 1885-87; Toronto, O., 1887—. Brother of Brownhill T., '72.

WILLIAM STEWART, Teacher, Oxford, O.

A. B., A. M. Superintendent of Oxford Public Schools.

HARLAN PAGE USTICK, Oculist, Portland, Ore.

A. B., A. M. M. D., Hahnn Med. Coll., 1883. Member of consulting staff of Baptist Hospital, Chicago, Ills.

JAMES VINCENT, Minister, Danbury, Conn.

A. B., A. M. Ordained Universalist minister, 1871. Pastor of Universalist churches at Mexico, N. Y., 1871-75; Barre Ver. 1875-80; Shirley, Mass., 1880-84; Calais, Me., 1884-91; Danbury, Conn., 1891—.

*MATTHEW WADE, Minister, Holton, Kan.

A. B. Was graduated from Union Theol. Sem., 1873. Ordained, June 8, 1875. Pastor of Pres. churches at Perry, Kan., 1874-75; Holton, Kan., 1875-77. Brother of Nehemiah, '69. Born, Ross, O. Oct, 18, 1848. Died, April 24, 1877.

*JOHN KEOWN YOUTSEY, Insurance, Newport, Ky.

A. B. Corporal, Co. H, 3rd Ky. Veteran Cavalry, 1864-65. Deputy Revenue Collector, Sixth Ky. district, 1870-71. Cashier, New York Equitable Life Assurance Co., Cincinnati, O., 1871-74. Died, Feb. 15, 1874.

*HARRY C. WOODROW, Cincinnati, O.

B. S. Son of David T., '34. Murdered in San Francisco, Cal., Feb. 9, 1892.

Class of 1871.

WILLIAM EDWARD ALLEN, Farmer, Wyoming, O.
B. S.

PHILIP GILBERT BERRY, Lawyer, Hamilton, O.

A. B., A. M. Admitted to the bar. Probate Judge of Butler Co., 1888-91.

ANDREW ROBINSON BOLIN, Lawyer, Circleville, O.

A. B., A. M. L L. B., Cincinnati Law School, 1873. President Board of City Examiners, 1877—.
Office, Rooms 1 and 2 Masonic Temple.

*LUKE CLARKE, Lawyer, . Columbus, O.

A. B. Sergeant, 13th U. S. Inf., 1861–63. Severely wounded at the Siege of Vicksburg, resulting in the loss of the use of his left arm. Promoted First Lieutenant for distinguished valor and retired for life on full pay. Admitted to the bar and practised law at Columbus, O. Killed in a railroad accident at Bucyrus, O., Dec., 1881.

JAMES RUTHERFORD COLLIER, Minister, Louisville, Ky.

A. B., A. M. Was graduated from Lane Sem., 1874. Ordained by Presbytery of Chillicothe, Sept. 9, 1874. Private, 168th Ohio Vol. Inf., 1864. Pastor of Pres. churches at Mason, O., 1874–79; Jackson, O., 1879–83; Louisville, Ky., 1883—.
Address, 1927 West Jefferson street.

SAMUEL HAMMEL FORMAN, Farmer, Carthage, O.

B. S. Member Board of Agriculture.

CLARK MADISON GALLOWAY, Physician, Xenia, O.

A. B., A. M. M. D., Ohio Med. Coll., 1877. Private, Co. E, 154th Ohio Vol. Inf., and Co. G, 181st Ohio Vol. Inf. Physician to Ohio Soldier's and Sailor's Orphans' Home. Medical Director, Department of Ohio, G. A. R.

WILLIAM SCOBEY GIFFEN, Lawyer, Hamilton, O.

A. B., A. M. LL. B., Cincinnati Law School, 1880.
Office, Reily Block.

JEREMIAH MARSTON HUNT, Physician, Lytle, O.

A. B., A. M. M. D., Cincinnati Med. Coll., 1873.

ROBERT EATON LOWRY, Lawyer, Portland, Ind.

B. S. A. M. Admitted to the bar, 1892. Private, 46th Ohio Vol. Inf., 1864. Teacher in Public Schools in Ohio and Indiana, 1865–68 and 1871– 85. County Surveyor of Preble Co., O., 1885–91. City Engineer of Eaton, O., 1886–91.

ALBERT MALDON MACKERLEY, Lawyer, Greenfield, O.

A. B., A. M. LL. B., Univ. of Michigan, 1875. Postmaster at Greenfield, O., 1886–90.

HENRY BROWN MCCLURE, Lawyer, Cincinnati, O.

A. B., A. M. Admitted to the bar, 1880. Principal Preparatory Department, 1872–73. Attended Universities of Gottingen and Leipsic, 1873–74. Principal Public Schools, Glendale, O., 1875–80. Mayor of Glendale, O. 1880—. Joint Author of "Dower and Curtesy Tables," 1882.
Residence, Glendale, O. Office, Carlisle Building.

DAVID ROSS MOORE, Minister, Logan, O.

A. B., A. M. D. D., Miami Univ., 1891. Was graduated from Lane Theol. Sem., 1874, and Princeton Theol. Sem., 1878. Ordained by Presbytery of Chillicothe, April 15, 1874. Pastor of Pres. churches at Venice, O., 1874-77; Brookville, Ind., 1878-86; Logan, O., 1886—. Son of William H, '41.

DAVID EDWIN PLATTER, Minister, St. Paul, Minn.

A. B., A. M. Was graduated from Lane Theol. Sem., 1874. Ordained by Morris and Orange Presbytery, July 22, 1874. Pastor of Pres. churches at Rockaway, N. J., 1874-80; Canton, O., 1880-89. Retired on account of ill health.
Address, 26 Schulte Block.

JAMES HOLLINGSWORTH PUNTENNEY, Columbus, O.

A. B.
Address, 83 West Fifth avenue.

WOODHULL SMITH SCHENCK, Navy Officer, Philadelphia, Pa.

B. S. Captain and Assistant Quarter-Master, U. S. Marine Corps.
Address, 216 South Second street.

FRANK FILLMORE SCOTT, Merchant, Ross, O.

A. B. Dealer in General Merchandise.

JAMES OLIVER SHIRAS, Electrician, Mobile, Ala.

A. B., A. M. Introduced the telephone into Cincinnati, O., and Roumania. Secretary of Merchants' Police, Cincinnati, O., for several years.

EBERLE DENNIS SMITH, Banker, Blanchester, O.

A. B., A. M. L L. B., Univ. of Mich., 1873. Principal of Public School, Blanchester, O., 1872. President of Blanchester Bank.

ISAAC NEWTON SNYDER, Farmer, Clifton, Ind.

B. S. A. M. Secretary Richland Lodge, No. 4020, Farmers' Mutual Benefit Association. Statistical Correspondent of the U. S. Department of Agriculture, 1882—.

ROBERT BREWSTER STANTON, Civil Engineer, Denver, Col.

A. B., A. M. Resident Engineer, Cincinnati Southern R. R. Division Engineer, Union Pacific R. R. At present Chief Engineer Denver, Colorado Canon & Pacific R. R. Son of President Robert L. Stanton.
R. R. Address, San Diego, Cal.

ANDREW JAY SURFACE, Teacher, San Jose, Cal.

A. B., A. M. Corporal, 156th Ohio Vol. Inf., 1863. Admitted to the bar, 1872 and practised law for several years. Attorney for the People's Building and Loan Association, Fort Bragg, Cal. Superintendent of Schools, Ironton, O., 1878-81; Liverpool, O., 1881-88. Prof. in the Primary Academical Department, Univ. of Pacific, 1888—.

JAMES PAULL TOWNSLEY, Merchant, Xenia, O.

A. B., A. M. Son of Thomas P, '36.

JOHN MARSHALL VAN DYKE, Physician, Mason, O.

A. B., A. M. M. D., Ohio Med. Coll., 1874.

JAMES PATTERSON ZIEGLER, Physician, Mount Joy, Pa.

M. E. A.M. M. D., Univ. of Penn., 1880. Surgeon for the Pennsylvania R. R. Co.

ELIAS REYNOLDS ZELLER, Farmer, Winterset, Iowa.

A. B., A. M. Private 167th Ohio Vol. Inf., 1864. City superintendent of Public Schools, Winterset, Iowa, 1873-78. Secretary of Iowa State Senate, 1884. County Superintendent of Schools, 1886-90. Farmer and stock-raiser.

Class of 1872.

ROBERT HENRY ADAMS,

A. B. Can not be traced. Last address known, Mission, Kan.

HORACE ANKENEY, Farmer, Alpha, O.

A. B., A. M. County Infirmary Director, 6 years. President of Board of Education of Beaver Township schools, 7 years. Trustee of Heidelberg Univ., Tiffin, O. Trustee, Financial Agent, and Treasurer, Heidelberg Theol. Sem. Director of Orphans' Homes of the Reformed Church in the U. S. Trustee of Miami Univ., 1887—. Brother of Albert, '68. *Vide*, Sketch and Portrait, "Miami Journal," Vol. II., No. 8.

SYLVESTER LYONS BISHOP, Civil Engineer, Chicago, Ills.

A. B., A. M. Son of Robert H, Jr., '31. Brother of George S, '67. Address, 1615 Wabash avenue.

SAMUEL FENTON CARY, JR., South America.

A. B. Sailed for South America four years ago and has not since been heard from.

MOSES BRANSON EARNHART, Lawyer, Columbus, O.

A. B., A. M. LL. B., Univ. of Michigan, 1874. Mayor of Troy, O., 1876-77. City Solicitor of same, 1877-78. Prosecuting Attorney for Miami Co., O., 1879-84. Republican candidate for Attorney-General of the State of Ohio, 1883.

BENJAMIN RILEY FINCH, Solicitor, Chicago Lawn P. O., Ills.

A. B., A. M. County Surveyor of Butler Co., O., 1885-88.

WILLIAM MALLORY FISHER, Lawyer, El Dorado, Kan.

A. B., A. M. Admitted to the bar, 1875. U. S. Commissioner, 1877. Deputy U. S. Internal Revenue Collector, 1883-85.

THOMAS FITZGERALD, Minister, Downsville, N. Y.

A. B., A. M. Ordained by the Pres. church at Newburg, N. Y., 1879. Pastor of Pres. churches at Montague, N. J., 1879-80; Branchville, N. J., 1881-82; Mount Hope, N. Y., 1883-84; Amity, N. Y., 1885-92; Downsville, N. Y., 1892—.

THOMAS MADISON GOSSARD, Minister, Forest Hill, Ind.

A. B., A. M. Was graduated from Lane Seminary, 1882. Licensed by Presbytery of Columbus, Sept., 1881. Ordained by Presbytery of Portsmouth, April, 1882. Pastor of Pres. churches at Red Oak and Decatur, O., 1882-90; Forest Hill, Ind., 1890—.

GEORGE EDWIN GOWDY, Minister, Eaton, O.

A. B., A. M. Was graduated from Lane Seminary, 1875. Ordained by Presbytery of Chillicothe, Dec. 8, 1876. Pastor of Pres. churches at Greenfield, O., 1876-78; Carlisle, O., 1878-91; Eaton, O., 1891—.

THOMAS HANNA, Lawyer, Cincinnati, O.

A. B., A. M. L L. B., Cincinnati Law School.
Office, 21 West Third street.

*SAMUEL MALLERT, Lawyer, Somerville, O.

A. B. Admitted to the bar, April 25, 1876. Retired to a farm near Somervlle, O., March, 1878, on account of ill-health. Born, Glasgow, Scotland, Aug. 5, 1850. Died, Chicago, Ills., July 24, 1879.

JOSEPH CLAYBAUGH MCKEE, Lawyer, San Francisco, Cal.

B. S. A. M. Editor of papers at Greensburg, Ind.; Indianapolis, Ind.; Richmond, Ind.; Toledo, O.; Indianapolis, Ind.; Harper, Kan.; Richfield, Kan.; 1872-87. Admitted to the bar, 1887. Judge of Municipal Court, Richfield, Kan., 1887-90.
Address, 137 Montgomery street.

*JOHN ANDERSON RANKIN, Lawyer, Colorado.

A. B., A. M. Admitted to the bar and practised law at Olathe, Kan. Went to Colorado on account of health and died in 1888.

BROWNHILL TIDBALL SHEELEY, Minister, Fredericksburg, O.

A. B., A. M. Attended Lane Sem., 1876-78. Ordained, June, 1880. Pastor of Pres. churches at Youngstown, O.; Scott, O.; Fredericksburg, O. Brother of Homer, '70.

*BRUCE FRAZER THOMAS, Lawyer, Vanceburg, Ky.

A. B. Attended Harvard Law School and Cincinnati Law School. Admitted to the bar, Oct., 1874. Died, Jan. 2, 1882.

MIAMI UNIVERSITY.   117

NATHAN EGBERT WARWICK,   Lawyer,   Toledo, O.

A. B., A. M. Admitted to the bar, 1873.
Address, 609 Madison street.

*ROGER WILLIAMS,   Student,   Paddy's Run, O.

A. B. Editor and proprietor, "Oxford Citizen," 1872-73. Studied at the Univ. of Göttingen, 1872-73, in order to equip himself more thoroughly for journalistic work. Died, June 24, 1873.

Class of 1873.

HOLLY RAPER BUCKINGHAM,   Lawyer,   Alto Pass, Ills.

A. B. LL. B., Univ. of Mich., 1875. Member General Assembly of Illinois, 1881-82. Brother of Alexander, '70.

FRANCIS ELLIS CALLICOTT,   Lawyer,   Shawneetown, Ills.

A. B., A. M. Admitted to the bar, 1879.

WILLIAM ALPHEUS CHARLES,   Insurance,   Portland, Ore.

A. B. Principal Public Schools, Graham, Mo., 1873-75; Maryville, Mo., 1875-81. Life Insurance Agent, Portland, Ore., 1881—.
P. O. Box, 453.

FRANCIS MARION COPPOCK,   Lawyer,   Cincinnati, O.

A. B., A. M. Ph. D., Heidelberg, Germany, 1876. LL. B., Cincinnati Law School, 1878. City Solicitor, Cincinnati, O., 1885-87. Author of "Coppock's Municipal Code of Ohio," 1890.
Office, 180 Walnut street.

THOMAS JEFFERSON DAGUE,   Minister,   Paulding, O.

A. B., A. M. Principal Salem Academy, 1873-76. Principal and Proprietor Dague's Collegiate Institute, Chillicothe, O., 1876-79; Wadsworth, O., 1879-83. Teacher Caldwell, O., 1883-85. Stated supply of Pres. church at Chippewa Lake, O., 1880-83. Pastor of Pres. churches at Caldwell, O., 1883-89; Delphos, O., 1889-91; Paulding, O., 1891—.

JUAN DOS PASSOS DAMASCENO,   Civil Engineer,   Para, Brazil.

B. S., C. E. Student Stevens' Institute of Technology, 1873-74. Draughtsman, Quintard Iron Works, New York City. Civil Engineer, Para, Brazil.

JOHN CHARLES FARBER,   Lawyer,   Frankfort, Ind.

A. B., A. M. Admitted to the bar, Jan. 4, 1876. City Solicitor of Frankfort, Ind., 1886—. Attorney for Big Four R. R. Co.
Address, 951 East Clinton street.

ALFRED COLQUITT FICKLIN,   Lawyer,   Charleston, Ills.

A. B. Attended Chicago Law School. Admitted to the bar, Jan., 1876. City Attorney of Charleston, Ills., 8 years.

*JACKSON HAWKINS GILMORE, Lawyer, Eaton, O.

A. B. L L. B., Cincinnati Law School, 1876. Attended Univ. of Va,, 1874–75. Died, Oct. 24, 1880.

HARRY WEBSTER HUGHES, Commission, Cincinnati, O.

A. B., A. M. Was engaged in banking business, Cincinnati, O.,'ten years. At present engaged in Flour and Grain Commission. Firm name, Smyrl, Armstrong, & Hughes.
Office, 59 West Fourth street. Residence, Glendale, O.

ALFRED AUGUSTUS LOVETT, Physician, Eaton, O.

A. B., A. M. M. D., Hahnemann Coll., Philadelphia, Pa., 1876.

*WILLIAM BARKALOW MCALPIN, Merchant, Cincinnati, O.

A. B. Wholesale Dry Goods Merchant. Firm name, McAlpin, Polk & Co. Born, Cincinnati, O., Oct. 11, 1851. Died, Dec. 30, 1880.

JOHN FOSTER MARTIN, Lawyer, Cincinnati, O.

A. B. L L. B., Cincinnati Law School, 1875.

GEORGE FRANCIS O'BYRNE, Lawyer, Brookville, Ind.

B. S. Admitted to the bar, 1879. Private, Co. H, 68th Ind. Vol. Inf.

DAVID HUSTON POTTENGER, Lawyer, Cincinnati, O.

A. B., A. M. B. L., Univ., of Va., 1875. Attorney for the Jones Bros. Electric Co.; Cincinnati Electrical Sub-way Co.; Corrugated Elbow Co.; T. P. Scott Lumber Co.; M. H. Garrity Co.; Metropolitan National Bank; McDougall Bath and Massage Co.; Roan Mountain Steel and Iron Co.
Office, United Bank Building, Third and Walnut streets.

*ROBERT F. RYMAN, Lawyer, Cincinnati, O.

A. B. L L. B., Cincinnati Law School. Lawyer and Real Estate Dealer. Born, Jan. 24, 1852. Died, May 14, 1888.

WILLIAM POLLOCK SHANNON, Teacher, Greensburg, Ind.

A. B., A. M. Teacher, Glendale, O., 1873–74; Greensburg, Ind., 1875–82. Superintendent of Public Schools, Greensburg, Ind., 1882—.

JOHN N. WALTON,

A. B. Last address known, Liberty, Ind. Mysteriously disappeared years ago and his whereabouts are not known by his own parents.

Class of 1888.

JACOB NEWTON BROWN, Lawyer, Atlanta, Ga.

A. B. L L. B., Cincinnati Law School, 1889. Son of Charles E, '54.
Office, Room 50, Old Capitol Building.

MIAMI UNIVERSITY.   119

KEARNEY PRUGH,   Teacher,   Gratis P. O., O.

A. B. Editor, "Miami Journal," 1886-87. Principal Public School, 1888-89. — —

HARRY WEIDNER,   Journalist,   Dayton, O.

B. S. A. M. Founded "Miami Journal," 1886. Editor of same, 1886-88. On reportorial staff of the "Dayton Daily times," and "Evening News," 1889—. Correspondent, "Chicago Herald." President Young Men's Jackson Club, 1890-91. Address, 28 East Garden street.

Class of 1889.

WILLIAM EUGENE CLOUGH,   Physician,   Akron, O.

A. B. M. D., Eclectic Med. Coll., Cincinnati, O., 1892. Attended Louisville Med. Coll., 1889-90; Bellevue Med. Coll., 1890-91.

ORLANDO BENNET FINCH,   Teacher,   Hamilton, O.

A. B. Editor "Miami Student," 1888-89. Principal Public School, Jones' Station, O., 1890—. Brother of Elmer B, '90.

WILBUR JOHN GREER,   Teacher,   Oxford, O.

A. B. Editor "Miami Student," 1888-89. Principal Preparatory Department, Miami Univ., 1890—.

JOHN HART MACREADY,   Physicián,   Cincinnati, O.

A. B. M. D., Ohio Med. Coll, 1892. Address, 29 Wesley avenue. Permanent address, Monroe, O.

WILLIAM EARL MORRIS,   Stock Raiser,   Liberty, Ind.

A. B. Editor "Miami Student," 1888-89. Now engaged in farming and stock raising.

WILLIAM JOHN RUSK,   Lawyer,   Oxford, O.

A. B. Editor "Miami Student," 1888-89. L L. B., Cincinnati Law School, 1891. Attended Univ. of Va. Law School, 1889. Mayor of Oxford, O., 1892—. *Vide*, Sketch and Portrait, "Miami Student," Vol. XI, No. 7.

SAMUEL WITHROW TOWNSEND,   Book-keeper,   Pueblo, Col.

A. B. Editor "Miami Journal," 1886 and 1888-89. Real Estate Agent, Pueblo, Colo., 1889-91. Book-keeper, Pueblo National Bank, 1891—.

Class of 1890.

CHARLES FREDERICK BROOKINS, Student of Theology, Eaton, O.

A. B. Editor "Miami Student," 1889-90, Student Kenyon Theol. Sem., Gambier, O., 1890—.

ELMER BARTON FINCH, Photographer, Oxford, O.

A. B. Brother of Orlando B., '89.

ALFRED MELVILLE GREER, Book-keeper, Cincinnati, O.

A. B. Attended Nelson's Commercial Coll., Cincinnati, O., 1890-91. With the L. M. Dayton Co., 1891—. Address, 98 Vine street.

PERRY WILSON JENKINS, Teacher, Sweet Water, Tenn.

A. B. Editor "Miami Journal," 1888-89; "Miami Student," 1889-90. Student at Cincinnati Law School, 1890-91. Prof. of Mathematics, Sweet Water Coll., Tenn., 1891—.

*ROSCOE F. MASON, Journalist, Oxford, O.

A. B. Reporter and proof-reader, "Dayton Evening Herald," June, 1890—Oct., 1890, when he was taken ill with typhoid fever. Died, Nov. 11, 1890.

JOHN SAMUEL MUDDELL, Clerk, Oxford, O.

A. B. Studied law at Hamilton, O., 1890-92. Clerk in Post-office, Oxford, O., 1892—.

CHRISTIAN PETER PANN, Minister, Riverside, Cal.

A. B. Ordained by the Christian church. Pastor of Christian church, Riverside, Cal., 1891—.

JOHN LINTON PHYTHIAN, Physician, Newport, Ky.

A. B. M. D., Louisville Med. Coll., 1891. Attended Ohio Med. Coll., 1890-91. Address, York street.

HOLWAY BREWER SMITH, Superintendent, Crown Hill, W. Va.

A. B. Assistant and Acting Superintendent, Crown Hill Coal Co., 1890-92.

Class of 1891.

WILLIAM AMOS BOURNE, Student, Contreras, O.

A. B. Post-graduate course in Mathematics, Johns Hopkins Univ., Baltimore, Md., 1891-92.

WILLIAM MATSON CHIDLAW, Teacher, Cleves, O.

A. B. Editor "Miami Student," 1889-90. Teacher in public school near Cleves, O., 1891-92.

ROBERT HARVEY COOK, Student of Medicine, Oxford, O.

A. B. Student at Ohio Med. Coll.

WALTER CONGER HARRIS, Student, Eaton, O.

A. B. Editor "Miami Journal," 1888–89; "Miami Student," 1890–91. Post-graduate student, Ohio State Univ., 1891—. Correspondent "Register," Eaton, O. Son of Andrew L, '60.

JAMES EDWIN LOUGH, Teacher, Eaton, O.

A. B. Teacher, Eighth Grade, Public Schools, Eaton, O., 1891–92.

WILLIAM HENRY POWERS, Teacher, Ada, O.

A. B. Editor "Miami Student," 1890–91. Teacher of Latin and Greek, Normal School, Ada, O., 1891. Post-graduate student at Harvard Univ., 1891–92.

JOHN HINCKLEY SMITH, Student of Law, Oxford, O.

A. B. Editor "Miami Student," 1888–91. Student, Law Department, Univ. of Mich., 1891—.

SAM STEPHENSON, Lawyer, Woods, O.

A. B. Editor "Miami Student, 1889–91. Studied law, Hamilton, O., 1891–92. Admitted to the bar, 1892. Will locate in Falls City, Montana.

WALTER LAWRENCE TOBEY, Journalist, Dayton, O.

A. B. Business Manager, "Miami Journal," 1886–88. Editor "Miami Student," 1888–91. On reportorial staff, "Dayton Evening Herald," 1891–92. Managing Editor, "The World," Dayton, O., 1892—.

CHARLES A. WILSON, Teacher, Nashville, Tenn.

A. B. Editor "Miami Student," 1890–91. Teacher in Academy, Nashville, Tenn., 1891—.

Class of 1892.

ROBERT ACTON HIESTAND, Eaton, O.

A. B.

ASBURY E. KROM, Springfield, Ind.

A. B. Editor, "Miami Student," 1889–91. Business Manager, "Miami Student, 1891–92.

EVERETT ANDERSON MACDONALD, Union City, Ind.

A. B. Editor, "Miami Journal," 1889–90; "Miami Student," 1890–91.

OKEY B. NOWLIN, Lawrenceburg, Ind.

A. B. Son of Ambrose E, '64.

HONORARY DEGREES.

[This list does not comprise the honorary degrees conferred upon Alumni or Former Students, since the sketches contain the same.]

A. B.

1845. GEORGE J. REED, Esq.
MASON D. P. WILLIAMS, Esq.

A. M.

1826. CHARLES MOORE CUNNINGHAM, Esq.
REV. JOSEPH PARKS CUNNINGHAM.
REV. JOHN HUDSON.
1827. REV. BAYNARD HALL.
REV. JOHN T. PRESSLY.
REV. WILLIAM SPARROW.
1828. PROF. JOSEPH TOMLINSON.
1831. WILLIAM A. LEAVY, Esq.
1834. REV. WILLIAM C. ANDERSON.
REV. SAMUEL P. PRESSLY.
REV. GREENBURY W. RIDGELY.
LUTHER SMITH, Esq.
1835. REV. SAMUEL McFARRON.
1839. REV. SAMUEL ROBERTS.

1846. CHARLES E. MATTHEWS, Esq.
STANLEY MATTHEWS, Esq.
SAMUEL L. SLACK, Esq.
WILLIAM L. SLACK, Esq.
1849. PROF. WILLIAM F. GEORGE.
1850. REV. J. M. GOSHORN.
JOHN J. LAYMON, Esq.
1851. LORIN ANDREWS, Esq.
M. F. COWDERY, Esq.
ASA D. LORD, Esq.
1853. PROF. A. FREESE.
PROF. JOHN LYNCH.
D. T. DE WOLF, Esq.
1854. REV. ELIAS H. SABIN.
1857. REV. EVAN DAVIES.
1858. REV. ANDREW J. REYNOLDS.
THOMAS WALLACE, Esq.
1859. CORNELIUS MOORE, Esq.
1861. REV. S. WEEKS.
JAMES HARVEY WILLIAMSON, Esq.
1864. REV. D. J. STARR.
1865. DR. W. P. THORNTON.
REV. J. C. TIDBALL.
1866. JUDGE SAMUEL BONNER,
1867. REV. N. R. KIRKPATRICK.
1871. REV. JOHN COOPER.
1891. PROF. WALTER RAY BRIDGMAN.
1891. MAXWELL VAN ZANDT WOODHULL, Esq.

D. D.

1827. Rev. James Hoge.
1836. Rev. John F. Crowe.
   Rev. William Sparrow.
1838. Rev. James Hay.
   Rev. Samuel Magaw.
   Rev. Joel Parker.
   Rev. Adam Thompson.
   Rev. George Young.
1841. Rev. Joseph Claybaugh.
   Rev. Samuel Crothers.
   Rev. Robert Palmer.
   Rev. Alexander Duncan.
1842. Rev. John William Baynes.
   Rev. Abijah Blanchard.
   Rev. John W. Yeomans.
1843. Rev. Alexander Ogilvie Beattie.
1846. Rev. William C. Anderson.
   Rev. William L. Breckenridge.
   Rev. Peter Mac Indoe.
1847. Rev. John W. Hall.
   Rev. Henry Hervey.
1850. Rev. D. X. Junkin.
1852. Rev. W. H. Gould.
   Rev. John C. Lowrie.
1853. Rev. J. C. Moffat.
1854. Rev. D. R. Kerr.
   Rev. S. R. Wilson.

1856. Rev. Hugh McMillan.
1858. Rev. B. J. Wallace.
1861. Rev. John M. Lowrie.
1862. Rev. Robert D. Harper.
       Rev. Robert Patterson.
       Rev. S. G. Speers.
1865. Rev. Theophilus A. Wylie.
1869. Rev. M. A. Hoge.
1885. Rev. S. H. McMullin.
1886. Rev. Prentiss De Veuve.
1887. Rev. Evan Herber Evans.
       Rev. William H. James.
1888. Rev. David Roberts.
1890. Rev. James H. Shields.
1891. Rev. Frank E. Miller.

LL. D.

1837. John W. Picket, Esq.
1841. Prof. Robert Cunningham.
1846. Joseph Bateman, Esq.
1850. Hon. John S. Hart.
1852. Hon. Joseph Estabrook.
1854. Rev. George Junkin.
1862. Dr. J. G. Flugel.
1864. Rev. E. D. McMaster.
1865. Hon. Salmon P. Chase.
1873. Hon. Henry Stanberry.
1888. Rev. William H. Roberts.
1890. Hon. James E. Campbell.
1891. Ethelbert Dudley Warfield, Esq.

INDEX.

ALPHABETICAL INDEX.

A

Abernethy, Allen	97
Abernethy, Henri M.	97
Abernethy, John J.	82
Adams, Robert H.	115
Allen, William E.	111
Anderson, Charles	12
Anderson, David S.	41
Anderson, Isaac	64
Anderson, James H.	24
Anderson, John A.	57
Anderson, William	13
Andrew, George L.	35
Andrews, Robert W.	90
Ankeney, Albert	103
Ankeney, Henry N.	83
Ankeney, Horace	115
Anthony, Joseph E.	43
Armstrong, Absalom G.	98
Armstrong, Thomas	7
Ashford, William T.	102
Aten, Aaron M.	73
Aten, John L.	64
Atherton, Gibson	57
Atkinson, Maynard C.	83
Austin, William H.	98
Ayers, Stephen C.	86

B

Bacon, James H.	3
Baird, John W.	70
Baker, J. Edward	90
Baker, James S.	104
Baker, John S.	54
Baldridge, Benjamin L.	44
Baldridge, Samuel C.	1
Baldwin, Edgar A.	83
Banning, Myran	94
Barnes, Charles	41
Barnett, Allen A.	53
Barnett, James	29
Barr, John	33
Barrere, Carlisle W.	100
Barrett, John	83
Battle, Joel A.	79
Beatty, William T.	61
Beckett, David C.	83
Beckett, William	43
Belch, James	107
Bell, Alexander P.	61
Bell, John W.	27
Bell, Josiah R.	110
Bell, Thomas C.	70
Bellville, William W.	33
Bennett, Martin C.	29
Bennett, Samuel T.	102
Berry, Albert S.	67
Berry, James J.	38
Berry, Philip G.	112
Bigham, D. L.	100
Billings, John S.	70
Birney, James	21
Bishir, Christopher	100
Bishop, Ebenezer B.	13
Bishop, George B.	4
Bishop, George S.	102
Bishop, John M.	35
Bishop, Lucius W.	102
Bishop, Robert H.	8
Bishop, Robert N.	92
Bishop, Sylvester L.	115
Blackburn, William E.	38
Blain, Wilson	18
Blount, John R.	33
Boatman, James C.	104

Bolin, Andrew R.	113
Bonham, John C.	49
Bonham, Lazarus N.	64
Bonner, James R.	13
Booth, Eli	51
Booth, Henry A.	47
Boude, John K.	55
Bourne, William A.	120
Boyd, Joseph Y.	27
Boyse, William M.	6
Brady, Joseph	51
Branham, John L.	35
Bratton, William S.	73
Brackenridge, Samuel Z.	86
Brice, Calvin S.	92
Brigham, Lucius A.	18
Brigham, Marcus, M.	9
Bright, Johnston E.	18
Broadbent, John W.	98
Broadbent, Oliver	100
Broadbent, Robert F.	98
Bronson, John G.	93
Brookes, James H.	57
Brookins, Charles F.	119
Brooks, Andrew M.	52
Brooks, Frank S.	107
Brooks, John K.	94
Brooks, Peter H.	104
Brooks, Robert F.	73
Brown, Benjamin H.	104
Brown, Charles E.	61
Brown, Jacob N.	70
Brown, Jacob N.	118
Brown, James L.	104
Brown, James M.	18
Brown, Josiah E.	61
Brown, M. A.	43
Brown, Matthew N.	104
Brown, Mitchell M.	33
Brown, Nathan M.	64
Brown, Robert J.	90
Brown, Robert P.	7
Brown, Robert S.	87
Bruce, James E.	64
Bruen, David H.	15
Buckingham, Alexander	110
Buckingham, Holly R.	117
Buckley, Dennis W.	13
Buell, James L.	38
Bullard, Ebenezer W.	15
Bundy, Eugene H.	107
Burgoyne, William M.	57
Burnet, Jacob	24
Burrowes, Thomas A.	50
Burrowes, William S.	44
Butler, Jacob	29
Byrkett, Ahijah R.	104

C

Caldwell, Caleb D.	57
Caldwell, David R.	79
Caldwell, James P.	70
Caldwell, John W.	3
Caldwell, Robert C.	6
Caldwell, William B.	18
Calhoun, Persius B.	36
Callicott, Francis E.	117
Cambern, Samuel M.	83
Campbell, John M.	33
Canby, Oliver S.	79
Carney, John	100
Carr, Nelson	110
Carson, James	57
Carson, William	47
Cartwright, Noah	73
Cary, Freeman G.	9
Cary, Samuel F.	18
Cary, Samuel F., Jr.	115
Caskey, James B.	9
Cathcart, Charles W. H.	53
Chalfant, Lafayette W.	41
Chamberlin, John R.	74
Chambers, Andrew G.	57
Chambers, Pascal H.	45
Charles, William A.	117
Cheshire, William W.	74
Chestnut, James G.	74
Chidlaw, Benjamin W.	13
Chidlaw, William M.	120
Childs, James H.	55
Christie, Robert	100
Christy, Robert	50
Christy, William H.	48
Churchill, Lucius C.	36
Clark, Benjamin F.	13
Clark, David	102
Clark, George K.	61
Clark, James	48
Clark, James H.	57
Clark, John R.	41
Clark, Robert C.	15
Clarke, Charles L.	107

Clarke, Luke.................................. 113	Curran, Ulysses T......................... 67
Clopper, Edward N....................... 87	Currie, Ebenezer............................ 87
Clough, William E........................ 119	Cushing, Courtland........................ 6
Cochran, William R...................... 9	Cushman, Isaac J........................... 74
Coke, Richard H........................... 13	

D

Cole, Eliphalet P.......................... 33	
Coleman, William.......................... 83	Dague, Thomas J........................... 117
Coler, Christian A......................... 74	Damasceno, Juan D. P................... 117
Colescott, John A.......................... 90	Dameron, Augustus S.................... 87
Collett, William R......................... 7	Dameron, Robert C........................ 33
Collins, James R............................ 113	Davies, Joseph P............................ 93
Collins, John A.............................. 38	Davies, Samuel W.......................... 79
Colmery, David R.......................... 61	Davis, Benjamin F......................... 107
Combs, James B............................ 52	Davis, Ferman D............................ 93
Conklin, Pierson C........................ 58	Davis, James.................................. 91
Connaway, Joseph W.................... 95	Davis, John J.................................. 98
Conover, Wilbur............................. 33	Davis, Joseph R.............................. 39
Cook, R. Harvey............................. 120	De Armond, James M.................... 71
Cooper, Daniel C........................... 79	Dennison, William......................... 19
Cooper, Daniel W.......................... 70	Denny, Harmar.............................. 55
Cooper, James................................ 67	Dewey, Charles............................... 45
Cooper, James H........................... 87	Dewey, Elijah F.............................. 83
Cooper, John.................................. 70	Dewey, James S.............................. 74
Coppock, Francis M....................... 117	Dial, Enoch G................................. 41
Corbin, Julius L............................. 104	Dickey, Theophilus L..................... 9
Corry, William M........................... 1	Dickson, William M....................... 48
Cortelyou, Thomas F..................... 62	Dills, James H................................ 79
Corwin, Quincy.............................. 90	Dodds, Ozro J................................. 87
Cory, Andrew J.............................. 64	Dougan, William T........................ 98
Cory, Benjamin.............................. 38	Drake, John W................................ 51
Cory, James M............................... 51	Drake, Robert T............................. 53
Courtwright, Calvin W.................. 93	Dubois, John T............................... 43
Covington, John I.......................... 110	Dubose, Virgil M............................ 27
Cowan, James P............................. 110	Dudley, Adolphus S....................... 74
Crabb, John M............................... 15	Duff, Jackson.................................. 30
Craig, Isaac E................................. 87	Duncan, John H............................. 33
Craig, John S.................................. 79	Duncan, Robert.............................. 24
Craighead, John P......................... 55	Dunlap, Alexander......................... 21
Craighead, R. D.............................. 100	Dunlap, Archibald S....................... 71
Craighead, William........................ 65	Dunn, Nathan P............................. 87
Crane, George................................. 53	Durham, William........................... 100
Crane, Stephen............................... 62	Durrell, Richard T.......................... 100
Crane, William E........................... 11	Dyche, George F............................. 62
Craven, John G.............................. 45	

E

Craven, Thomas............................. 39	
Crawford, Alexander M................. 74	Earnhart, Moses B......................... 115
Crawford, Samuel E...................... 98	Earnist, Charles W........................ 107
Crawford, William B..................... 33	Edwards, John............................... 91
Crissman, George T....................... 83	Effinger, Michael........................... 24
Crothers, John M........................... 21	Elam, John B.................................. 110
Crozier, John.................................. 51	Elder, John..................................... 34

Elliott, Ebenezer N............... 7
Elliott, James C............... 104
Elliott, James H............... 93
Ellis, Alston............... 102
Ellis, Anderson N............... 95
Eltzroth, William F............... 107
Erlougher, John M............... 45
Evans, Daniel H............... 79
Evans, Edward N............... 110
Evans, Frank D............... 88
Evans, Henry O............... 103
Evans, J. Rush............... 95
Evans, Nelson W............... 95
Evans, William E............... 107
Evans, William H............... 88
Ewing, Philemon B............... 30

F

Faran, James J............... 9
Farber, John C............... 117
Faries, Isaiah............... 48
Farr, Henry H............... 103
Feighan, John W............... 110
Ferguson, James............... 71
Ferguson, Pickney M............... 74
Ferguson, William F............... 4
Ficklin, Alfred C............... 117
Finch, Benjamin R............... 115
Finch, Elmer B............... 120
Finch, Orlando B............... 119
Finney, James R............... 83
Fisher, Elam............... 111
Fisher, William M............... 116
Fisk, Charles H............... 93
Fithian, Washington............... 45
Fitzgerald, Thomas............... 116
Fletcher, Albert M............... 21
Flory, Aaron M............... 75
Forman, Samuel H............... 113
Foster, Charles............... 21
Foster, James B............... 75
Foster, Peregrine D............... 24
Francis, Favid............... 62
Franklin, Amherst............... 98
Frazier, James A............... 45
Fullerton, Erskine B............... 93
Fullerton, Hugh S............... 91
Fullerton, George H............... 75
Fullerton, Joseph S............... 67
Fullerton, Thomas A............... 58
Furrow, Benjamin D............... 53

G

Galbraith, Robert C............... 58
Golloway, Albert G............... 8
Galloway, Clark M............... 113
Galloway, Henry P............... 4
Galloway, James E............... 43
Galloway, Samuel............... 13
Gamble, James N............... 6
Garrigus, John M............... 4
Garvin, James H............... 98
Garvin, Thomas D............... 61
Gassaway, Nicholas G. R............... 3
Gerard, Clinton W............... 104
Geyer, Mahlon F............... 95
Gibson, James K............... 108
Gibson James R............... 30
Giffen, William S............... 113
Gilchrist, James............... 39
Gilchrist, John............... 36
Gilchrist, Robert............... 100
Gill, Heber............... 98
Gillet, Jerome T............... 50
Gilmer, Daniel............... 19
Gilmore, Charles W............... 48
Gilmore, Jackson H............... 118
Glenn, John J............... 67
Goble, John............... 39
Goode, James S............... 45
Goodman, Henry H............... 24
Goodwin, R. J. M............... 71
Gordon, Gilbert............... 24
Gordon, John M............... 24
Gordon, Neal M............... 24
Gordon, Thomas B............... 34
Gossard, Thomas M............... 116
Gowdy, George E............... 116
Gowdy, George W............... 36
Graham, George B............... 21
Graham, James W............... 22
Graham, John M............... 27
Graham, John M............... 75
Graham, William A............... 93
Graham, William M............... 27
Grand—Girard, Herdman E............... 108
Graves, Allen T............... 25
Graves, Samuel............... 45
Gray, Daniel L............... 1
Greer, Alfred M............... 120
Greer, Horace E............... 95
Greer, Wilbur J............... 119

Gregg, George A............ 19
Gregg, William............ 8
Groesbeck, Herman J............ 15
Groesbeck, William S............ 15
Guy, Edward A............ 75

H

Hageman, George............ 98
Hageman, Simon A............ 99
Hair, James A............ 88
Haire, Thomas............ 42
Hall, Benton J............ 65
Halley, Samuel B............ 30
Halliday, George V............ 91
Halsey, Joseph P............ 8
Hamilton, A. W............ 39
Hamilton, William,............ 100
Hancock, Walter D............ 108
Hanes, David............ 43
Hanna, John............ 67
Hanna, Samuel T............ 75
Hanna, Thomas............ 116
Harbine, John T............ 91
Hardin, Charles H............ 36
Harding, Lyman............ 74
Harney, John H............ 3
Harris, Andrew L............ 84
Harris, Horatio J............ 19
Harris, John H............ 67
Harris, Joseph............ 84
Harris, Rufus K............ 30
Harris, Walter C............ 121
Harrison, Benjamin............ 55
Haskell, Thomas N............ 54
Haslett, George N............ 14
Hay, Lawrence G............ 50
Haynes, Henry L............ 101
Hays, William............ 65
Hearne, Thomas C............ 52
Hearst, John W............ 14
Helm, Henry T............ 58
Henderson, John M............ 91
Heron, John M............ 44
Herron, John W............ 45
Hiatt, John M............ 88
Hibben, James S............ 39
Hibben, Joseph M............ 104
Hibben, Samuel............ 58
Hibbett, Theophilus C............ 62
Hiestand, Robert A............ 121
Hill, John E............ 88

Hillis, William H............ 99
Hilts, Charles............ 46
Hitchcock, James K............ 16
Hittell, John S............ 42
Hocker, James D............ 30
Holbrook, Craft C............ 101
Holliday, William A............ 6
Hollingsworth, William R............ 88
Hollyday, Robert H............ 27
Hollyday, Wilson C............ 25
Holmes, James............ 58
Holmes, Louis D............ 105
Holmes, William............ 22
Honnell, William H............ 58
Horr, Versalius............ 42
Howard, George A............ 62
Howell, James B............ 25
Hueston, Matthew............ 53
Hughes, Harry W............ 118
Hughes, Isaac M............ 65
Hughes, James A............ 55
Hughes, Melanchton............ 95
Hughes, Thomas E............ 65
Humphreys, William S............ 19
Hunt, Franklin M............ 58
Hunt, Jeremiah M............ 113
Hunt, John S............ 58
Hunt, Samuel F............ 96
Hunter, William............ 39
Hussey, John............ 62
Hussey, Lutellus............ 67
Huston, Robert M. L............ 103
Hutchison, John C............ 68
Hutchison, William A............ 93
Hutchison, W Clark............ 71

I

Iddings, Daniel W............ 39

J

Jackson, H. Parks............ 79
Jamison, John M............ 108
Jamison, William............ 39
Jenkins, Peny W............ 120
Jeter, Fielding R. A............ 46
John, Robert N............ 75
Johns, John J............ 34
Johnson, Henry C............ 99
Johnson, Henry H............ 34
Johnson, James W............ 34
Johnson, Theodore............ 11

Johnston, David... 62
Johnston, James F... 27
Johnston, John B... 105
Johnston, Miles... 95
Johnston, William... 62
Jones, Abner F... 76
Jones, Bruce P... 105
Jones, Daniel D... 48
Jones, James R... 99
Jones, Thomas A... 3
Jordon, Isaac M... 71
Junkin, Anthony C... 55
Junkin, George... 39
Junkin, John M... 36
Justice, Horace H... 88

K

Kelly, Dennis N... 71
Kemper, D. Rice... 99
Kendall, Clark... 46
Kennedy, Gilbert... 28
Kenner, Duncan F... 10
Kerr, James W... 42
Kerr, John F... 28
Kerr, Samuel C... 59
Kessling, Henry L... 62
Killen, John T... 62
Kirkpatrick, James D... 46
Kleinschmidt, Edward H... 101
Knox, John R... 30
Krom, Asbury E... 121
Kumler, J. P. E... 59
Kyle, David C... 88
Kyle, Joshua R... 80

L

Lancaster, Hugh... 22
Lane, Isaac S... 55
Lapham, Levi... 16
Lathrop, Abner S... 53
Lathrop, Henry J... 68
Laughead, William C... 46
Laws, Samuel S... 51
Layman, John M... 53
Leake, J. Bloomfield... 48
Leathers, Bowling S... 19
Lee, Harvey... 111
Lee, William... 108
Lewis, Addison S... 108
Lewis, Sohn C... 84

Liggett, James D... 44
Lindley, John W... 53
Linton, David... 30
Little, Isaiah... 51
Lockhart, John M... 105
Lockwood, William L... 76
Logan, John P... 96
Long, James... 36
Long, Robert K... 44
Lough, James E... 121
Loughridge, Robert M... 25
Lovett, Alfred A... 118
Lowe, Jacob D... 59
Lowe, John G... 28
Lowe, Ralph P... 6
Lowe, William B... 65
Lowes, Abraham B... 84
Lowes, James A. I... 36
Lowrie, James A... 54
Lowrie, Samuel T... 56
Lowry, Charles Fox... 9
Lowry, Robert E... 113
Ludlow, William S... 91
Lyle, John A... 25
Lyle, William C... 6
Lyons, Robert L... 105
Lyons, Spencer C... 44
Lytle, George M... 76

M

Mac Dill, John B... 65
MacDonald, Everett A... 121
Mack, David... 37
Mackerly, Albert M... 113
Macready, John H... 119
Magill, Charles B... 76
Magoffin, Thomas... 108
Major, Daniel S... 10
Mallert, Samuel... 116
Maltby, Frederick... 63
Manning, James T... 65
Manspeaker, Andrew... 30
Marshall, James B... 4
Marshall, John... 88
Marshall, Joseph H... 59
Marshall, Robert M... 108
Marshall, Samuel T... 34
Marshall, Thomas B... 88
Martin, Charles W... 10
Martin, David D... 34

Martin, John F. 188
Martin, William S. 37
Mason. Roscoe F. 120
Matson, John A. 5
Matson, William D. 19
Matthews, Samuel R. 54
Maxwell, John C. 30
May, Martin 80
McAfee, Isaac W. 99
McAlpin, William B. 118
McArthur, James R. 51
McAuley. William H. 16
McCague, John 28
McCague, Joseph W. 31
McCarty, Benjamin M. 84
McCaughan, Charles T. 25
McCaw, David 28
McClanahan, A. W. 44
McClave, Jessie T. 105
McCleary, Daniel 40
McCleery, Samuel 16
McClelland, Samuel I. 105
McClelland, Thomas J. 106
McClenahan, John 76
McClung, David W. 63
McClung, John N. 68
McClung, Leonidas H 108
McClure, Henry B. 113
McClurg, Alexander C. 59
McCoy, John 22
McCoy, Samuel F. 31
McCracken, George W. 99
McCracken, Henry M. 71
McCracken, John S. 31
McCracken, Samuel W. 10
McCrea, Adam 40
McCrery, Joseph 16
McDill, James W. 59
McDill, John 7
McDonald, David K. 14
McDonald, Duncan 80
McDonald, James S. 80
McDonald, Laughlin 22
McDonald, Matthew 40
McFarland, Armour J. 76
McFarland, James M. 111
McFarland, Joseph 80
McGaw, James A. P. 68
McGregor, James W. 94
McGuire, Henry L. 48
McKee, Joseph C. 116

McKee, Samuel 72
McKesson, John A. 16
McKinley, Samuel 80
McKinney, Alexander 16
McKinney, Colin 19
McKinney, William H. 72
McKitrick, Ebenezer S. 111
McLain, Alvan L. 105
McLain, James L. 105
McLain, William 10
McLandburgh, Henry J. 80
McLauren, Hugh 11
McMaken, Joseph J. 111
McMechan, John 3
McMillan, A. James 59
McMillan, Daniel A. 105
McMillan, Gavin R. 48
McMillan, John 50
McMillan, Robert 63
McMillan, Samuel H. 80
McNair, William S. 60
McNutt, Joseph G. 60
McRae, John J. 16
McRae, Malcolm J. 11
McSurely, William J. 68
Means, William B. 188
Mecum, Burton A. 100
Meeks, John A. 14
Merrick, E C. 46
Miller, Benjamin F. 68
Miller, Franklin E. 96
Miller, John H. 16
Miller, John M. 68
Miller, Joseph 31
Millikin, Joseph 80
Millikin, Minor 63
Millikin, Thomas 28
Mills, Benjamin 37
Mills, John M. 37
Mills, Thornton A. 8
Mitchell, Claudius N. 94
Mixer, William M. 96
Molyneaux, William J. 50
Monfort, Isaac W. 49
Monfort, Joseph G. 17
Montgomery, Clark B. 99
Moore, David R. 114
Moore, James W. 109
Moore, James Z. 103
Moore, John R. 109
Moore, Robert 76

Moore, Samuel M 37
Moore, Philip N 111
Moore, William A 31
Moore, William B 42
Moore, William H 37
Morehead, Samuel J 19
Morey, J. Elwood 103
Morgan, Pollard M 60
Morris, Aaron H 106
Morris, Austin 88
Morris, Benjamin F 11
Morris, Isaac B 91
Morris, John W 89
Morris, Samuel T 40
Morris, William E 119
Morrison, John I 5
Morrison, Marion 49
Morrison, Robert 52
Morrison, William M 60
Morrow, David 56
Morrow, Henry F 84
Morrow, Jeremiah 10
Morrow, Joseph A 76
Morrow, Josiah 81
Mosgrove, William F 40
Muddell, John S 120
Mulford, Asa 84
Murdock, David 96
Murphy, Duncan 25
Murphy, Robert C 46

N

Nall, Robert 10
Nauerth, George V 91
Naylor, Arthur R 37
Naylor, James M 101
Nelson, James A 17
Newman, Omar 65
Noble, Henry C 46
Noble, John 60
Nowlin, Ambrose E 96
Nowlin, Okey B 121
Nutter, John A 101

O

O'Byrne, George F 118
O'Conner, Joseph S 46
Ogden, George C 94
Ogle, Jacob W 47
Ogle, John 37
Oldfather, Jeremiah M 109

Olds, Chauncey N 22
Oliver, Joseph C 109
Oliver, M. Wade 50
Orr, James M 81
Orr, John 47
Orr, John R 89
Osborne, William K 50
Owens, James W 92
Owens, William 63

P

Pabody, Ezra 84
Pack, Arnaldo F 40
Paddack, Alexander 37
Page, Henry F 31
Pann, Christian P 120
Parker, Samuel W 5
Parker, Tudor H 77
Parks, James W 28
Parks, Robert H 31
Parks, William H 28
Parsons, George M 26
Patterson, James B 77
Patterson, James R 77
Patton, G. Randolph 60
Patton, John F 40
Patton, William W 40
Patton, William Y 40
Pease, Walter B 54
Peck, George B 72
Peck, Hiram D 92
Peck, Morris 92
Peirce, Jeremiah H 19
Pence, Abram M 84
Pendery, Thomas L 69
Peyton, R. L. Y 38
Phythian, John I 120
Picard, Federick J 106
Pierson, Aaron H 5
Pinkerton, John W 69
Platter, Cornelius C 85
Platter, David E 114
Pollock, Garnett A 77
Pope, Charles D 22
Porter, James B 72
Porter, Joseph 20
Porter, William A 3
Porter, William L 89
Pottenger, David H 118

Potter, Elisha P.	63	Russell, Moses	26
Potter, George W.	85	Ryan, Michael C.	31
Powers, William H.	121	Ryman, Robert F.	118
Pressly, David	31		
Pressly, Ebenezer E.	1		

S

Pressly, James P.	2	Sackett, Milton A.	29
Prestley, William H.	56	Sargeant, H. W.	103
Prugh, Kearney	119	Saunders, Richardson C.	32
Pugh, George E.	34	Sawyer, James F.	14
Pugsley, Jacob	81	Sayer, William D.	26
Puntenney, James H.	114	Sayler, J. Riner	85
		Sayler, Milton	56

Q

		Sayler, Nelson	72
Quinn, James	109	Schenck, John S.	92
		Schenck, Robert C.	4

R

		Schenck, Robert C., Jr.	97
		Schenck, Woodhull S.	114
Ramsey, Samel M.	96	Scobey, Frank H.	77
Rankin, John A.	116	Scott, David C.	111
Rea, Francis	14	Scott, Edward S.	112
Rea, George S.	28	Scott, Frank F.	114
Reber, Samuel	26	Scott, John J.	38
Reid, Whitelaw	69	Scott, Samuel P.	101
Reid, William H.	66	Shaffer, William V.	111
Reiley, John A.	40	Shannon, William P.	118
Reily, James	7	Sheeks, Benjamin	99
Reynolds, James	2	Sheeley, Brownhill T.	116
Reynolds, John A.	81	Sheeley, Homer	112
Reynolds, John P.	29	Sheeley, Virgil G.	94
Reynolds, Wilberforce	89	Sheil, George K.	41
Rigdon, Francis D.	29	Shellabarger, Samuel	38
Robertson, William W.	17	Shepherd, Hervey B.	20
Robinson, George F.	106	Shepherd, Isaac N.	8
Robinson, John M.	111	Sheppard, Samuel C.	99
Roby, John B.	111	Shields, Edward P.	63
Rodgers, J. Harrison	60	Shinkle, Bradford	97
Rogers, Andrew W.	54	Shiras, James O.	114
Rogers, Ardivan W.	54	Shirk, Harvey J.	49
Rogers, Thomas H.	69	Shockley, Henry M.	66
Rogers, William H.	20	Shotwell, William	44
Rogers, William S.	20	Shuey, A. M.	101
Ronald, W. J.	92	Sickels, Isaac C.	81
Root, Oliver W.	77	Sidell, George A.	106
Rosamond, James	14	Sillars, William	20
Ross, Andrew	22	Simpson, George W.	81
Ross, Joseph C.	60	Simpson, James	5
Ross, Lewis W.	56	Sloan, William S.	89
Rowan, Alexander H.	94	Smeltzer, William V.	77
Rowe, Edward L.	96	Smith, David B.	97
Runkle, Benjamin P.	72	Smith, Eberle D.	114
Rusk, William J.	119	Smith, Edmund	20

Smith, John Hinckley..................121
Smith, Holway B. 120
Smith, James G........................... 35
Smith, J McLain.......................... 81
Smith, John A............................. 20
Smith, John B............................. 77
Smith, John R............................. 72
Smith, Kirby..............................109
Smith, L. Orestes......................... 32
Smith, Otis C.............................101
Smith, Palmer W.......................... 97
Smith, Ransford........................... 66
Smith, Richard H.......................... 35
Smith, Robert C........................... 26
Smith, Samuel M.......................... 23
Smith, William............................ 89
Smith, William C.......................... 69
Smith, William M.......................... 26
Smith, Windsor A.......................... 23
Snow, Henry............................... 29
Snyder, Isaac N...........................114
Spence, John Q............................106
Spence, William B......................... 20
Spencer, Frank A.......................... 85
Stagg, Warren............................. 49
Stanbery, William......................... 26
Stanton, Robert B.........................114
Steel, John W............................. 60
Steele, David............................. 72
Steele, John C............................ 11
Steele, Joseph D.......................... 34
Steele, Robert W.......................... 35
Steele, Walter............................ 35
Steen, Moses D. A.........................101
Stephenson, Sam...........................121
Sterrett, Alexander....................... 50
Stevens, Algernon S....................... 52
Stevens, Edward B......................... 42
Stevens, Lawrence M....................... 66
Stevenson, Joseph H....................... 81
Stevenson, Robert......................... 47
Stewart, Charles.......................... 51
Stewart, David M.......................... 14
Stewart, George H......................... 32
Stewart, Jonathan......................... 63
Stewart, Robert E......................... 49
Stewart, Samuel G.........................106
Stewart, William H........................112
Stoddard, Henry........................... 63
Stone, Jared M............................ 17
Stormont, Samuel R........................ 81

Stout, Joseph............................. 41
Strain, David J........................... 69
Strong, Hiram............................. 49
Strong, R. O..............................103
Sturdevant, Charles....................... 12
Sullivan, Algernon S...................... 47
Surface, Andrew J.........................114
Swan, Benjamin C.......................... 47
Swan, James N............................. 52
Swan, George.............................. 32
Swan, George W............................ 32
Swim, Thomas F............................ 32
Swing, David.............................. 56

T

Tappan, David S........................... 97
Taylor, Edward L.......................... 85
Taylor, Henry............................. 47
Taylor, Henry C........................... 99
Taylor, James............................. 69
Taylor, William........................... 69
Taylor, William M......................... 32
Telford, Alexander........................ 66
Telford, Charles L........................ 23
Temple, John B............................ 23
Thomas, Alfred............................ 26
Thomas, Benjamin F........................ 73
Thomas, Bruce F...........................116
Thomas, Thomas E.......................... 17
Thomas, Walter S.......................... 85
Thompson, John C.......................... 42
Thompson, Nathaniel J..................... 77
Thompson, William......................... 11
Thomson, James............................ 2
Thomson, John S........................... 2
Thomson, William M........................ 5
Thornton, Anthony......................... 18
Thornton, H. C............................ 94
Thornton, Joseph L........................ 73
Thornton, Paul F.......................... 82
Thruston, Dickinson P..................... 78
Thruston, Gates P......................... 66
Tiffany, James E.......................... 41
Tiffany, John J........................... 52
Titus, Joseph B........................... 78
Tobey, Walter L...........................121
Todd, David W............................. 85
Todd, James S............................. 97
Tolbert, William H........................109
Tomlinson, J. C........................... 42
Torbert, James............................ 44

Torrey, John L................................ 12
Townsend, Samuel W...................119
Townsley, James P......................115
Townsley, Thomas P.................... 23
Trembly, John M........................... 53
Trevor, William M........................ 61
Turner, Thomas............................ 12
Turner, William D........................ 12
Turrell, William S....................... 41
Tuttle, Joel.................................... 73
Twitchell, Jerome......................... 23

U

Ure, David M................................ 78
Ure, Walter................................... 82
Ustick, Harlan P.........................112
Ustick, Hugh S............................. 61

V

Vail, Jonathan B..........................106
Van Ausdal, Isaac........................ 41
Vance, Calvin F........................... 38
Van Dyke, John M......................115
Van Dyke, John P........................ 2
Van Eaton, John.......................... 42
Van Matre, Henry....................... 89
Vincent, James............................112

W

Wade, Matthew...........................112
Wade, Nehemiah.........................109
Wakefield, John C....................... 89
Walker, Faye...............................107
Walker, Joseph............................ 56
Walker, Silas B............................ 42
Wall, Henry H.............................. 12
Wallace, David A......................... 49
Wallace James A......................... 89
Wallace, John.............................. 32
Wallace, Joseph S....................... 4
Wallace, William A..................... 82
Waller, James B........................... 23
Walton, John N............................118
Wampler, John M........................ 43
Ward, Edgar M............................ 78
Ward, Thomas B......................... 66
Warren, Charles D...................... 85
Warwick, Nathan E....................117
Wasson, Samuel Y......................102
Waterman, Charles..................... 52

Watkins, Nivison......................... 20
Weakley, Herbert H..................... 78
Weaver, John S............................ 2
Weaver, Michael.........................103
Webb, John A.............................. 86
Weede, Nathaniel C.................... 7
Weidner, Harry...........................119
Welch, James............................... 73
Wells, Francis M......................... 47
Whallon, Thomas........................ 21
White, A M................................... 26
Whiteside, John A....................... 89
Whittaker, Horace S..................107
Whittaker, James T..................... 94
Wiley, J. H.................................... 90
Wilkerson, Burwell G................. 86
Wilkins, W. F...............................109
Williams, Alexander R............... 73
Williams, Edward P.................... 78
Williams, John S......................... 29
Williams, Mark............................ 78
Williams, Meade C...................... 90
Williams, Roger..........................117
Williams, Thomas....................... 64
Wilson, Charles A......................121
Wilson, John................................ 14
Wilson, John M........................... 52
Wilson, Robert W........................ 35
Wilson, Spencer H...................... 86
Winstead, Jacob P......................109
Winters, William H..................... 94
Wintersmith, Charles G............. 11
Witherby, Oliver S...................... 23
Wood, Charles S.........................102
Woodbridge, John M.................. 26
Woodrow, David T....................... 18
Woodrow, Harry C......................112
Woodruff, Edward....................... 2
Woodruff, Henry M..................... 64
Woodruff, Thomas J................... 97
Woodruff, William B................... 8
Woods, John................................ 86
Woods, William C....................... 15
Worden, James A........................ 90
Worth, James.............................. 3
Wright, Cyrus M......................... 86
Wright, Edward W....................... 21
Wright, Irvin B............................ 90
Wright, James P......................... 43
Wright, Wellington..................... 73
Wright, William.......................... 54

Wright, Williamson...... 15
Wyatt, R. Calvin...... 82
Wyman, John N...... 103
Wyatt, James C...... 82

Y

Yaryan, John L...... 86
Young, Alexander H...... 82
Young, James L...... 12
Young, James M...... 32
Young, John C...... 32

Young, John N...... 27
Young, Samuel O...... 32
Young, William P...... 35
Youtsey, John K...... 112

Z

Zeigler, James P...... 115
Zeller, Elias R...... 115
Zeller, Jacob A...... 69

FORMER STUDENTS.

FORMER STUDENTS.

A.

ROBERT NEWTON ADAMS, Minister, Minneapolis, Minn.

Attended Miami Univ., 1859-61. D. D., Miami Univ., 1887. Attended Western Theol. Sem. Ordained, April, 1870. Private, Co. C, 20th Ohio Vol. Inf., 1862. Promoted subsequently to Captain, Major, Lieutenant-Colonel, Colonel, and Brigadier-General. Pastor of Pres. churches at Ottawa, Kan., 1871-75; Waverly, O., 1876-80; Fergus Falls, Minn., 1880-86; Synodical Missionary, 1886—. Address, 327 Hennepin avenue.

*****HENRY ALLEN,** Minister, Hoboken, N. J.

Attended Miami Univ., 1842-43. Ordained by First Presbytery of Ohio, April, 1847. Pastor of United Pres. churches at Hopkinsville, O., 1847-55; Iowa City, Ia., 1856-60; Union, Ills., 1860-65; Hoboken, N. J., 1865-67. Died, Dec.. 25, 1867.

*****JOHN DAVIESS ALLEN,** Owensboro, Ky.

Attended Miami Univ., 1870-71. Unintentionally killed by a party of masked men, Aug., 1873.

FRANK ALLYN, Lawyer, Tacoma, Wash.

Attended Miami Univ., 1864-65. Admitted to the bar, 1870. Practised law at Keokuk, Ia., 1870-87. City Attorney of Keokuk, Ia., and County Attorney of Lee County. Removed to Tacoma, Wash., 1887. Appointed Associate Justice, Washington Terr., 1887. Elected Superior Judge of Pierce Co., 1889.

*****RICHARD CLOUGH ANDERSON,** Manufacturer, Dayton, O.

Attended Miami Univ., 1846-48. Manufacturer of Agricultural Implements. Died, 1878.

CHARLES FREDERICK ANDRESS, Clerk, Cincinnati, O.

Attended Miami Univ., 1868-69.
Address. 134 West Seventh street.

JOHN ARNOLD, Physician, Rushville, Ind.

Attended Miami Univ., 1830-34. M. D.

B.

JESSE LOCKHARDT BAIRD, Physician, Fincastle, O.
Attended Miami Univ., 1871-73. A. B., Hamilton Coll., 1877. M. D.

SAMUEL C. BALDRIDGE, Minister, Linn, Ills.
Attended Miami Univ., 1843-44. A. B. Hanover Coll., 1849. A. M., same, 1852. Pastor of Pres. church at Friendsville, Ind., 1853-82. Principal Friendsville Sem., 22 years. Chaplain, 11th Reg. Mo. Vols., 1861-62. Author of numerous works and correspondent of the "Interior."

AARON DWIGHT BALDWIN, Editor, Chicago, Ills.
Attended Miami Univ., 1870-71. L. L. B., Univ., of Mich., 1873. Editor "Chicago Journal of Commerce." Address, 1016 W. Adams street.

ANSON SHERWOOD BALDWIN, Lawyer, North Platte, Neb.
Attended Miami Univ., 1866-68. Admitted to the bar, 1870. Member Lower House, Nebraska Legislature, 1881-83. Receiver, U. S. Land office, 1890—.

FAY BALDWIN, Banker, Greenfield, O.
Attended Miami Univ., 1871-73. Cashier of Bank.

JAMES FOSTER BARBOUR, Banker, Maysville, Ky.
Attended Miami Univ., 1862-63. A. B., Centre Coll., 1864. Cashier of Maysville Bank.

JAMES HERVEY BARBOUR, Physician, Falmouth, Ky.
Attended Miami Univ., 1846-47. M. D., Ohio Med. Coll., 1852.

JAMES C. BEARD, Artist, . New York, N. Y.
Attended Miami Univ., 1853-55. Artist, Judge Building. Address, 110 Fifth avenue.

DANIEL PICKEN BEATON, Agent, Oxford, O.
Attended Miami Univ., 1859-60. Private, Co. A, 86th Ohio Vol. Inf., 1862. Company M, 2nd Ohio Cavalry, 1862-64. Wounded at Monticello, Ky., June 9, 1863, resulting in the loss of the right foot. Postmaster, Oxford, O., 1865-88. Mayor of Oxford, 1888-92. Agent U. S. Express, 1892—.

CHARLES K. BECKETT, Ranchman, Sterling, Kan.
Attended Miami Univ., 1868-70.

*WILLIAM F. BECKETT, Farmer, Westchester, O.
Attended Miami Univ., 1864-66. Died, 1878.

MIAMI UNIVERSITY.

SHALER BERRY, Student, Newport, Ky.
Attended Miami Univ., 1885-87; Harvard Univ., 1887—.

WILLIAM BIRNEY, Lawyer, Washington, D. C.
Attended Miami Univ., 1836-37. A. M., Indiana State Univ. LL. B., Cincinnati Law School. Served in U. S. A., 1861-65, beginning as Captain and brevetted Brigadier-General, 1865. Judge, Alachua Co., Florida. Attorney for the District of Columbia, four years. Attorney for Washington Market Co. Author of "James G. Birney and His Times," "Genesis of the Republican Party," etc.
Address, 458 Louisiana avenue.

EDWARD S. BISHOP, Banker, Sargent, N. Dak
Attended Miami Univ., 1872-73.

LEONARD WESTCOTT BISHOP, Physician, Batavia, O.
Attended Miami Univ., 1845-46. M. D., Ohio Med. Coll., 1854. Member 64th General Assembly of Ohio. U. S. Examiner of Pensions.

ROBERT H. BISHOP, JR., Farmer, Mankato, Kan.
Attended Miami Univ., 1865-69.

*JAMES BLACK, Minister, Cincinnati, O.
Attended Miami Univ., 1827-28. Ordained, April, 1841. Pastor of Pres. churches at Monroe, O., 1841-46; Cincinnati, 1846-59; Feesburg, O., 1859-61. Missionary, Cincinnati, O., 1861-70. Pastor, Cincinnati, O., 1870-79. Died, June 29, 1881.

JOHN W. BLOOMFIELD, Lawyer, Paducah, Ky.
Attended Miami Univ., 1858-59. Admitted to the bar. Private, Co. G, 11th Ind. Vol. Inf., U. S. A., 1861-65. Judge, Paducah City Court, 4 years.

ANDREW BLUME, Lawyer, Boston, Mass.
Attended Miami Univ., 1861-62. Member Massachusetts Legislature.

*JOSEPH HEARST BONNER, Physician, Rosebud, Ala.
Attended Miami Univ., 1836-37. M. D., Charleston Med. Coll., 1846. C. S. A. Volunteer, 1863. Member County Board of Revenues. Died, 1884.

WILLIAM HENDERSON BONNER, Merchant, Eaton, O.
Attended Miami Univ., 1887-89. Engaged in hardware business.

HENRY BUCKNER BOUDE, Minister, Pleasant Hill, Mo.
Attended Miami Univ., 1852-53. A. B., Center Coll., 1857. D. D., Arkansas Coll. Ordained, 1860. Pastor of Pres. churches at Gallatin, Tenn., 1860-72; Columbus, Miss., 1872-75; Paris, Tex., 1875-78; Kansas City, Mo., 1881-83 Evangelist, Pleasant Hill, Mo., 1883—. President Austin Coll., Tex., 1878-81.

MIAMI UNIVERSITY.

JOHN ANDREW BOWER,   Minister,   Caldwell, O.

Attended Miami Univ., 1859-61. A. M., Monmouth Coll. Private, 74th Ohio Vol. Inf., 1861-65. Ordained, 1872. Pastor of churches at Hayesville, O., 1872-75; Fredericktown, O., 1875-76; Barton, Md., 1876-78; Bloomington, Ills., 1878-84; Van Wert, O., 1884-87; Rock Hill, O., 1887-90; Caldwell, O., 1890—.

LIVY BLAIR BOYD,   Coal Merchant,   Hillsboro, O.

Attended Miami Univ., 1867-68. President of the Fluhart Coal and Mining Co.

ABRAHAM BROWER,   Lawyer,   Fernbank, O.

Attended Miami Univ., 1838-40. Practiced law in Lawrenceburg, Ind., 11 years; Cincinnati, O., 32 years.

*SAMUEL SAWYER BROWER,   Student,   Lawrenceburg, Ind.

Attended Miami Univ., 1861-62. Died, March 9, 1872.

SYLVANUS A. BROWER,   Farmer,   Corwin, O.

Attended Miami Univ., 1843.

HENRY LEWIS BROWN,   Minister,   Merrill, Wis.

Attended Miami Univ., 1851-55. Principal High School, Oxford, O., 1861-64. Was graduated from Lane Sem., 1867. Pastor of Pres., churche at Marion, Ind., 1867-69; Peru, Ind., 1869-70; Omro, Wis., 1870-76; Reedsville, Wis., 1876-79; Lodi, Wis., 1879-83; Omro, Wis., 1883-88, Merrill, Wis., 1888—.

*JAMES POLK BROWN,   U. S. Army,   Dayton, O.

Attended Miami Univ., 1860. Second Lieutenant, 15th U. S. Inf., 1863. Brevet First Lieutenant, 1863. First Lieutenant, 1864. Captain, 1867. Died, St. Louis, Mo., June 9, 1875.

WALDO F. BROWN,   Farmer,   Oxford, O.

Attended Miami Univ., 1855. Lecturer before Farmers Institutes.

CHARLES PAUL BROWN,   Student of Dentistry,   Cincinnati, O.

Attended Miami Univ., 1887-90.
Residence, College Hill, O.

LORING BUNDY,   Book-keeper,   Chicago, Ills.

Attended Miami Univ., 1868-69; Indiana State Univ., 1869-70. Banker, New Castle, Ind., 1872-82. On Editorial Staff, "Indianapolis Sentinel," 1882-83. Grain Merchant, Indianapolis, Ind., 1883-87 Banker, Williamsport, Ind., 1887-89. Book-keeper, 1889—.
Address, Corner Lake and Michigan avenues.

JAMES WILLIAM BURGESS, Salesman, Williamstown, Ky.

Attended Miami Univ., 1886-88.

WILLIAM W. BYERS, Manufacturer, Terre Haute, Ind.

Attended Miami Univ., 1864-65. Principal Young Ladies School, Greencastle, Ind., 1870-74. Principal High School, Terre Haute, Ind., 1881-89. Deputy City Treasurer, 1889-91. Engaged in manufacture of gas.

C.

LYCURGUS MARSHALL CARMICHAEL, Clerk, Rushville, Ind.

Attended Miami Univ., 1869-72. Was engaged in wholesale business in Indianapolis, Ind., 3 years.

ARCHIBALD ARGYLE CARNAHAN, Lawyer, Concordia, Kan.

Attended Miami Univ., 1856-58. Admitted to the bar, 1860. Private, Co. C, 2nd Kansas Vol. Inf., 1861-63. State Senator from Seventh District of Kansas, 1863-71. Judge of Twelfth Judicial District of Kansas, 1871-82. Receiver of Public Moneys and Disbursing Agent of the U. S., Concordia, Kan., 1886—.

EDWARD HENRY CHADWICK, Lawyer, Shelbyville, Ind.

Attended Miami Univ., 1871-73. A. B., Dartmouth Coll. Admitted to the bar, 1879. City Attorney of Shelbyville, Ind., 1889-91.
Address, 48 E. Mechanic street.

WILLIAM HENRY CHAMBERLIN, Journalist, Cincinnati, O.

Attended Miami Univ., 1858-61. A. M., Miami Univ., 1886. Sergeant, Co. B, 20th Ohio Vol. Inf., 1861. First Lieutenant, Captain, Major, 81st Ohio Vol. Inf., 1861-64. Law Reporter, Cincinnati "Gazette," 1866-72. City Editor of same, 1872-79. Agent, Associate Press, Cincinnati, O., 1879—. Author "History of 81st Ohio Vol. Inf., 1865. and sketches of War History.
Address, N. W. corner of Fourth and Vine streets.

FRANK CHANCE, Lawyer, Urbana, O.

Attended Miami Univ., 1858-60. Admitted to the bar, 1863. Private, Co. D, 13th Ohio Vol. Inf. First Lieutenant, Co. H, 86th Ohio Vol. Inf., 1862-63. U. S. Navy, 1863-64. Solicitor for P. C. & St. L. R. R., 1869-83; C. St. L. & P., 1883-90.

*BENJAMIN E. CHESTNUT, Farmer, Chillicothe, O.

Attended Miami Univ., 1856-57. Died, May, 1872.

BENJAMIN F. CHIDLAW, Contractor, Cleves, O.

Attended Miami Univ., 1866-67.

JOHN CHIDLAW, Farmer, Cleves, O.
Attended Miami Univ., 1862-63.

*SAMUEL H. CLARK, Student, Hamilton, O.
Attended Miami Univ., 1855-57. Died, 1857.

JEFFERSON H. CLAYPOOL, Lawyer, Connersville, Ind.
Attended Miami Univ., 1870-73; Univ. of Va., 1874-75. Admitted to the bar, 1878. Member Indiana House of Representatives, 1888—. President of the Connersville Natural Gas Company.

CHARLES BAILEY CLEGG, Street Railway, Dayton, O.
Attended Miami Univ., 1861-63. Private, 131st Ohio Vol. Inf., 1864. President of the Oakwood Street Railway Co. Address, Central Block.

JOHN T. CLEVELAND, Physician, Cincinnati, O.
Attended Miami Univ., 1862-63. A. B., Centre Coll., 1863. M. D., Ohio Med. Coll., 1868. Demonstrator of Anatomy, 1870-71. Address, 474 West Seventh street.

EDWARD NATHAN CLINGMAN, Lawyer, Cincinnati, O.
Attended Miami Univ., 1872-73. A. B., Univ. of Cincinnati, 1880. U. S. Gauger, Cincinnati, O., 1882-84. Republican Senator from Hamilton Co., 70th General Assembly of Ohio, 1891—. Address, 27 Johnston Building.

JERE M. COCHRAN, Journalist, Wyoming, O.
Attended Miami Univ., 1864. A. B., Farmer's Coll., 1865. Associate Editor, Cincinnati "Commercial Gazette, 1874-91. Editor and Proprietor, "Miami Valley News," 1891—.

CHARLES HILTS COLBURN, Pine Bluff, Ark.
Attended Miami Univ., 1871-73.

HENRY BLANCHARD COLBURN, Real Estate, Bedford City, Va.
Attended Miami Univ., 1869-70; Prussian School of Mines, 1872-74. Mining Engineer, 1875-83. Now engaged in real estate business.

WILLIAM JUDKINS COMLY, Artist, New York, N. Y.
Attended Miami Univ., 1856-59.
Address, 15 West Twentieth street.

*OBADIAH MILLER CONOVER, Lawyer, Madison, Wis.
Attended Miami Univ., 1843. A. B. Coll. of New Jersey, 1844. L L. D., Wisconsin, Univ., 1878. Prof. of Ancient Languages, Univ. of Wisconsin, 1852-58. Supreme Court Reporter, 1864-84. Died, 1884.

*CHARLES ANDERSON CORRY,   Student,   Cincinnati, O.
Attended Miami Univ., 1887-89. Died, March, 1889.

*WILLIAM MCMILLAN CORRY,   Cincinnati, O.
Attended Miami Univ., 1886-87 and 1889. Died, Feb., 1891.

RICHARD CORSON,   Teacher,   Middletown, O.
Attended Miami Univ., 1855-56.

*WILLIAM HENRY CORWIN,   Physician,   Lebanon, O.
Attended Miami Univ., 1846-47. A. B., Dennison Coll. I. L. B., Cincinnati Law School, 1853. M. D., Med. Coll., 1868. Secretary of Legation to Mexico, 1861-64. Charge d' affairs of the same, 1864-66. Died, March 12, 1880.

QUINTON CORWINE,   Lawyer,   New York, N. Y.
Attended Miami Univ., 1859-61; Harvard Univ., 1865-66. Admitted to the bar, 1868. Private, Co. E. 137th Ohio Vol. Inf., 1861. Captain, 1864. Practised law at Cincinnati, O., 1868-71; Washington, D. C., 1871-81; N. Y., 1881—. Assistant U. S. District Attorney, 1868-70.
Address, 2 Wall street.

*SAMUEL FULTON COVINGTON, Insurance,   Madisonville, O.
Attended Miami Univ., 1837-38. Admitted to Indiana bar. Editor and Proprietor "Indiana Blade," Rising Sun, 1845. Established "Daily Courier," Madison, Ind., 1847. Member Indiana Legislature, 1847-49. President of Cincinnati Chamber of Commerce, two terms; of Board of Trade, two terms, and of Board of Aldermen, one term, Cincinnati. Vice President of National Board of Trade for many years. President of the Globe Insurance Co., Cincinnati, 1865-87, and honorary Vice President until death. Inventor. First suggested traveling postmasters, and weather bureau system of reports. Advocate of, and constant writer for newspapers on political and economic subjects. Specialty: the improvement and protection of inland navigation. Had in preparation a history of Cincinnati at time of death. Father John I., '70. Born, Rising Sun, Ind., Nov, 12, 1819. Died, Dec. 26, 1889.

CHARLES S. COWAN,   Physician,   Fort Jones, Cal.
Attended Miami Univ., 1872-73. M. D., Miami Med. Coll., 1880.

JOHN SNYDER COX,   Merchant,   West Chester, O.
Attended Miami Univ., 1868-72.

JOSEPH COX,   Lawyer,   Glendale, O.
Attended Miami Univ., 1837-39. A. M., Miami Univ., 1890. L L. B.; Cincinnati Law School, 1844. Captain Cavalry, U. S. Army, 1862. Prosecuting Attorney of Hamilton Co., 1856-57. Judge Common Pleas Court, Hamilton Co., O., 1867-82. Judge First Circuit Court of Ohio, 1884-. Author of "Life of General W. H. Harrison," "Sketches of Justices of the Supreme Court of the U. S.," "Historical Sketch of Miami Valley," etc. Has delivered many public orations and addresses.

MIAMI UNIVERSITY.

*ISRAEL LORING CRAFT,   Lawyer,   Rising Sun, Ind.

Attended Miami Univ., 1860–61. Enlisted in U. S. Army and served, 1861–64. Died, Oct. 19, 1864.

ROBERT EMMET CRAIG,   Cotton Merchant,   New Orleans, La.

Attended Miami Univ., 1860–61. First Lieutenant, 15th Miss. Inf., C. S. A., 1861–65. President New Orleans Water Works Co. Address, 222 Gravier street.

WILLIAM CUMBACK,   Lawyer,   Greensburg, Ind.

Attended Miami Univ., 1847–48. L L. B., Cincinnati Law School, 1851. Member U. S. House of Representatives, 1854–56. Paymaster, U. S. Army, 1861–65. Member Indiana State Senate, 1865–67. President of the Senate and acting Lieutenant-Governor, 1866–67. Lieutenant-Governor of Indiana, 1868–70. Collector of Internal Revenues, 1870–83. Has since been engaged in lecturing.

D.

SAMUEL T. DANNER,   Farmer,   Newton, Kan.

Attended Miami Univ., 1860–61. Private, Co. K, 37th Ind. Vol. Inf., 1861–63. First Lieutenant, Co. A, 12th U. S. Colored Inf., 1863–64, County Superintendent of Public Instruction, Harvey Co., Kan., 1881–83 and 1887–91.

JOHN M. DAVIDSON,   Lawyer,   Cheyenne, Wyoming.

Attended Miami Univ., 1862–66. Admitted to the bar, 1868. Private, 167th Ohio Vol. Inf., 1864. Superintendent Public School, Aurora, Ind., 1867–68. Practised law at Hamilton, O., 1868–69 and 1870–80; Fort Collins, Colo., 1882–89; Cheyenne, Wyoming, 1889—. Mayor of Fort Collins, Colo., 1884–85. Member Colorado Legislature, 1888–89.

JOSEPH C. DAVIDSON,   Lafayette, Ind.

Attended Miami Univ., 1866–68.

*ROBERT B. DAVIDSON,   Lawyer,   Xenia, O.

Attended Miami Univ., 1865–68. Admitted to the bar, 1869. Private and First Lieutenant, 35th Ohio Vol. Inf., 1862–65. Died, Oct. 28, 1889.

FRANK DAVIS,   Clerk,   Cincinnati, O.

Attended Miami Univ., 1865–66. Clerk in Cincinnati Post-office.

SILAS ADDISON DAY,   Lawyer,   Kanapolis, Kan.

Attended Miami Univ., 1860–62. A. B., Hanover Coll., 1863. A. M., same, 1866. Admitted to the bar, 1866. Private, 20th Ind. State Inf., 1862. Editor and Proprietor, "Daily Times," Fort Scott, Kan., 1881–84.

CHARLES P. DENNIS, Dentist, Portsmouth, O.
Attended Miami Univ., 1857-58. Dentist.

*ARCHER C. DICKERSON, Minister, Bowling Green, Ky.
Attended Miami Univ., 1826-28. D. D. Licensed, 1832. Ordained by the Presbytery of Clinton, Miss., 1834. Pastor of Pres. church in Northern Mississippi, 1834-39; Bowling Green, Ky., 1839-51. Home Missionary of Central Kentucky, 1851-91. Died, Dec. 22, 1891.

*CYRUS EWING DICKEY, Lawyer, Memphis, Tenn.
Attended Miami Univ., 1854-56. Admitted to the bar, 1856. Adjutant, 11th Ills. Vol. Inf., U. S. A., 1861. A. A. G. on staff of General Lew Wallace, afterwards on the staff of General T. E. Ransom. Killed in the Banks' Red River Expedition, 1863.

CLARENCE DICKINSON, Student, Evanston, Ills.
Attended Miami Univ., 1888-89; Northwestern Univ., 1890—.

PARKER DICKSON, Lawyer, Cincinnati, O.
Attended Miami Univ., 1870-73. A. B., Dartmouth Coll. Admitted to the bar, 1876. Assistant District Attorney, 1877-81. Adjusting Attorney, Queen and Cresent R. R.
Address, 35 West Fourth street.

CALVIN WASSON DIGGS, Insurance, Winchester, Ind.
Attended Miami Univ., 1860. Private, U. S. A., 1863-65. Loan and Insurance Agent.

*ROBERT DILL, Student, Hillsboro, O.
Attended Miami Univ., 1858-60. Died, Feb. 3, 1860.

*GODWIN VOLNEY DORSEY, Physician, Piqua, O.
Attended Miami Univ., 1825-27. M. D., Ohio Med. Coll., 1836. Ohio State Treasurer, 1862-63. Member Ohio Constitutional Convention, 1873. Trustee of Miami Univ., 1854-72. Died, 1890.

ALBERT MILTON DOYLE, Real Estate, Lynchburg, Va.
Attended Miami Univ., 1864-66. Secretary of the Rivermont Land Company.

PETER DRAYER, Merchant, Johnsville, O.
Attended Miami Univ., 1860-63.

THADDEUS CLAY DRULEY, Minister, Stafford, Conn.
Attended Miami Univ., 1861-63 and 1866-68. Private, Co. A, 16th Ohio Vol. Inf., 1862. Private, Co. I. 106th Regular, 1863. Sergeant, Co. C., 9th Ind. Cav., 1863-65. Minister in the Universalist Church.

E.

AUGUSTUS WESLEY ECKERT, Lawyer, Toledo, O.

Attended Miami Univ., 1855-56. First Lieutenant, 167th Ohio National National Guards, 1861-65.

JAMES N. ECKMAN, Banker, Pawnee City, Neb.

Attended Miami Univ., 1861-63 and 1864-65. Private, 9th Army Corps, 1863-64. Mayor of Pawnee City, Neb., 2 years. President First National Bank.

SILAS FULTON EDGAR, Physician, Zanesville, O.

Attended Miami Univ., 1853-56. M. D., Pulte Med. Coll., 1873. Hospital Steward, U. S. A., 1861-65.

ROBERT PATTERSON EFFINGER, Lawyer, Peru, Ind.

Attended Miami Univ., 1843-45. Admitted to the bar, 1848. Attorney for Wabash R. R.; L. E. & W. R. R.; P. C. & St. L. R. R., and Citizen's National Bank. Judge of the Circuit Court.

EDWIN EMERSON, Student, Ithaca, N. Y.

Attended Miami Univ., 1887-88.

JOHN PRESTON ERNST, Banker, Covington, Ky.

Attended Miami Univ., 1863-64. President of the Northern Bank of Kentucky.

MARCUS GASTON EVANS, Lawyer, Chillicothe, O.

Attended Miami Univ., 1872-73. A. B., Wooster Univ., 1877. A. M., same, 1880. Prosecuting Attorney for Ross Co., O., 1885—.

F.

CYRUS FALCONER, Physician, Hamilton, O.

Attended Miami Univ., 1826-27. Has practiced medicine at Hamilton, O., since 1832.

*JEROME B. FALCONER, Hamilton, O.

Attended Miami Univ., 1861-62. Sergeant, Co. C, 93rd Ohio Vol. Inf., 1861-62. Mortally wounded at the battle of Stone River, Dec. 31, 1862.

*JOHN WOODS FALCONER, Lawyer, Hamilton, O.

Attended Miami Univ., 1859-61. Admitted to the bar, 1864. Volunteer, 3rd Ohio Vol. Inf., 1861. Captain, Co. A, 41st U. S. Colored troops, 1864-65. Mortally wounded at Appomatox, April 9, 1865. Died, Farmville, Va., April 21, 1865.

WILLIAM ELLIOT FINDLEY, Architect, Fremont, O.

Attended Miami Univ., 1869-70. Was editor at Xenia, O.; Middletown, O.; and Franklin, O., for many years.

*CHARLES BURNETT FITZPATRICK, Lawyer, Modesto, Cal.

Attended Miami Univ., 1867. Admitted to the bar. Died, Aug. 5, 1880.

*WILLIAM HARPER FOSTER, Teacher, Morning Sun, O.

Attended Miami Univ., 1885-86. A, B., Indiana State Univ. Taught public school in Southern Indiana. Died, 1890.

*ALBERT ROBERT FYE, Merchant, St. Joseph, Mo.

Attended Miami Univ., 1870-73. Killed by cars, Dec. 29, 1888.

G.

ISAAC NEWTON GARD, Physician, Greenville, O.

Attended Miami Univ., 1824-28. M. D., Ohio Med. Coll., 1831. Member Ohio House of Representatives, 1841-42. Member Ohio State Senate, 1857-58.

*LEVI R. GARD, Farmer, Fair Haven, O.

Attended Miami Univ., 1853-54. Died, June, 1891.

*GEORGE FAIRLAMB GARROD, Druggist, Kansas City, Mo.

Attended Miami Univ., 1885-86. Died, Oct. 21, 1888.

CHARLES W. GATH, Undertaker, Hamilton, O.

Attended Miami Univ., 1869-70.

*SAMPSON GATH, Undertaker, Oxford, O.

Attended Miami Univ., 1859-61 and 1865. Served in the 47th Ohio Vol. Inf., 1861-65. Died, May 10, 1888.

SAMUEL C. GLOVER, Lumber Merchant, Grand Haven, Mich.

Attended Miami Univ., 1858-61. Private, Co. A, 39th Ohio Vol. Inf., 1861-63. First Lieutenant of same, 1863-64. Captain of same, 1864-66. Appointed Major, 1866. Postmaster, Grand Haven, Mich., 1882-85. Secretary and Treasurer of Grand Haven Lumber Co. Contributor to "Forest and Stream."

THOMAS LEWIS GOFF, Tobacco Merchant, Shelbyville, Ky.

Attended Miami Univ., 1889-91.

CHARLES LONGMOOR GRANT, Physician, Louisville, Ky.

Attended Miami Univ., 1886-88. M. D., Jefferson Med. Coll., 1890. Assistant Demonstrator Anatomy and Surgery, Kentucky School of Medicine, 1890—.
Address, 1504 West Chestnut street.

HENRY HORACE GRANT, Physician, Louisville, Ky.

Attended Miami Univ., 1872-73. B. S., Centre Coll., 1875. A. M., same, 1882. M. D., Jefferson Med. Coll., 1878. Lecturer on Operative Surgery, Kentucky School of Medicine. Trustee of the State Asylum.
Address, 1916 Market street.

WILLIAM EDWARD GRANT, Physician, Louisville, Ky.

Attended Miami Univ., 1865-66. M. D., Louisville Med. Coll., and Jefferson Med. Coll. Lecturer on Physiology, Kentucky School of Medicine, until 1891. Demonstrator of Anatomy in same institution, 1891—.
Address, 721 West Jefferson street.

*ENOCH M. GORDON, Teacher, Eaton, O.

Attended Miami Univ., 1853-54. Color Sergeant, 75th Ohio Vol. Inf., 1861-63. Killed in battle.

*HARVEY WILLIAM GRAHAM, Druggist, Lacrosse, Wis.

Attended Miami Univ., 1862-66. A. B., Monmouth Coll., 1867. Private, Co. A, 186th Ohio Vol. Inf. Died, Oct. 8, 1869.

MITCHELL MATHEW GRAHAM, Artist, Carrollton, Mo.

Attended Miami Univ., 1862-66. Private, Co. A, and Co. K, 86th Ohio Vol. Inf., 1862.

*MOSES PEED GREEN, Lawyer, Hannibal, Mo.

Attended Miami Univ., 1838-41. Admitted to the bar. Died, 1870.

EDWARD HERBERT GREER, Salesman, Oxford, O.

Attended Miami Univ., 1885-87.

ANDREW JANUARY GRUNDY, Farmer, Lebanon, Ky.

Attended Miami Univ., 1862-63. A. B., Centre Coll., 1863. Principal of High School, Maysville, Ky., 1864-68. Teacher at Terre Haute, Ind., 1870-72. Farmer and Stock-raiser, 1877—. Trustee of Danville Theol. Sem.

LEWIS B. GUNCKEL, Lawyer, Dayton, O.

Attended Miami Univ., 1846-47. Member Ohio State Legislature.
Address, 6 North Main street.

PATRICK H. GUNCKEL, Lawyer, Minneapolis, Minn.

Attended Miami Univ., 1863-65. Admitted to the bar, 1871. Practised law at Dayton, O., 1871-83; Minneapolis, Minn., 1883—. Address, 1614 Second avenue.

DAVID WADE GUY, Lawyer, Oxford, O.

Attended Miami Univ., 1854-59. Was graduated from Princeton Coll. L L. B., Cincinnati Law School.

WILLIAM EDWARD GUY, Merchant, St. Louis, Mo.

Attended Miami Univ., 1853-63. Sergeant, 86th Ohio Vol. Inf., 1862.

H.

SAMUEL GILBERT HAIR, Real Estate Broker, Chicago, Ills.

Attended Miami Univ., 1856-61. Real Estate and Loan. Address, 4417 Lake Avenue.

JOHN SPOHN HALDERMAN, Physician, Zanesville, O.

Attended Miami Univ., 1840-41. M. D., Starling Med. Coll., 1854. Address, 30 Orchard street.

JOHN W. HALL, JR., Teacher, Covington, Ky.

Attended Miami Univ., 1847-48. Superintendent of Public Schools, Covington, Ky.

ROBERT CALVIN HAMILTON, Physician, Coultersville, O.

Attended Miami Univ., 1868-69. M. D. Prof. of Principles of Medicine and Physics, Physio-Medical Insitute, Chicago, Ills.

CHARLES HANNA, Cincinnati, O.

Attended Miami Univ., 1870-71.

RICHARD HICKMAN HANSON, Lawyer, Paris, Ky.

Attended Miami Univ., 1834-36. L L. B., Transylvania Law School, 1840. Member of Legislature of Kentucky, 1846-47 and 1863. Member Constitutional Convention, 1849. Commonwealth Attorney, 6 years.

THOMAS HARBINE, Lawyer and Banker, Fairbury, Neb.

Attended Miami Univ., 1839-41. Lieutenant-Colonel, 25th Missouri Militia, 1861-63. Appointed Colonel and resigned, 1863. Member Maryland Constitutional Convention, 1850. Prosecuting Attorney of Washington Co.. Md., 1852-56. Mayor of St. Joseph, Mo., 1862-63. State Senator of Missouri, 1866-70. President of Harbine Bank, Fairbury, Neb., and First National Bank, Nelson, Neb.

*JAMES H. HART, Lawyer, Piqua, O.

Attended Miami Univ., 1835-37. Admitted to the bar. Adjutant, 71st Ohio Vol. Inf., U. S. A., 1861. Lieutenant-Colonel, April, 1863. Brevet-Brigadier-General, 1865. Died, 1867.

*JOSEPH STUBBS HARTER, Lawyer, Canton, O.

Attended Miami Univ., 1856-60. A. B., Kenyon Coll. Captain, Co. E, 115th Ohio Vol. Inf., U. S. A., 1861-63. Killed, Aug. 26, 1863.

JOHN JAMES HAYDEN, Lawyer, Washington, D. C.

Attended Miami Univ., 1837-38. L L. B., Harvard Law School, 1841. Member Indiana Legislature, 1856-57. Judge of Court of Common Pleas, 1859-60. Address, 929 K street, N. W.

DAVID JACKSON HEASTON, Lawyer, Bethany, Mo.

Attended Miami Univ., 1857-58. Admitted to the bar, 1858. Colonel, 57th Regiment, Missouri Vols. U. S. A., 1862-63. Probate Judge, Harrison Co., Mo., 1861-63. State Senator, 4th district of Mo., 1878-82. Editor, "Bethany Watchman," 1872-84.

WILLIAM ROSSMAN HENDERSON, Minister, St. Louis, Mo.

Attended Miami Univ., 1861-62. A. B., College of New Jersey, 1867. A. M., same, 1870. D. D., Center College, 1891. Studied theology at Princeton and McCormick. Ordained, April, 1876. Pastor of Pres. churches at Danville, Ky.; Harrodsburg, Ky.; St. Louis, Mo., and Omaha, Neb. Prof. Greek and Latin, Bellvue, Coll., Neb., 1885-86. Now Editor of the "Central West."

CHARLES MCGUFFEY HEPBURN, Lawyer, Cincinnati, O.

Attended Miami Univ., 1872-73. A. B., Davidson Coll., 1878. L L. B., Univ. of Va., 1881. Tutor in Davidson Coll., 1881-82. Practised law, Cincinnati, O., 1883—. U. S. Commissioner. Editor, "Beta Theta Pi." Address, 99 West Fourth street.

*SAMUEL HERON, Lawyer, Connersville, Ind.

Attended Miami Univ., 1847-48. Admitted to the bar. Died, Nov. 17, 1860.

STANLEY W. HIGGINS, Merchant, Duluth, Minn.

Attended Miami Univ., 1865-68.

THEODORE HENRY HITTELL, Lawyer, San Francisco, Cal.

Attended Miami Univ., 1845-48. A. B., Yale, 1849. Admitted to the bar, 1852. State Senator of California, 1880-82. Author of "History of California," 2 volumes, 1885; and numerous other books. Address, 808 Turk street.

*ROBERT S. HOLT, Lawyer, Yazoo City, Miss.

Attended Miami Univ., 1835-36. Admitted to the bar. Died, May 27, 1867.

ABDALLAH M. HOWE, Physician, Fair Haven, O.
Attended Miami Univ., 1868–69. M. D., Ohio Med. Coll., 1877.

A. E. HUBBARD, Banker, Eaton, O.
Attended Miami Univ., 1854–56. Cashier, Preble County National Bank,' Eaton, O.

ROBERT DAVID HUGGINS, Physician, West Alexandria, O.
Attended Miami Univ., 1855–56. M. D., Cincinnati Coll. of Medicine and Surgery, 1859. Coroner of Preble Co., O., 1882–88.

*CHARLES MARION HUGHES, Lawyer, Lima, O.
Attended Miami Univ., 1853–55. A. M., Miami Univ., 1890. L L. B., Cincinnati Law School, 1859. First Lieutenant, Co. A, 20th Ohio Vol. Inf., and Captain, Co. H, 81st Ohio Vol. Inf. Probate Judge of Shelby Co., 1864–70. Prosecuting Attorney of Allen Co., 1874–78. Common Pleas Judge, 1879–89. Died, 1891.

ALEXANDER F. HUME, Lawyer, Hamilton, O.
Attended Miami Univ., 1847–48. Admitted to the bar. Judge of Common Pleas Court, 1876–84.

HARRY CLINTON HUME, Civil Engineer, Portland, Ore.
Attended Miami Univ., 1872–73. A. B., Ohio Wesleyan Univ., 1875. Was Editor of the "Butler County Democrat," for several years.

*JOHN RANDOLPH HUNT, Manufacturer, Trenton, N. J.
Attended Miami Univ., 1860–61. Private, 20th Ohio Vol. Inf., U. S. A., 1861–62. Adjutant and First Lieutenant, 81st Ohio Vol. Inf., 1862–65. Brevet Major. Treasurer of the Trenton Woolen Company. Died, Glendale, O., Feb. 3, 1890.

JAMES NELSON HUSTON, Banker, Connersville, Ind.
Attended Miami Univ., 1865–67. Studied law 2 years. Studied medicine at Bellevue Med. Coll. 1 year. MemberIndiana House of Representatives 1880–84. Member Indiana State Senate, 1885–89.Chairman Republican State Committee of Indiana, 1886–88. Delegate at large to Republican National Convention, 1888. Appointed U. S. Treasurer, April 1, 1889. Resigned, April 25, 1891.

GEORGE ANDREW HUTCHISON, Minister, Baker City, Ore.
Attended Miami Univ., 1857–60. A. B., Monmouth Coll., 1862. Ordained, 1864. Pastor of Pres. churches at North Platte, Neb.; Eureka, Kan.; San Francisco, Cal.; Baker City, Ore.

I.

HORACE A. IRVIN, Manufacturer, Dayton, O.
Attended Miami Univ., 1871–72. Manufacturer of paint. Address, 213 Boulevard.

JOHN N. IRWIN, Lawyer, Phœnix, Arizona

Attended Miami Univ., 1862–65. Governor of Arizona Territory.

WELLS M. IRWIN, Lawyer, Keokuk, Ia.

Attended Miami Univ., 1868–69. Admitted to the bar.

J.

JAMES NEWTON JAMISON, Farmer, Roxabell, O.

Attended Miami Univ., 1872–73. Book-keeper, Merchants' and Farmers' Bank, Frankfort, O. Now a farmer and stock raiser.

*JAMES SMITH JELLEY, Lawyer, Rising Sun, Ind.

Attended Miami Univ., 1837–41. Admitted to the bar. Major, 83rd Indiana Vol. Inf., U. S. A., 1862–65. Wounded at the battle of Arkansas Post. U. S. Commissioner, Leavenworth, Kan., 1865–73. Practised law at Rising Sun, Ind., 1845–62 and 1873–86. Died, March 20, 1886.

JAMES RENWICK JOHNSTON, Farmer, New Alexandria, Pa.

Attended Miami Univ., 1856–57; Univ. of Mich., 1857–58. Sergeant, Co. I, 18th Indiana Vol. Inf., 1861–65. Wounded in the battle of Winchester, Sept. 19, 1864. Farmer.

WILLIAM WYLIE JOHNSTON, JR., Merchant, Wichita, Kan.

Attended Miami Univ., 1870–73. Wholesale Dry Goods Merchant. Firm name, Johnston, Larimer Dry Goods Co.

EDWARD H. JONES, Lawyer, Hamilton, O.

Attended Miami Univ., 1889–90. L L. B., Cincinnati Law School, 1891. Secretary Board of Elections.

ROBERT T. JONES, Farmer, Columbus City, Ia.

Attended Miami Univ., 1853–56. County Supervisor of Louisa Co., Ia., 1880–86. Farmer and stock dealer.

ZACHARY TAYLOR JONES, Farmer, Billingsville, Ind.

Attended Miami Univ., 1872–73.

K.

GEORGE LEWIS KALB, Minister, Bellefontaine, O.

Attended Miami Univ., 1843–45 and 1846–48. A. B., Centre Coll., Ky. A. M., Wittenberg Coll. D. D., Wooster Univ. Ordained, May 31, 1853. Pastor of Pres. churches at Circleville, O., 1852–63; Bellefontaine, O., 1863—.

ISRAEL HALLOCK KELLEY, Manufacturer, Springfield, O.

Attended Miami Univ., 1854-56. Granite dealer. Secretary of Marble and Granite Dealers Association of Ohio, 1889—. Address, 40 North Factory street.

CHARLES I. KEELY, Dentist, Hamilton, O.

Attended Miami Univ., 1868-69.

*GEORGE WASHINGTON KEELY, Dentist, Oxford, O.

Attended Miami Univ., 1838-41. D. D. S., Ohio Coll. of Dental Surgery, 1853. President, American Dental Association. Prof. "Irregularities of the Teeth," Ohio Coll. of Dental Surgery. Trustee of Miami Univ., 1869-84. Died, Aug. 24, 1888.

ANDREW CARR KEMPER, Physician, Cincinnati, O.

Attended Miami Univ., 1850-52. A. B., Centre Coll., 1855. A. M., same, 1867. A. M., Miami Univ., 1869. M. D., Ohio Med. Coll., 1866. Captain and Assistant Adjutant General on staff of General Halleck, 1861-65. Author of several pamphlets and addresses. Address, 101 Broadway.

MARTIN VAN BUREN KENNEDY, Merchant, Zanesville, O.

Attended Miami Univ., 1861-63. First Sergeant, Co. G, 129th Ohio Vol. Inf., 1863-64. First Lieutenant, Co. L, 8th U. S. Colored Artillery, 1864-65. Book and Stationery Merchant. Address, 70 Woodlawn avenue.

WILLIAM SLOANE KENNEDY, Litterateur, Belmont, Mass.

Attended Miami Univ., 1867-73. A. B. Yale, 1875. Special contributor to New York "Critic," Boston "Herald," Boston "Transcript," Boston "Index," "Literary World," etc. Author of "Life of John G. Whittier," "Life of Longfellow," "Life of O. W. Holmes," "Sketch of Edward Everett Hale," etc. Address, Concord avenue.

NEWTON REED KIRKPATRICK, Minister, Ft. Gay, W. Va.

Attended Miami Univ., 1845-47 and 1848-49. Licensed by Chillicothe Presbytery, June 9, 1852. Ordained, June 22, 1854. Pastor of United Pres. churches at Caledonia, Ind., 1854-56; White Grove, Ills., 1866-71. Missionary in Kentucky, 1871-85. Joined the Pres. church, 1885. Pastor of Pres. church at Ft. Gay, W. Va.

JEREMIAH M. KLINGER, Civil Engineer, Plymouth, Ind.

Attended Miami Univ., 1853-55. County Surveyor, 1862-65 and 1872-78 and 1884-86. Engineer of the City of Plymouth, Ind. Located the Indiana Pacific and other railroads.

GEORGE KRAMER, Farmer, Oxford, O.

Attended Miami Univ., 1864-66. Merchant, Chicago, Ills., 1867-78. Farmer, near Oxford, O., since 1878.

THEODORE R. KUMLER, Stock Raiser, Oxford, O.
Attended Miami Univ., 1861-63. Secretary of Magie Swine Breeder's Co. Trustee of Miami Univ., 1889—.

WALTER SCOTT KUMLER, Oxford, O.
Attended Miami Univ., 1868-69. Was Mayor of Oxford.

*WILLIAM FESTUS KUMLER, Merchant, Oxford, O.
Attended Miami Univ., 1856-60. Private, Co. A, 167th Ohio Vol. Inf. Dry Goods Merchant. Died, March 21, 1870.

L.

LAWRENCE MILLIKIN LARSH, Official, Hamilton, O.
Attended Miami Univ., 1868-69. Farmer, Eaton, O., 1869-74. Accountant, Hamilton, O., 1874-91. Mayor of the City of Hamilton, 1891—.

ABRAM S. LEE, Retired, Oxford, O.
Attended Miami Univ., 1852-53.

GEORGE M. LEE, Merchant, Oxford, O.
Attended Miami Univ., 1872-73. Was engaged in the hardware business.

BENJAMIN LE FEVRE, Lawyer, Maplewood, O.
Attended Miami Univ., 1858-59. Private, U. S. A., 1861-65. U. S. Consul, Nuremberg, Germany, 1867-69. Member of U. S. House of Representatives, 1879-86.

MARC WINFIELD LEWIS, Civil Engineer, Duluth, Minn.
Attended Miami Univ., 1885-86. Assistant City Engineer, 1887—.

*WILLIAM R. LIDDELL, Trinity, La.
Attended Miami Univ., 1859-60. First Lieutenant, staff of Gen. I. Scott, C. S. A., 1861-63. Killed at the battle of Chickamauga, Sept. 19th, 1863.

JAMES REYNOLDS LINN, Lawyer, Toledo, O.
Attended Miami Univ., 1850-51. Mayor of Toledo, O. Prosecuting Attorney of Putnam Co., O. Editor and proprietor, "Sidney Empire," 1854. Address, 3 Trinity block.

JAMES MARCELLUS LOGAN, Physician, Kansas City, Mo.
Attended Miami Univ., 1867-69. M. D., Ohio Med. Col., 1874. Private, Co. D, 93rd Ohio Vol. Inf., 1862-65.
Address, 1303 East Eighth street.

ARCH LONGWORTH, Milford, O.
Attended Miami Univ., 1862-63. Private, U. S. A., 11 months.

*WELLINGTON LOUCKS, Lawyer, Peoria, Ills.
Attended Miami Univ., 1844-45. Studied law and served as County Judge for many years. Died, Aug. 24, 1890.

*JAMES MADISON LOUGH, Campbellstown, O.
Attended Miami Univ., 1860-62. Private, 20th Ohio Vol. Inf., 3 months. Sergeant, 86th Ohio Vol. Inf., 4 months. Lieutenant, 2nd Ohio Vol. Cav. Died from wounds received at the battle of Cedar Creek, Va., Nov. 12, 1864.

WILLIAM HENRY LOUGH, Farmer, Eaton, O.
Attended Miami Univ., 1853-54 and 1856-59. Co. C, 2nd Ind. Vol. Cav., 1861-64. Wounded, resulting in loss of left arm. County Recorder of Preble Co., O., 1863-72. Secretary of Central Branch, National Home for Disabled Volunteer Soldiers, Dayton, O., 14 years.

LEMOINE LOWE, Chicago, Ills.
Attended Miami Univ., 1867-68.

AMBROSE WILLIAM LYMAN, Journalist, Helena, Mont.
Attended Miami Univ., 1867-69. On reportorial staff, "Cleveland Leader," 1872-74; "New York Tribune," 1875-76; "New York Sun," 1876-89. Editor and General manager, "Helena Independent," 1889—.

M.

DAVID MACDILL, Minister and Teacher, Xenia, O.
Attended Miami Univ., 1845-48. A. B. Centre Coll.,1848. A. M., same, 1851. D. D.,Monmouth Coll. Pastor of United Pres. churches at Cherry Fork, O., 1853-76. Prof. of Philosophy,Monmouth Coll., 1876-85. Prof. of Apologetics,Xenia Theol. Sem., 1885—. Author of "Bible, a Miracle."

LOUIS DRAKE MANNING, Lawyer, Batavia, O.
Attended Miami Univ., 1853-55. Admitted to the bar, 1858. U. S. Navy, 1864-65.

SAMUEL M. MARKLE, Real Estate, St. Joseph, Mo.
Attended Miami Univ., 1844-48.

*HUMPHREY MARSHALL, Lawyer, Louisville, Ky.
Attended Miami Univ., 1827-28. Was graduated from West Point, 1832. Served in the Black Hawk Expedition, 1833. Admitted to the bar, 1835. Captain, Kentucky Militia, 1836; Major, 1838; Lieutenant-Colonel, 1841; Colonel, 1846. Served in the Mexican War. Member of U. S. House of Representatives, 1849-52. U. S. Minister to China, 1852-54. Member of Congress, 1855-59. Brigadier-General, C. S. A., 1861-63. Member Congress of the Confederacy. One of the first Confederates whose disabilities as a citizen were removed by Congress. Died, March 28, 1872.

162   MIAMI UNIVERSITY.

*WILLIAM PATTERSON MARSHALL,   Lawyer,   Keokuk, Ia.
Attended Miami Univ., 1868-69. Admitted to the bar, 1874. Sheriff of Lee Co., Ia., 1875 and 1887-91. Died, Prescott, Ia., Feb. 12, 1891.

*FREDERICK WILLIAM MARVIN,   Student,   St. Paul, Minn.
Attended Miami Univ., 1857-60. Died, March 3, 1860.

*LOUIS MASON,   Farmer,   Lawrenceburg, Ind.
Attended Miami Univ., 1862-63. Private, 76th Ind. Vol. Inf. Died, 1869.

RODNEY MASON,   Lawyer,   Detroit, Mich.
Attended Miami Univ., 1841-42. A. B., Jefferson Coll., 1844. Patent Lawyer.

THOMAS MATTINSON,   Civil Engineer,   South Charleston, O.
Attended Miami Univ., 1886-88.

JAMES RIJOR MAYO,   Lawyer,   Chillicothe, O.
Attended Miami Univ., 1885-86. Admitted to the bar, 1888.

HORATIO BURGOYNE MCBRIDE,   Minister,   Golden Gate, Cal.
Attended Miami Univ., 1866. A. B., Monmouth Coll., 1869. Pastor of Pres. churches at Pioche, Nev., 1873-74; Ione, Cal., 1875-77; Colusa, Cal., 1875-77; Tehama, Cal., 1877-79; Ukiah, Cal., 1879-85; Healdsburg, Cal. 1885-91; Golden Gate, Cal., 1891—.

*JAMES MCCLELLAN,   Physician,   Middletown, O.
Attended Miami Univ., 1842-45. M. D., Ohio Med. Coll. Died, 1862.

JAMES THOMAS MCCLELLAN,   Merchant,   Tallulah, La.
Attended Miami Univ., 1871-72.

JOHN MCCLELLAN,   Lawyer,   Middletown, O.
Attended Miami Univ., 1841-43. Admitted to the bar, 1854. Member Ohio State Legislature, 2 years.

WILLIAM C. MCCLURE,   Banker,   East Saginaw, Mich.
Attended Miami Univ., 1861-63. Private, 86th Ohio Vol. Inf., 1863-65. Banker, Lumberman and Manufacturer. Address, 403 South Washington avenue.

JOSEPH L. MCCRACKEN,   Merchant,   Huntsville, Ala.
Attended Miami Univ., 1869-72. Lumber Merchant.

JOHN BEECRAFT MCFARLAN, Manufacturer, Connersville, Ind.

Attended Miami Univ., 1886-87.

BENJAMIN SPENCER MCFARLAND, Teacher, Olathe, Kan.

Attended Miami Univ., 1857-60. A. M., Miami Univ., 1888. Superintendent Sidney Public Schools, 1862-63. Prof. of Mathematics, Western Military School, Dayton, O., 1865-69. Superintendent Public Schools, Olathe, Kan., 1869-72 and 1883-92. County Superintendent Public Instruction, Johnson Co., Kan., 1873-83.

WILLIAM HUGH MCFARLAND, Teacher, Columbus, O.

Attended Miami Univ., 1871-73. Superintendent of Public Schools, Quincy, Ills., 1876-79; Yellow Springs, O., 1884-85. Principal of Garfield School, Columbus, O.
Address, 1063 East Long street.

ALEXANDER MCGUFFEY, Lawyer, Cincinnati, O.

Attended Miami Univ., 1826-31. Admitted to the bar and has since practised in Cincinnati, O.

JAMES CHARLES MCMECHAN, Physician, Cincinnati, O.

Attended Miami Univ., 1861-65. M. D., Ohio Med. Coll., 1868. Physician to St. Mary's Hospital. Trustee of Miami Univ., 1877-78.
Address, 367 West Seventh street.

WADE MCMILLAN, Student of Medicine, Cincinnati, O.

Attended Miami Univ., 1885-87. Student of Medicine, Miami Med. Coll.
Address, Walnut Hills.

HARRY E. MEAD, Manufacturer, Dayton, O.

Attended Miami Univ., 1871. Engaged in the manufacture of paper.

JAMES C. MEARS, Salesman, Cincinnati, O.

Attended Miami Univ., 1886-87.
Address, Avondale.

*A. H. MILLER, Teacher, White Cloud, Kan.

Attended Miami Univ., 1854-55. Died, 1891.

EDWARD HAMILTON MILLER, Merchant, Portland, Ore.

Attended Miami Univ., 1869-70. Secretary of Knapp, Burrell & Co., Portland, Ore.

*JOSEPH WARREN MILLER, Journalist, London, Eng.

Attended Miami Univ., 1855-58. Captain and assistantant Adjutant General, 45th Ills. Vol. Inf., 1861-65. Wounded at Pittsburg Landing. Contributor to "London Times." Died, Dec. 26, 1875.

MARTIN B. MILLER, Lawyer, Winchester, Ind.

Attended Miami Univ., 1857-58. Admitted to the bar, 1861. Second Lieutenant, 1861-62. Captain Co. E, 84th Ind. Vol. Inf., 1862-64. Lieutenant Colonel, same, 1865. Special Examiner in Pension Office, 1886-89.

WILLIAM H. H. MILLER, Lawyer, Washington, D. C.

Attended Miami Univ., 1859-60. Admitted to the bar and practiced law at Indianapolis, Ind., until 1889. Attorney General of the U. S. 1889—.

*MURRAY G. MILLIKIN, Hamilton, O.

Attended Miami Univ., 1865-66. Date of death unknown.

JOSEPH L. MOLYNEAUX, Farmer, Oxford, O.

Attended Miami Univ., 1854-58. Private, Co. A, 167th Ohio Vol. Inf., 1864.

*DAVID MONROE, Student of Law, Xenia, O.

Attended Miami Univ., 1868-69. Died, April 10, 1879.

AARON EYLAR MOORE, Lawyer, Cincinnati, O.

Attended Miami Univ., 1872-73. A. B., Hamilton Coll., 1876. Admitted to the bar, 1877.
Address, 271 Main street.

CHARLES MASSIETTE MOORE, U. S. Storekeeper, Owensboro, Ky.

Attended Miami Univ., 1870. Merchant, New York City, 1870-78. Since 1878, U. S. Storekeeper. Owensboro, Ky.

EDWARD EVERETT MOORE, Farmer, Bowling Green, Mo.

Attended Miami Univ., 1867-70.

HENRY LYNN MOORE, Real Estate Broker, Minneapolis, Minn.

Attended Miami Univ., 1873. A. B., Dartmouth Coll., 1877. A. M., same, 1880. Real Estate and Insurance.
Address, 3132 Hennepin avenue.

THOMAS W. MOORE, Lawyer, Hamilton, O.

Attended Miami Univ., 1838-39 and 1842-43. Admitted to the bar and has practised in Hamilton, O., for many years.

WILLIAM P. MOORE, County Auditor, Bowling Green, Mo.

Attended Miami Univ., 1870-73.

MIAMI UNIVERSITY. 165

HENRY LEE MOREY, Lawyer, Hamilton, O.

Attended Miami Univ., 1857-59. Attended Indianapolis Law School and was admitted to the bar. Private, 20th Ohio Vol. Inf., 1861. Captain, 75th Ohio Vol Inf., 1862-65. Was Prosecuting Attorney for Butler county and City Solicitor of Hamilton, O. Member U. S· House of Representatives, 1881-85 and 1889-91.

JAMES EDWARD MORRIS, Physician, Liberty, Ind.

Attended Miami Univ., 1852-54. A. M., Miami Univ,, 1886. M. D., Starling Med. Coll., 1857; Bellvue Med. Coll., 1874. U. S. Examining Surgeon, 1861-64, Member and President Union District Medical Association. Preeminent Member American Medical Association. President Union county National Bank.

ROBERT EMMET MORRIS, Real Estate Broker, Washington, D. C.

Attended Miami Univ., 1873. L L. B., Columbia Law School, 1880. Real Estate and Insurance Broker. Address, 700 Fourteenth street, N. W.

JOHN C. MORRISON, Farmer, Eldon, Mo.

Attended Miami Univ., 1851-56. Clerk in Asylum, Olathe, Kan., 1870. Warden, Kansas State Penitentiary, 1881-86.

*ROBERT C. MORRISON, Teacher, Olathe, Kan.

Attended Miami Univ., 1849-50. Died, 1878.

*JAMES MORROW, Minister, Tildin, Ills.

Attended Miami Univ., 1828-29. Pastor of United Pres. churches at Washington, Ills., 1849-61. Home Missionary, Tildin, Ills., 1861-84. Died, Oct. 27, 1884.

*OLIVER PERRY MORTON, Lawyer, Indianapolis, Ind.

Attended Miami Univ., 1842-45. Admitted to the bar, 1847, and practised law at Centerville, Ind. Circuit Judge, 1852-54. One of the founders of the Republican Party. Elected Lieutenant Governor of Ind., 1860, and became acting Governor upon the election of Governor Henry S. Lane to the U. S. Senate. Re-elected in 1864. Took an active part in the support of the Union. Member U. S. Senate, 1873-77. Died, Nov. 1, 1877.

JAMES CHARLES MOUNT, Banker, Connersville, Ind.

Attended Miami Univ., 1885-87. Cashier of Connersville Bank.

EDMUND HARRIS MUNGER, Lawyer, Xenia, O.

Attended Miami Univ., 1845-48. A. B., Centre Coll., 1848. Admitted to the bar, 1851. Teacher in Private Academy, 1848-49. Judge Court of Common Pleas, 1868-72. Address, 231 King street.

N.

JOHN WILLOCK NOBLE,   Lawyer,   Washington, D. C.

Attended Miami Univ., 1845-49. A. B., Yale Coll., 1851. L L. D., Miami Univ., 1889. Admitted to the bar and practised law at Keokuk, Ia., until 1866. Colonel of cavalry, U. S. A., 1861-65. For meritorious service promoted to Brigadier General. Removed to St. Louis, 1866. U. S. District Attorney, 1866-70. Secretary of the Interior, President Harrison's Cabinet, 1889—.

O.

*WILLIAM WOODRUFF OLDS,   Columbus, O.

Attended Miami Univ., 1859-60. Adjutant, 42nd Ohio Inf., U. S. A., 1861-62. Captain, Co. A, 42nd Ohio Vol. Inf. Killed near Point Gibson, Miss., May 1, 1863.

*WARNER SYMMES OLIVER,   Merchant,   Cincinnati, O.

Attended Miami Univ., 1853-56. Died, May 30, 1874.

JOHN K. O'NEAL,   Lawyer,   Lebanon, O.

Attended Miami Univ., 1840-42. Admitted to the bar. Judge Circuit Court.

ALEXANDER T. ORMOND,   Teacher,   Princeton, N. J.

Attended Miami Univ., 1869-70. A. B., Princeton Coll. Ph. D. Prof. of Logic and Metaphysics, College of New Jersey.

CHARLES L. OSBORN,   Columbus, O.

Attended Miami Univ., 1861-62.

JOHN GARD OXER,   Farmer,   Campbellstown, O.

Attended Miami Univ., 1860-61. Corporal, Co. H, 156th Ohio Vol. Inf., 1864.

*LEVI HARRISON OXER,   Teacher,   Campbellstown, O.

Attended Miami Univ., 1857-59. Died, March, 1864.

P.

WILLIAM W. PAGE,   Lawyer,   Portland, Ore.

Attended Miami Univ., 1854-56. Prosecuting Attorney, 4th Oregon District, 1860-62. Circuit Judge, 1862-64.

*JOHN MACCLEARY PARKS,   Physician,   Hamilton, O.

Attended Miami Univ., 1830-34. M. D., Ohio Med. Coll. Died, May 1, 1890. — -

OAKEY V. PARRISH,   Insurance,   Hamilton, O.

Attended Miami Univ., 1860-63; Ohio Wesleyan Univ., 1863-64. Private, 167th Ohio Vol. Inf.

JOHN MORRISON PARSHALL,   Planter,   Tallahasse, Fla.

Attended Miami Univ., 1863-65. Manager, Wholesale department of Giles Bros. Jewelry Co., Chicago, Ills., 1866-89. Removed to Tallahassee, 1889.

JOHN HENRY PATTERSON,   Manufacturer,   Dayton, O.

Attended Miami Univ., 1864-66. A. B., Dartmouth Coll., 1867. Private, 131st Ohio Vol. Inf., 3 months. Manufacturer of Cash Registers. President of the National Cash Register Co.
Address, First and Ludlow streets.

S. J. PATTERSON,   Coal Merchant,   Dayton, O.

Attended Miami Univ., 1861-62. Dealer in Coal and Coke.
Address, Sixth and Ludlow Streets.

EDWIN TYLER PECK,   Cashier,   Berkeley, Cal.

Attended Miami Univ., 1855-58. Private, 2nd Ky., Vol. Inf., 1862-65. Bookkeeper and Cashier, Holt Bros., 30-32 Main street, San Francisco, Cal.

*JAMES ERNEST PLATTER,   Minister,   Winfield, Kan.

Attended Miami Univ., 1864-66. A. B., Ohio Wesleyan Univ., 1867. Was graduated from Princeton Theol. Sem., 1870. Pastor of Pres. churches at Sandy Hill, N. Y., 1870-73; Winfield, Kan., 1873-83. Died, June, 1883.

*BENJAMIN PIERSON PORTER,   Planter,   Cuba Station, Ala.

Attended Miami Univ., 1841-42. Member Alabama Legislature, 1853-54. Died. Dec. 16, 1878.

SAMUEL HENRY POWE,   Manufacturer,   Winchester, Miss.

Attended Miami Univ., 1839-41. Member Mississippi Legislature, 1854-56. First Lieutenant and Captain 13th Miss. Inf., C. S. A., 1861-63. First Lieutenant Miss. Battalion Cavalry, 1863-65. President Board of School Commissioners, Wayne Co., Miss., 1876-78.

*JOHN NEWTON PRESSLY,   Minister,   Grandview, Ia.

Attended Miami Univ., 1831-33. Studied theology at Due West. Ordained by Indiana Presbytery, June 27, 1838. Pastor of United Pres. churches at Bethesda, Shiloh, and Richland, Ind., 1838-51; Lafayette, Ind., 1851-56; Albia and Service, Ia., 1858-62. Stated Supply at Indianola, Ia., 1857-58; Grandview, Ia., 1862-66. Died, Aug. 22, 1866.

FINLEY BIGGER PUGH, Manufacturer, Indianapolis, Ind.

Attended Miami Univ., 1871-72; Univ. of Mich., 1872-74. Druggist, Rushville, Ind., 1875-87. Removed to Indianapolis, Ind., 1887.

Q.

JAMES L. QUINN, Physician, Eaton, O.

Attended Miami Univ., 1860-61. Private, Co. D, 156th Ohio Vol. Inf., 1864. M. D., Miami Med. Coll., 1869. Resident Physician, Cincinnati Hospital, 1869-70. Member Eaton Board of Pension Examiners, 1891.

R.

*GEORGE J. RABB, Physician, Linn Co., Kan.

Attended Miami Univ., 1861-63. Lieutenant, 2nd Mo. Artillery, 1863-65. M. D., StLouis Med. Coll., 1866. Died, Feb. 11, 1889.

*JOHN WILLIAM RABB, Lawyer, Lafayette, Ind.

Attended Miami Univ., 1854-55. A. B., Wabash Coll., 1859. Admitted to the bar, 1860. Captain, Co. I, 7th Ind. Vol. Inf., 1861. Captain 2nd Indiana Battery, 1862. Major, 2nd Mo. Regiment of Artillery, 1863. Died, Jan. 20, 1868.

FRANCIS KELLOGG RAYMOND, Court Reporter, Winfield, Kan.

Attended Miami Univ., 1866-71. Official Court Reporter.

JAMES ERASTUS REED, Stock-raiser, Towner, N. Dak.

Attended Miami Univ., 1868-70. Merchant, Middletown, O., 1872-83. Stockraiser, Towner, N. Dak., 1883—. Member First Legislature of North Dakota.

*HUGH THOMPSON REID, Lawyer, Keokuk, Ia.

Attended Miami Univ., 1834-36. Admitted to the bar. Colonel, 15th Iowa Vol. Inf., U. S. A., 1862-63; Brigadier-General, 1863. Resigned, 1864. President Des Moines Valley R. R. Died, Aug. 21, 1874, from wounds received at Shiloh.

GEORGE L. REINHARD, Lawyer, Rockport, Ind.

Attended Miami Univ., 1866-68. Admitted to the bar, 1869. Private, Co. I., 15th Ind. Vol. Inf., 1861-64. Prosecuting Attorney for Spencer County, Ind., 1876-80. Judge of 2nd Judicial district, 1882—. Term expires, 1894.

SUTTON CLAY RICHEY, Banker, Oxford, O.

Attended Miami Univ., 1854-55. Druggist, Oxford, O., 1857-91. Treasurer of Miami Univ., 1869—. Treasurer of the Village of Oxford, 1874—. President First National Bank.

MIAMI UNIVERSITY.   169

*DAVID RINEHART, Farmer, Eaton, O.
Attended Miami Univ., 1852-54. Died, Sept., 1859.

*HARRY LACY ROBBINS, Merchant, Falmouth, Ky.
Attended Miami Univ., 1870-72. Hardware Merchant. Died, April 24, 1881.

ISAAC ROBERTSON, Lawyer, Hamilton, O
Attended Miami Univ., 1837-39. Admitted to the bar and has practised law continuously at Hamilton, O.

*LOSADO RODGERS, Student, Piqua, O.
Attended Miami Univ., 1850-51. Died, Nov. 11, 1851.

*EDWARD H. ROSSMAN, Student, Hamilton, O.
Attended Miami Univ., 1853-55. Died, Sept. 19, 1855.

*STEPHEN CLEGG ROWAN, U. S. Navy Officer, Washington, D. C.
Attended Miami Univ., 1825-26. Appointed Shipman, U. S. Navy, 1826. Passed Midshipman, 1832. Cruised in the "Vandalia" during the Seminole war. Appointed Lieutenant, 1837; Commander, 1845. Executive officer of the sloop "Cyane" during the Mexican war. Commander of "Pawnee," 1861-62. Appointed Commodore in command of "New Ironsides," 1862-66. Vice-Admiral, 1870. Died, March 31, 1890.

S.

JOHN ELBERT SATER, Lawyer, Columbus, O.
Attended Miami Univ., 1872-73; Marietta Coll., 1873-75. Admitted to the bar.

EDSON M. SCHRYVER, Merchant, Baltimore, Md.
Attended Miami Univ., 1861-62. Private and Second Lieutenant, U. S. A., 1862-66. Grain Merchant. President Flour Exchange, 1885-86. President Police Commission of Baltimore. President Board of Trade.

ORANGE WATSON SCHULTZ, Merchant, Oxford, O.
Attended Miami Univ., 1885-88. Engaged in Hardware business.

JOHN S. SCOBEY, Lawyer, Greensburg, Ind.
Attended Miami Univ., 1841-43. Admitted to the bar, 1844. Colonel, 68th Ind. Vol. Inf., 1861-63. Prosecuting Attorney, 1847-58. Indiana State Senator, 1852. Democratic Presidential Elector, 1876.

JOHN NEAL SCOTT, Lawyer, Port Townsend, Wash.
Attended Miami Univ., 1850-55 and 1857. Captain, 79th Ind. Vol. Inf., 1862-64. Major of same, 1864-65. Judge City Court, Indianapolis, Ind., 1867-69.

WILLIAM THOMAS SCOTT, Farmer, Collinsville, O.

Attended Miami Univ., 1869-73. A. B., Princeton Coll., 1874. Farmer.

HARRY FORD SCUDDER, Student of Medicine, Cincinnati, O.

Attended Miami Univ., 1889-91. Student, Eclectic Medical Coll., Cincinnati, O., 1891—.
Address, 228 Court street.

JOHN M. SCUDDER, Physician, Cincinnati, O.

Attended Miami Univ.,'1842. M. D. Established the Eclectic Medical Coll. of Ohio, and is President of the same. Author of several well known medical works.
Address, 228 Court street.

WALTER GREENOUGH SHANNON, Life Insurance, Eaton, O.

Attended Miami Univ., 1885-87. Treasurer, Equitable Life Assurance Society, Cincinnati, O., 1888-90. Agent, Eaton, O., 1890—.

GEORGE W. SHAW, Manufacturer, Dayton, O.

Attended Miami Univ., 1838-41.
Address, Third and Perry streets.

*JOHN HORATIO SHEPHERD, Lawyer, Tonica, Ills.

Attended Miami Univ., 1858-61. First Lieutenant, 104th Illinois Vols., 1861. Adjutant, 9th Kentucky Vols., 1862-65. Wounded at the battle of Chickamauga. L L. B., Univ. of Mich., 1867. Treasurer of La Salle Co., Ills., 1870-71. Died, 1872.

CALEB A. SHERA, Banker, Oxford, O.

Attended Miami Univ., 1868-69 and 1870-72. Cashier, First National Bank.

CLARENCE EDGAR SHOOK, Solicitor, Dayton, O.

Attended Miami Univ., 1886-88. Solicitor, "Evening News," Dayton, O., 1892—.

JOHN W. SHORT, Teacher, Liberty, Ind.

Attended Miami Univ., 1865-69. A. M., Miami Univ., 1886. Private, 83rd Ohio Vol. Infantry., 1862-65. Wounded at Sabine Cross Roads, April 8, 1864. Superintendent of Public School, Liberty, Ind.

WILLIAM H. SIMMS, Banker, Dayton, O.

Attended Miami Univ., 1853-56. President Dayton National Bank. Stockholder, Huffman Publishing Company, Third Street Railway, Dayton Stock Yards Association, and various other stock companies.

ELIHU CALVIN SIMPSON,   Minister,   Hamilton, O.

Attended Miami Univ., 1868–69. A. M., Westminster Coll. Ordained, May 5, 1874. Pastor of United Pres. churches at Richmond, Ind., 1874-81. Hamilton, O., 1881—.

CHARLES B. SIMRALL,   Lawyer,   Cincinnati, O.

Attended Miami Univ., 1860–62. Admitted to the bar and has practised continuously in Cincinnati, O. Residence, Covington, Ky.

*CALEB BLOOD SMITH,   Lawyer,   Indianapolis, Ind.

Attended Miami Univ., 1825-26. Admitted to the bar, 1828. Practised law at Connersville, Ind., 1828–43; Indianapolis, Ind., 1850–60. Established and edited "The Sentinel," 1832. Member Indiana Legislature, 2 terms. Member U. S. House of Representatives, 1843-49. President of the National Republican Convention, Chicago, Ills., 1860. Secretary of the Interior in President Lincoln's Cabinet, 1861-62. Appointed U. S. District Judge, Dec., 1862. Died, Jan. 7, 1864.

CULBERTSON JONES SMITH,   Lawyer,   Hamilton, O.

Attended Miami Univ., 1868–70. Admitted to the bar, 1876. Prosecuting Attorney for Butler County.

*S. MITCHELL SMITH,   Journalist,   Columbus, O.

Attended Miami Univ., 1867-68. Died, March 7, 1878.

WILSON B. SMITH,   Farmer,   Seven Mile, O.

Attended Miami Univ., 1863–64 and 1864–67. Private, U. S. A., 1864.

DAVID BASSET SNOW,   Lawyer,   Ottawa, Ills.

Attended Miami Univ., 1856–59 and 1860–62. Sergeant, Co. K, 83rd Ohio Vol. Inf., 1862–65. L L. B., Cincinnati Law School, 1867.

JOSEPH CROCKER SNOW,   Minister,   Haverhill, Mass.

Attended Miami Univ., 1855–57. A. B., A. M., Tufts Coll. D. D., St. Lawrence Univ. Ordained, Oct. 1858. Chaplain, 23 Maine Vol. Inf., 1862–63. Pastor of Presbyterian churches at Norway, Maine, 5 years; Auburn, N. Y., 14 years; Newark, N. J., 3 years; Haverhill, Mass., 9 years. President of Westbrook Seminary and Female College, Deering, Maine, 3 years.

EDWARD LUSH SOUTHGATE,   Minister,   Newport, Ky.

Attended Miami Univ., 1859–62. Private 3rd Ky. Battalion C. S. A., 1862-63. Methodist Minister.

FRANK HILL SOUTHGATE,   Physician,   Newport, Ky.

Attended Miami Univ., 1885-87. M. D., Ohio Med. Coll., 1892.

*COLIN SPENCE, Physician, Clermont Co., O.

Attended Miami Univ., 1832. Practised medicine, Clermont Co., O., 1840–92. Died, Jan. 11, 1892.

WALTER LOWRIE SPENCE, Teacher, Sidney, O.

Attended Miami Univ., 1871–73. A. B., Wooster Univ., 1876. A. M., same, 1877. Teacher of public schools at Pleasant Run, O., 1878–80; Shelby Co., O., 1880—.

JAMES RUDOLPH SPIVEY, Druggist, Oxford, O.

Attended Miami Univ., 1886–88; Purdue Univ., 1889–91.

JOHN MCMILLAN STEVENSON, Minister, New York, N. Y.

Attended Miami Univ., 1832–35. A. B., Jefferson Coll., 1836. D. D. Studied theology at Lane Seminary. Principal Preparatory Department, Kenyon Coll., 1837. Licensed as a minister in the Pres. church, 1840. Prof. of Greek, Ohio Univ., 1841–42. Pastor of Pres. church at Troy, O., 1842–46; New Albany, Ind., 1849–57. Elected Secretary of the American Tract Society, June 20, 1857 and is still in this position. Trustee of Miami Univ., 1845–49. Author of "A Memoir of Rev. Thomas Marquis;" "Toils and Triumphs of Colportage."

*MARION MARQUIS STEVENSON, Teacher, Bellefontaine, O.

Attended Miami Univ., 1857–58. Teacher in Greenfield Academy, 1858–61. Entered U. S. A., 1861. Mortally wounded at Rich Mountain, W. Va., July 11, 1861. Died, Beverly, Va., July 23, 1861.

JOHN WILLIAMS STODDARD, Manufacturer, Dayton, O.

Attended Miami Univ., 1854–56. A. B., Princeton Coll., 1858. Manufacturer of Agricultural Implements. Address, Dayton View.

HARRY LEFEVRE STROHM, Lawyer, Kansas City, Mo.

Attended Miami Univ., 1869–73. Admitted to the bar, 1877. County Attorney of Kingham County, Kan., and Judge of the Criminal Court. Address 1028–29 New York Life Building.

T.

FRANK TALLMADGE, Stockman, Columbus, O.

Attended Miami Univ., 1870–72. Address, 35½ N. High street.

*THOMAS A. TAYLOR, Lawyer, Connersville, Ind.

Attended Miami Univ., 1869–72. L L. B., Univ. of Mich., 1874. Editor "Connersville News." Died, Kansas City, Mo., June, 1882.

ALFRED ADDISON THOMAS, Lawyer, Chicago, Ills.

Attended Miami Univ., 1864-65. A. B., Dartmouth Coll., 1867. Private, 4th Battalion, Ohio Cavalry, 1864. Admitted to the bar. City Solicitor of Dayton, 1872-75. Removed to Chicago, 1887.

ALFRED CLARENCE THOMAS, Student, Cincinnati, O.

Attended Miami Univ., 1887-88. Student, Boston School of Technology, 1890—.
Address, 137 Walnut street.

*WILLIAM IRVING THOMAS, Lawyer, Troy, O.

Attended Miami Univ., 1860. Private, Co. H, 11th Ohio Vol. Inf., 1862-65. Died, 1866.

FRANK GARDINER THOMPSON, Lawyer, Eaton, O.

Attended Miami Univ., 1872-73. Admitted to the bar.

THOMAS VOLNEY THORNTON, Lawyer, Bedford, Ind.

Attended Miami Univ., 1867-68. A. B., Hanover Coll., 1869. L L. B., Indiana State Univ., 1871. Clerk of Circuit Court, 1884-92. General Manager of the Chicago and Bedford Stone Co.

LINDORF D. L. TOSH, Lawyer, Argentine, Kan.

Attended Miami Univ., 1868-70. A. B., Univ. of Kansas, 1873. Admitted to the bar, 1876.

*GEORGE SMITH TRIMBLE, · Hillsboro O.

Attended Miami Univ., 1867-68; Kenyon Coll., 1868-70. Died, March 20, 1879.

WILLIAM ERNEST TRUSLOW, Banker, Charleston, W. Va.

Attended Miami Univ., 1866-67. A. B., Washington and Lee, 1869. Banker.

U.

JOSEPH URMSTON, Civil Engineer, Reily, O.

Attended Miami Univ., 1887-88.

V.

JOHN NEWTON VAN DEMAN, Lawyer, Washington C. H., O.

Attended Miami Univ., 1863-65. Admitted to the bar, February, 1877. Local Attorney, C. H. & D. R. R.

MILTON VERNON, Fruit Grower, Los Angeles, Cal.

Attended Miami Univ., 1855-56. Chief Clerk in Subsistence department, U. S. A., 1864-66. Fruit grower.
Address, Station C.

ROBERT STEVENSON VOORHIS, Lawyer, New York, N. Y.

Attended Miami Univ., 1847-48. A. B., Centre Coll., 1850. L L. B., Cincinnati Law School, 1852. Prof. of Medical Jurisprudence, Med. Coll. of Missouri, 1867-69; St Louis Coll. of Physicians, 1867-69. Major and Judge Advocate General Missouri Militia, 1861.
Address, 56 Wall street.

W.

ERWIN DICKEY WALKER, Minister, Poplar Bluff, Mo.

Attended Miami Univ., 1869-73. A. M., Wooster Univ. Studied theology at Lane Sem. Ordained, Oct., 1877. Pastor of Presby. churches at Peabody, Kan., 1877-89; Abilene, Kan., 1889-91; Poplar Bluff, Mo., 1891—.

ISAAC NEWTON WALKER, Lawyer, Lebanon, O.

Attended Miami Univ., 1872. Admitted to the bar. Mayor of Lebanon, 1889—. Trustee of the Central Ohio Insane Asylum.

JOHN MONTGOMERY WAMPLER, Druggist, Richmond, Ind.

Attended Miami Univ., 1870-73. M. D., Miami Med. Coll. Deputy Collector, Internal Revenue Office, Sixth District of Indiana. President Board of Health. Assistant Surgeon, U. R., K. of P.
Address, 730 Main street.

*JAMES DURBIN WARD, Lawyer, Lebanon, O.

Attended Miami Univ., 1838-40. Admitted to the bar. Prosecuting Attorney of Warren Co., O., 1845-51. Member State Legislature, 1852-53. Major, Lieutenant-Colonel, and Colonel, 17th Ohio Vol. Inf., 1861-65. Brevetted Brigadier-General on account of meritorious service and distinguished bravery at Chickamauga. Wounded at the battle of Chickamauga, Sept. 19, 1863. U. S. District Attorney, 1866-68. State Senator, 1870-71. Attorney for N. Y. P. and O. R. R., 1870-86. Trustee of Miami Univ., 1875-86. Died, May 22, 1886.

*JAMES WARNOCK, Lawyer, Cincinnati, O.

Attended Miami Univ., 1845-48. A. B., Centre Coll., 1849. Admitted to the bar. First Lieutenant, 2nd Ohio Vol. Inf., 1861-64. Wounded at Lookout Mountain, Nov. 24, 1863. Promoted to Captain, Jan. 31, 1863. Died, July 2, 1872.

LEWIS D. WATSON, Banker, Houston, Tex.

Attended Miami Univ., 1855-56.

PERRY W. WEIDNER, Book-keeper, Dayton, O.

Attended Miami Univ., 1888–89. Bookkeeper, Staniland, Merkle & Staniland.
Address, Ware Block.

JOHN B. WELLER, JR., Lawyer, San Francisco, Cal.

Attended Miami Univ., 1865–66. Admitted to the bar.
Address, 213 Turk street.

*WALTER O. WELLS, Teacher, Oxford, O.

Attended Miami Univ., 1868–73. A. B., Princeton Coll., 1874. Prof. of Mathematics in Prof. R. H. Bishop's Latin School. Assistant Secretary, Cincinnati Type Foundry, 3 years. Died, May 6, 1880.

GEORGE REUBEN WENDLING, Lecturer, Washington, D. C.

Attended Miami Univ., 1861–63; Chicago Univ., 1863–66. Admitted to the bar, 1868. Practised law at Shelbyville, Ills., 1868–80. Editor of "Central Illinois Times," 1869. City Attorney of Shelbyville, 1871–72. Member Constitutional Convention, 1870. Author of a number of lectures on Modern Skepticism, one of which, "A Reply to Ingersoll from a Quaker Standpoint," was published in book form. Other lectures, "Saul of Tarsus," "Stonewall Jackson," "Popular Delusions," "Hamlet and His Interpreters," "Voltaire," "Is Death the End?"

J. P. WIDNEY, Physician, Los Angeles, Cal.

Attended Miami Univ., 1861–62. A. M., Univ. of Cal. M. D., Univ. of Cal. Dean of the College of Medicine, Univ. of Southern Cal.

*ZENAS FISK WILBER, Lawyer, Denver, Col.

Attended Miami Univ., 1858–60. A. B., Kenyon Coll., 1860. Admitted to the bar, 1861. Major of Fourth Colored Infantry. Entered Patent Office, 1876. Chief Examiner, Electrical Department, 1882. Died, Aug. 22, 1889.

A. G. WILSON, Lawyer, Dayton, O.

Attended Miami Univ., 1865–66. Admitted to the bar. Practised law at Xenia, O., and Dayton, O.

FRANK LAWSON WILSON, Physician, Greenfield, O.

Attended Miami Univ., 1871–72. M. D.

MOSES FLEMING WILSON, Lawyer, Cincinnati, O.

Attended Miami Univ., 1862. L L. B., Cincinnati Law School, 1865. Prosecuting Attorney, Police Court of Cincinnati, 1869–71. Judge of Police Court, 1877–81. Author of Criminal Code of Ohio. Judge of Superior Court, Cincinnati, O., 1891.

ROBERT A. WILSON, Monmouth, Ills.

Attended Miami Univ., 1872–73.

176   MIAMI UNIVERSITY.

*WILLIAM M. WILSON,   Lawyer,   Greenville, O.

Attended Miami Univ., 1826-29. Admitted to the bar. Member Ohio State Senate, 1846-48. Judge of Court of Common Pleas. Died, June 15, 1864.

JOHN M. WITHROW,   Physician,   Cincinnati, O.

Attended Miami Univ., 1870-73. A. B., Ohio Wesleyan Univ., 1877. Superintendent Public Schools, Germantown, O., 1877-78; Eaton, O., 1878-82. M. D., Ohio Med. Coll., 1884. Assistant Prof. of Gynecology, Ohio Med. Coll. Trustee of Miami Univ., 1884—. *Vide*, Portrait and Sketch, "Miami Journal," Vol. II, No. 8.
Address, 291 West Fourth street.

*WILLIAM WOODBRIDGE,   Merchant,   Marietta, O.

Attended Miami Univ., 1836-37. Died, July 9, 1876.

MAXWELL VAN ZANDT WOODHULL, Lawyer, Washington, D. C.

Attended Miami Univ., 1860-62. A. M., Miami Univ., 1890. Studied law at Columbia Law School. Captain and Aide de Camp, 8th Army Corps, 1862. Adjutant-General, General David Tyler's staff, 1862. Adjutant-General, General Wallace's staff, 1863. Major and Assistant Adjutant-General, Army of Tenesee, 1864. Lieutenant-Colonel, 75th Army Corps, 1865. Brevet-Colonel, 1866. Assistant Secretary, U. S. Legation, London, England, 1871-72. Chief of Division, Consular Bureau, department of State, 1878-80.
Address, 2033 G street.

*EDWARD M. WRIGHT,   Soldier,   Washington, D. C.

Attended Miami Univ., 1860-62. Was graduated from West Point, 1866. Second Lieutenant, U. S. Regular Army, 1866-74; First Lieutenant, 1874-76; Captain, 1876-80. Died, April 24, 1880.

*RICHARD YATES,   Statesman,   Springfield, Ills.

Attended Miami Univ., 1828-30. A. B., Illinois Coll., 1838. Member Illinois Legislature, 1842-50. Member U. S. House of Representatives, 1850-54. Governor of Illinois, 1860-64. Member U. S. Senate, 1865-71. Died, St. Louis, Mo., Nov. 23, 1873.

DIRECTORY.

RESIDENCE DIRECTORY.

ALABAMA.
HUNTSVILLE.
Joseph L. McCracken, Merchant.
MOBILE.
James O. Shiras, Electrician.

ARIZONA.
PHŒNIX.
John N. Irwin, Lawyer.

ARKANSAS.
PALESTINE.
Thomas C. Magoffin, Merchant.
PINE BLUFF.
Charles H. Colburn.
STUTTGART.
Nathan M. Brown, Horticulturist.

CALIFORNIA.
ARCATA.
James S. Todd, Minister.
BERKELEY.
Edwin T. Peck, Cashier.
ELSINORE.
Samuel M. Cambern, Lawyer.
FORT JONES.
Charles S. Cowan, Physician.
FRESNO.
James M. Cory, General Business.
GOLDEN GATE.
Horatio B. McBride, Minister.

IONE.
John Wallace, Minister.
LOS ANGELES.
Joseph C. Oliver, Broker.
Milton Vernon, Fruit Grower, Station C.
J. P. Widney, Physician.
MESSINA.
Benjamin L. Baldridge, Minister.
MONROVIA.
David R. Colmery, Minister.
OAKLAND.
Nelson Carr, Teacher.
James G. Chestnut, Lawyer.
David Morrow, Minister.
PASADENA.
Thomas D. Garvin, Minister.
RIVERSIDE.
Henry O. Evans, Civil Engineer.
John E. Hill.
Christian P. Pann, Minister.
SAN DIEGO.
Oliver S. Witherby, Lawyer, 1106 D street.
SAN FRANCISCO.
John S. Hittell, Journalist, 1216 Hyde street.
Theodore H. Hittell, Lawyer, 808 Turk street.
Joseph C. McKee, Lawyer, 137 Montgomery street.
John B. Weller, Jr., Lawyer, 213 Turk street.
James A. Whiteside, Agent, 105 Taylor street.

SAN JOSE.
Jacob N. Brown, Physician,
  29 East Santa Clara street.
Benjamin Cory, Physician,
  97 South First street.
Andrew J. Surface, Teacher.

SAN RAFAEL.
James S. McDonald, Minister.

SANTA ANA.
Henry A. Booth, Minister.

SANTA BARBARA.
Henry Stoddard, Real Estate.

SANTA MONICA.
John B. Roby.

SOUTH PASADENA.
John M. Graham, Minister.

WESTMINSTER.
Anthony C. Junkin, Minister.

WOODBRIDGE.
Moses D. A. Steen, Minister.

COLORADO.

DENVER.
Thomas N. Haskell, Minister,
  1643 Sherman avenue.
Isaac W. Monfort, Minister,
  2435 Grant avenue.
William S. Sloan, Solicitor,
  Care, "Rocky Mountain News."
Robert B. Stanton, Civil Engineer.
Nathaniel J. Thompson, Farmer,
  2229 Clarkson street.
William M. Thomson, Minister,
  1355 Inslee street.
William Allen Wallace, Broker,
  429 East Bayard street.

FORT COLLINS.
Alston Ellis, Teacher.

LONGMONT.
George T. Crissman, Minister.

PUEBLO.
Samuel W. Townsend, Book-keeper.

CONNECTICUT.

DANBURY.
James Vincent, Minister.

STAFFORD.
Thaddeus C. Druley, Minister.

DISTRICT OF COLUMBIA.

BROOKLAND.
Irvin B. Wright, Lawyer.

GEORGETOWN.
Thomas A. Fullerton, Minister.

WASHINGTON.
John S. Billings, Physician,
  U. S. Surgeon General's Office.
William Birney, Lawyer,
  458 Louisiana avenue.
John K. Boude, Physician,
  905 R street, N. W.
William W. Cheshire, Examiner,
  105 Eleventh street, S. E.
Robert Christy, Lawyer,
  1606 Seventeenth street, W. N. W.
Benjamin Harrison, Lawyer,
  White House.
John J. Hayden, Lawyer,
  929 K street, N. W.
James Long, Teacher,
  900 K street, N. W.
William H. H. Miller, Lawyer,
  U. S. Attorney-General.
William B. Moore, Statistician,
  Health Department.
Robert E. Morris, Real Estate,
  700 Fourteenth street, N. W.
John W. Noble, Lawyer,
  Secretary of the Interior.
Samuel Shellabarger, Lawyer.
Alfred Thomas, Clerk,
  Treasury Department.
George R. Wendling, Lecturer.
Alexander R. Williams, Merchant,
  615 Seventh street, N. W.
Maxwell Van Z. Woodhull, Lawyer,
  2033 G street.

FLORIDA.

JACKSONVILLE.
William H. Christy, Lawyer,
  57 West Adams street.

KISSIMMEE.
Lawrence M. Stevens, Minister.

SANFORD.
William H. Evans, Physician.

SWITZERLAND.
Charles L. Clarke.

TALLAHASSE.
John M. Parshall, Planter.

TAMPA.
James W. Graham, Minister.

GEORGIA.
ATLANTA.
William T. Ashford, Merchant,
    258 Peachtree street.
Jacob N. Brown, Lawyer,
    Room 50, Old Capitol Building.

ILLINOIS.
ALTO PASS.
Holly R. Buckingham, Lawyer.

BUCKLEY.
Jesse T. McClave, Farmer.

CAMP GROVE.
John B. McDill, Physician.

CARTHAGE.
David Mack, Lawyer.

CHARLESTON.
Alfred C. Ficklin, Lawyer.

CHICAGO.
Aaron D. Baldwin, Editor,
    1016 W. Adams street.
Sylvester L. Bishop, Civil Engineer,
    1615 Wabash avenue.
John G. Bronson, Broker,
    235 Michigan avenue.
Alexander Buckingham, Lawyer,
    164 Madison street.
Loring Bundy, Book-keeper,
    Corner Lake and Michigan avenues.
Calvin W. Courtwright, Minister,
    4033 Vincennes avenue.
James A. Hair, Broker,
    4823 Lake avenue.
Samuel G. Hair, Broker,
    4417 Lake avenue.
Benton J. Hall, Lawyer,
    25 and 26 Honore Building.
Henry T. Helm, Lawyer,
    189 LaSalle street.
Joseph B. Leake, Lawyer,
    218 Cass street.
John C. Lewis, Superintendent,
    4138 Ellis avenue.
Lemoine Lowe.
Robert L. Lyons, Lawyer,
    172 LaSalle street.
Alexander C. McClurg, Publisher,
    60 Lake Shore Drive.
Austin Morris, Lawyer,
George V. Nauerth, Lawyer,
    340 Dearborn street.
Abram M. Pence, Lawyer,
    550 North State street.

John P. Reynolds, Lawyer,
    468 LaSalle avenue.
David Swing, Minister,
    66 Lake Shore Drive.
Alfred A. Thomas, Lawyer.

CHICAGO LAWN.
Benjamin R. Finch, Solicitor.

DESPLAINES.
Heber Gill, Minister.

DU QUOIN.
John R. Smith, Coal Merchant.

EVANSTON.
Clarence Dickinson, Student.

GALENA.
David Clark, Minister.

GREENVILLE.
Asa Mulford, Farmer.

JERSEYVILLE.
Allen A. Barnett, Physician.

KANKAKEE.
William H. Prestley, Minister.

LINN.
Samuel C. Baldridge, Minister.

MALTA.
John R. Johnston, Minister.

MENDOTA.
Garnet A. Pollock, Minister.

METROPOLIS.
Benjamin C. Swan, Minister.

MONMOUTH.
John J. Glenn, Lawyer.
Thomas H. Rogers, Teacher.
Robert A. Wilson.

MT. CARMEL.
Joseph H. Stevenson, Minister.

OQUAWKA.
Wilberforce Reynolds, Clerk.

OTTAWA.
David B. Snow, Lawyer.
Joseph Stout, Physician.

PARIS.
James A. Nelson, Teacher.

PEKIN.
William Stanbery, Lawyer.

PEORIA.
Samuel I. McClelland, Merchant.
516 Perry street.

RANTOUT.
Samuel Graves, Teacher.

SHAWNEETOWN.
Francis E. Callicott, Lawyer.
Alexander H. Rowan, Lawyer.

SHELBYVILLE.
Anthony Thornton, Lawyer.

SPRINGFIELD.
Andrew M. Brooks, Teacher.

SULLIVAN.
Joseph B. Titus, Lawyer.

VIRDEN.
John M. Robinson, Minister.

VIRGINIA.
David J. Strain, Minister.

INDIANA.

ALQUINA.
Pinckney M. Ferguson, Farmer.

ANDERSON.
Oliver Broadbent, Physician.

BEDFORD.
Thomas V. Thornton, Lawyer.

BILLINGSVILLE.
Zachary T. Jones, Farmer.

BROOKVILLE.
Fielding R. A. Jeter, Farmer.
William H. Moore, Minister.
George F. O'Byrne, Lawyer.

CLIFTON.
Isaac N. Snyder, Farmer.

CONNERSVILLE.
Jefferson H. Claypool, Lawyer.
John B. McFarland, Manufacturer.
James N. Huston, Banker.
James C. Mount, Banker.

CRAWFORDSVILLE.
William H. Tolbert.

DUBLIN.
Robert N. John, Minister.

ELSTON.
Franklin M. Hunt, Farmer.

FOREST HILL.
Thomas M. Gossard, Minister.

FORT WAYNE.
Edward P. Williams, Merchant.

FRANKFORT.
John C. Faber, Lawyer.

GREENCASTLE.
Aaron H. Morris, Minister.

GREENSBURG.
William Cumback, Lawyer.
William P. Shannon, Teacher.
John S. Scobey, Lawyer.

HANOVER.
Jeremiah M. Oldfather, Minister.

INDIANAPOLIS.
James P. Cowan, Minister,
315 N. East street.
John Babb Elam, Lawyer,
300 Park avenue.
Finley B. Pugh, Manufacturer.

LA FAYETTE.
Joseph C. Davidson.
Jacob A. Zeller, Teacher.

LA GRANGE.
Thomas Edgar Hughes, Minister.

LA PORTE.
George L. Andrew, Physician.

LAWRENCEBURG.
Ambrose E. Nowlin, Farmer.
Okey B. Nowlin.

LIBERTY.
Joseph W. Connaway, Lawyer.
James E. Morris, Physician.
William E. Morris, Stock Raiser.
John W. Short, Teacher.

LOGANSPORT.
Edward S. Scott, Minister.
Henry C. Thornton, Lawyer.
Williamson Wright, Lawyer.

MADISON.
John Long Aten, Minister.

NEW CASTLE.
Eugene H. Bundy, Lawyer.
PERU.
Robert P. Effinger, Lawyer.
PLYMOUTH.
Jeremiah M. Klinger, Civil Engineer.
PORTLAND.
Robert E. Lowry, Lawyer.
PRAIRIETON.
Jacob W. Ogle, Farmer.
PRINCETON.
Samuel R. Stormont, Minister.
RICHMOND.
Isaac M. Hughes, Minister,
    323 North Ninth street.
Thomas J. McClelland, Minister,
    311 N. Eighth street.
Isaac B. Morris, Lawyer.
John M. Wampler, Druggist.
John L. Yaryan, Lawyer.
ROCKPORT.
George L. Reinhard, Lawyer.
RUSHVILLE.
John Arnold, Physician.
Lycurgus M. Carmichael, Clerk.
SHELBYVILLE.
Edward H. Chadwick, Lawyer.
SPRINGFIELD.
Asbury E. Krom.
TERRE HAUTE.
William W. Byers, Manufacturer.
UNION CITY.
Everett A. MacDonald.
VERNON.
James Gilchrist, Minister.
WINCHESTER.
Calvin W. Diggs, Insurance.
Martin B. Miller, Lawyer.

INDIAN TERRITORY.
SOUTH MCALLISTER.
Henry L. Haynes, Lawyer.

IOWA.
BOONE.
William B. Means, Broker.
CHEROKEE.
John C. Hutchison, Minister.
COLUMBUS CITY.
Robert T. Jones, Farmer.
COUNCIL BLUFFS.
Lewis W. Ross, Lawyer,
    203-204 Merriam block.
CRESTON.
James W. McDill, Lawyer.
DES MOINES.
John J. Davis, Lawyer,
    1169 Twenty-second street.
DUBUQUE.
George Crane, Lawyer.
GLENWOOD.
Peregrine D. Foster, Merchant.
KEOKUK.
Wells M. Irwin, Lawyer.
Robert M. Marshall, Lawyer.
Samuel T. Marshall, Lawyer.
MEDIAPOLIS.
Joseph H. Marshall, Minister.
RED OAK.
Cornelius C. Platter, Farmer.
SALEM.
James Welsh, Minister.
SIGOURNEY.
William R. Hollingsworth, Editor.
WASHINGTON.
James B. Combs, Physician.
James Henry Elliott, Minister.
David C. Kyle, Civil Engineer.
WINTERSET.
Charles T. McCaughan, Minister.
Elias L. Zeller, Farmer.

KANSAS.
ALMA.
James M. McFarland, Land Owner.
ARGENTINE.
Lindorf D. L. Tosh, Lawyer.

BELOIT.
John G. Craven, Minister.

BIRD CITY.
Edgar A. Baldwin, Farmer.

CONCORDIA.
Archibald A. Carnahan, Lawyer.

ELDORADO.
William M. Fisher, Lawyer.

EMPORIA.
Edward N. Evans, Lawyer.
Aaron M. Flory, Lawyer.
Michael Weaver, Lawyer,
    806 Cottonwood street.

HOWARD.
William H. Reid, Minister.

HUTCHINSON.
Christopher Bishir, Nurseryman.
James L. Buell, Minister.

IOLA.
James P. Wright, Minister.

KANAPOLIS.
Silas A. Day, Lawyer.

LANE.
John C. Wakefield, Druggist.

LYONS.
John R. Bell.
William H. Hillis, Minister.

MANKATO.
George S. Bishop, Banker.
Robert H. Bishop, Jr., Farmer.

MEADE.
Benjamin Mills, Minister.

MOUND VALLEY.
James H. Clark, Minister.

NEWTON.
Samuel T. Danner, Farmer.

NORTONVILLE.
Wellington Wright, Minister.

OLATHE.
Benjamin S. McFarland, Teacher.

OSWEGO.
John N. McClung, Minister.

OTTAWA.
Amherst Franklin, Lawyer.
John P. Logan, Physician.

PLYMOUTH.
Samuel T. Bennett, Farmer.

ST. JOHN.
William H. Honnell, Minister.

SPEAREVILLE.
Henry M. Shockley, Minister.

STERLING.
Charles K. Beckett, Ranchman.
George W. Potter, Physician.

THOMPSONVILLE.
Matthew N. Brown, Farmer.

TOPEKA.
Samuel G. Stewart, Physician.

WASHINGTON.
George Hageman, Minister.

WICHITA.
William W. Johnston, Jr., Merchant.
James M. Naylor, Teacher.

WINFIELD.
Francis K. Raymond, Court Reporter.

KENTUCKY.

COVINGTON.
John P. Ernst, Banker.
Charles H. Fisk, Lawyer.
John W. Hall, Jr., Teacher.

FALMOUTH.
James H. Barbour, Physician.

FERN CREEK.
Noah Cartwright, Farmer.
William M. Morrison, Teacher.

KUTTAWA.
Charles Anderson, Lawyer.

LEBANON.
Andrew J. Grundy, Farmer.
John C. Maxwell, Physician.

LOUISVILLE.
James R. Collier, Minister,
    1927 West Jefferson street.
Charles L. Grant, Physician,
    1504 West Chestnut street.

Henry H. Grant, Physician,
  1916 Market street.
William E. Grant, Physician,
  721 West Jefferson street.
Samuel McKee, Lawyer,
  216 Fifth street.

MAYSVILLE.
John F. Barbour, Banker.

MT. STERLING.
John S. Williams, Lawyer.

NEWPORT.
Albert S. Berry, Lawyer.
Shaler Berry, Student.
John L. Phythian, Physician.
Oliver W. Root, Lawyer.
Edward L. Southgate, Minister.
Frank H. Southgate, Student.

OWENSBORO.
Charles M. Moore, U. S. Storekeeper.

PADUCAH.
John W. Bloomfield, Lawyer.

PARIS.
Washington Fithian, Physician.
Richard H. Hanson, Lawyer.

PEWEE VALLEY.
Henry M. Woodruff, Merchant.

SHELBYVILLE.
Thomas L. Goff, Tobacco Merchant.

WILLIAMSTOWN.
James William Burgess, Salesman.

LOUISIANA.

NEW ORLEANS.
Robert E. Craig, Cotton Merchant.

TALLULAH.
James T. McClellan, Merchant.

MARYLAND.

BALTIMORE.
Edson M. Schryver, Merchant.
  Care, Board of Trade.

MASSACHUSETTS.

BELMONT.
William S. Kennedy, Litterateur,
  Concord avenue.

BOSTON.
Andrew Blume, Lawyer.
George B. Peck, Minister,
  38 Humphreys street.

HAVERHILL.
Joseph C. Snow, Minister.

MICHIGAN.

BATTLE CREEK.
James S. Baker, Merchant.

BENTON HARBOR.
William Hamilton, Horticulturist.

BIG RAPIDS.
Elijah F. Dewey, Lawyer.

DETROIT.
James S. Dewey, Lawyer,
  66 Joy street.
James D. Liggett, Minister,
  715 Fourth avenue.
Rodney Mason, Lawyer.

EAST SAGINAW.
William C. McClure, Banker.
  403 South Washington avenue.

GRAND HAVEN.
Samuel C. Glover, Merchant.

GRAND RAPIDS.
Herdman E. Grand-Girard, Druggist,
  128 Monroe street.

NILES.
William T. Dougan, Physician.

MINNESOTA.

DULUTH.
Stanley W. Higgins, Merchant.
Marc W. Lewis, Civil Engineer.

HASTINGS.
Alexander Telford, Minister.

HOWARD LAKE.
David Murdock, Minister.

LAKE CITY.
George R. Patton, Physician.

MINNEAPOLIS.
Robert N. Adams, Minister,
  327 Hennepin avenue.
Isaiah Faries, Minister,
  527 South Seventh street.
Patrick H. Gunckel, Lawyer,
  1614 Second avenue.

Lawrence G. Hay, Minister,
   43 Fifteenth street, N.
James W. McGregor, Minister.
Henry L. Moore, Real Estate,
   3132 Hennepin avenue.
Ezra F. Pabody, Druggist,
   28 Thirteenth street.
Alfred M. Shuey, Manufacturer,
   Century Building.

PINE BEND.
Frederick Maltby, Farmer.

REDWOOD FALLS.
D. L. Bigham.

ST. PAUL.
Robert Christie, Minister.
David E. Platter, Minister,
   26 Schulte Block.
John Woods, Minister,
   Merriam Park.

WABASHA.
John William Steel, Lawyer,
   Corner Peirce and Second streets.

MISSISSIPPI.

BILOXI.
Joseph R. Davis, Lawyer.

MISSISSIPPI CITY.
James P. Caldwell, Lawyer.

STARKVILLE.
Marion Morrison, Minister.

WINCHESTER.
Samuel H. Powe, Manufacturer.

MISSOURI.

AVILLA.
John K. Brooks, Physician.

BETHANY.
David J. Heaston, Lawyer.

BOWLING GREEN.
Edward E. Moore, Farmer.
William P. Moore, Auditor.

CARROLLTON.
Mitchell M. Graham, Artist.

CARTHAGE.
Robert F. Brooks, Physician.

DEEPWATER.
William Coleman, Minister.

ELDON.
John C. Morrison, Farmer.

FULTON.
Robert Morrison, Minister.
William W. Robertson, Minister.

GRAHAM.
Ferman D. Davis, Teacher.

INDEPENDENCE.
John McCoy, Manufacturer.

KANSAS CITY.
Samuel S. Laws, Minister,
   Centropolis Hotel.
John Marcellus Logan, Physician,
   1303 East Eighth street.
Joseph A. Morrow, Minister,
   1603 Penn street.
Omar Newman, Broker,
   Sheidley Building.
Harry Lefevre Strohm, Lawyer,
   1028-29 New York Life Building.
William F. Wilkins, Physician,
   1907 Holmes street.

MARYVILLE.
John S. Schenck, Lawyer.

MEXICO.
Charles H. Hardin, Lawyer.
Daniel A. McMillan, Teacher.

PLEASANT HILL.
Henry B. Boude, Minister.

POPLAR BLUFF.
Erwin D. Walker, Minister.

SCHELL CITY.
Isaac Coe Sickels, Farmer.

SEDALIA.
Burwell G. Wilkerson, Lawyer,
   322 West Seventh street.

ST. CHARLES.
John Jay Johns, Farmer.

ST. JOSEPH.
Samuel M. Markle, Real Estate.

ST. LOUIS.
James Hall Brookes, Minister,
   4429 Pine street.
Joseph S. Fullerton, Lawyer.
William E. Guy, Merchant.
William R. Henderson, Minister.
Philip North Moore, Geologist.
   55 Laclede Building

Robert Moore, Civil Engineer,
61 Vandwenter Place.
William H. Parks, Minister,
1122 Chambers street.
Meade C. Williams, Minister,
Care "The Mid-Continent."

WARRENSBURG.
Andrew Watts Rogers, Lawyer.

WARSAW.
James R. Jones, Lawyer.

WESTPORT.
John C. Bonham, Minister.

MONTANA.

HELENA.
Ambrose W. Lyman, Journalist.

NEBRASKA.

FAIRBURY.
Thomas Harbine, Banker.

NORTH PLATTE.
Anson S. Baldwin, Lawyer.

OMAHA.
Louis D. Holmes.

PAWNEE CITY.
James N. Eckman, Banker.

NEW JERSEY.

ALPINE.
Ben Pratt Runkle, Soldier.

FREEHOLD.
Andrew G. Chambers, Minister.

MONT CLAIR.
James K. Hitchcock, Lawyer.

NEWTON.
Alexander H. Young, Minister.

PATERSON.
Franklin E. Miller, Minister.

PERTH AMBOY.
Arthur R. Naylor, Minister.

PRINCETON.
Alexander T. Ormond, Teacher.

NEW YORK.

AMSTERDAM.
Joshua R. Kyle, Minister,
61 Arch street.

CENTER WHITE CREEK.
James E. Bruce, Minister.

DOWNSVILLE.
Thomas Fitzgerald, Minister.

ITHACA.
Edwin Emerson, Student.

KILL BUCK.
Ebenezer W. Bullard, Minister.

NEW YORK.
James C. Beard, Artist,
110 Fifth avenue.
William J. Comly, Artist,
15 Twentieth street.
John Cooper, Merchant,
146 West Forty-third street.
Quinton Corwine, Lawyer,
2 Wall street.
John I. Covington, Insurance,
45-47-49 Cedar street.
John P. Craighead, Lawyer,
Tribune Building.
Harmar Denny, Priest,
30 West Sixteenth street.
Henry M. MacCracken, Minister,
84 Irving Place.
William M. Mixer, Manufacturer,
113 West Twenty-fifth street.
William J. Molyneaux, Lawyer.
James B. Patterson.
Whitelaw Reid, Editor,
Tribune Building.
Milton Sayler, Lawyer,
316 West Twenty-third street.
William M. Smith, Lawyer,
207 West Forty-fourth street.
John McM. Stevenson, Minister.
Robert S. Voorhis, Lawyer,
56 Wall street.
Edgar M. Ward, Artist,
West Tenth street.
William H. Winters, Lawyer,
Post-office Building.

OTISVILLE.
William S. Humphreys, Teacher.

PUTNAM.
John A. Reynolds, Minister.

NORTH DAKOTA.

DEVIL'S LAKE.
John T. Killen, Minister.

SARGEANT.
Edward S. Bishop, Banker.

TOWNER.
James E. Reed, Stock-raiser.

OHIO.

ADA.
William H. Powers, Teacher.

AKRON.
William E. Clough, Physician.

ALPHA.
Albert Ankeney, Farmer.
Horace Ankeney, Farmer.

BATAVIA.
Leonard W. Bishop, Physician.
Lucius W. Bishop, Physician.
Lewis D. Manning, Lawyer.

BELLEFONTAINE.
George L. Kalb, Minister.

BLANCHESTER.
Eberle D. Smith, Banker.

BLUE ASH.
William Johnston, Physician.

BOURNEVILLE.
William Taylor, Farmer.

CALCUTTA.
James N. Swan, Minister.

CALDWELL.
John Bower, Minister.

CAMDEN.
James S. Ferguson, Physician.

CAMPBELLSTOWN.
John G. Oxer, Farmer.

CARTHAGE.
Samuel H. Forman, Farmer.

CEDARVILLE.
Samuel M. Ramsey, Minister.

CHILLICOTHE.
Marcus G. Evans, Lawyer.
William E. Evans, Lawyer.
Robert C. Galbraith, Minister.
John R. Mayo, Lawyer.
Samuel F. McCoy, Lawyer.
James C. Quinn, Banker.

CINCINNATI.
Charles F. Andress, Clerk,
   134 West Seventh street.
Stephen C. Ayres, Oculist,
   64 West Seventh street.
Myron Banning, Coal Merchant,
   Allen Building.
Charles E. Brown, Lawyer,
   27 Johnston Building.
Charles P. Brown, Student,
   27 Johnston Building.
William M. Burgoyne, Merchant,
   69 West Third street.
John W. Caldwell, Lawyer,
   11 Temple Bar.
William Carson, Physician,
   138 East Third street.
John R. Chamberlin, Journalist,
   11 Prospect street, Mt. Auburn.
William H. Chamberlin, Journalist,
   N. W. Corner of Fourth and Vine Sts.
John T. Cleveland, Physician,
   474 West Seventh street.
Edward N. Clingman, Lawyer,
   27 Johnston Building.
Francis M. Coppock, Lawyer,
   180 Walnut street.
Benjamin F. Davis, Lawyer,
   489 Central avenue.
Frank Davis, Clerk,
   Postoffice.
Parker Dickson, Lawyer,
   35 West Fourth street.
Richard T. Durrell, Lawyer,
   332 Richmond street.
Charles W. Earnist, Lawyer,
   43 Wiggins Block.
Anderson N. Ellis, Physician,
   213 Findlay street.
James J. Faran, Lawyer,
   122 East Third street.
Clinton W. Gerard, Lawyer,
   215 Woodburn avenue, Walnut Hills.
Alfred M. Greer, book-keeper,
   98 Vine street.
William S. Groesbeck, Lawyer.
Edward A. Guy, Evangelist,
   10 Hopkins street.
Simon A. Hageman, Physician,
   524 McMillan street.
George V. Halliday, Manufacturer,
   41 Elm srreet.
Charles Hanna.
Thomas Hanna, Lawyer,
   21 West Third street.
Lyman Harding, Teacher.
Charles M. Hepburn, Lawyer,
   99 West Fourth street.
John W. Herron, Lawyer,
   69 Pike street.
Harry W. Hughes, Commission,
   59 West Fourth street.
Samuel F. Hunt, Lawyer,
   Fifth and Main streets.
Miles Johnston, Lawyer,
   271 Main street.

MIAMI UNIVERSITY.

Andrew C. Kemper, Physician,
    101 Broadway.
D. Rice Kemper, Manufacturer.
Edward H. Kleinschmidt, Lawyer,
    Corner Main and Court streets.
William S. Ludlow, Broker,
    77 Garfield place.
John H. Macready, Physician,
    29 Wesley avenue.
David W. McClung,
    Government Building.
Henry B. McClure, Lawyer,
    Carlisle Building.
Alexander McGuffey, Lawyer.
James C. McMechan, Physician,
    367 West Seventh street.
Wade McMillan, Student,
    Walnut Hills.
James C. Mears, Salesman,
    Avondale.
Joseph G. Monfort, Minister,
    178 Elm street.
Clark B. Montgomery, Lawyer.
Aaron E. Moore, Lawyer,
    271 Main street.
George C. Ogden, Physician,
    Price Hill.
Melancthon W. Oliver, Lawyer,
    Price Hill.
Alexander Paddock, Lawyer,
    17½ West Third Street.
Hiram D. Peck, Lawyer,
    32 McGregor avenue.
Morris Peck, Accountant,
    United Bank Building.
David H. Pottenger, Lawyer,
    Third and Walnut streets.
J. Riner Sayler, Lawyer,
    Grand Hotel.
Nelson Sayler, Lawyer,
    58 West Third street.
Harry F. Scudder, Student,
    228 Court street.
John M. Scudder, Physician,
    228 Court street.
Bradford Shinkle, Grocer,
    Second street.
Charles B. Simrall, Lawyer.
George H. Stewart, Physician,
    Tusculum.
Alfred C. Thomas, Student,
    137 Walnut street.
Henry Van Matre, Lawyer,
    22½ East Fourth street.
Horace S. Whittaker, Merchant,
    34 Chamber of Commerce.
James T. Whittaker, Physician,
    100 West Eighth street.
Moses F. Wilson, Lawyer,
    21 West Third street.
John M. Withrow, Physician,
    291 West Fourth street.
Cyrus M. Wright, Dentist,
    277 West Seventh street.

CIRCLEVILLE.

Andrew R. Bolin, Lawyer.
Adam McCrea, Insurance Agent.
Jacob P. Winstead, Lawyer.

CLEVELAND.

John M. Henderson, Lawyer,
    219 Superior street.
Milton A. Sackett, Minister,
    40 Cornell street.

CLEVES.

Benjamin F. Chidlaw, Contractor.
Benjamin W. Chidlaw, Minister.
John Chidlaw, Farmer.
William M. Chidlaw, Teacher.

CLIFTON.

Addison S. Lewis, Civil Engineer.

COLLEGE HILL.

Charles E. Brown, Lawyer.
Charles P. Brown, Student.
Samuel F. Cary, Lawyer.

COLLINSVILLE.

William T. Scott, Farmer.

COLUMBUS.

Carlisle Barrere, Lawyer,
    571 East Town street.
Frank S. Brooks, Coal Merchant,
    253 East State street.
Moses B. Earnhart, Lawyer.
Erskine B. Fullerton, Physician,
    131 East State street.
Andrew L. Harris, Lawyer,
    Lieutenant Governor's office.
William Jamison, Lawyer,
    121 South Sixth street.
Dennis N. Keeley, Manufacturer,
    634 East Rich street.
William H. McFarland, Teacher,
    1063 East Long street.
Charles L. Osborn.
George M. Parsons, Lawyer.
Frederic J. Picard, Civil Engineer,
    66 Jefferson avenue.
James H. Puntenney, Merchant,
    83 West Fifth avenue.
John E. Sater, Lawyer.
Frank A. Spencer, Minister,
    628 Franklin avenue.
Frank Tallmadge, Stockman,
    35½ N. High street.
Edward L. Taylor, Lawyer.
Henry C. Taylor, Lawyer,
    1400 East Broad street.

CONTRERAS.

William A. Bourne, Student.

CORWIN.

Sylvanus A. Brower, Farmer.

DARRTOWN.
Joseph Harris, Farmer.

DAYTON.
Charles B. Clegg, Street Railway,
    Central Block.
Quincy Corwin, Lawyer,
    Beckel Hotel.
William Craighead, Lawyer,
    449 West Second street.
Joseph P. Davies, Manufacturer,
    First and Ludlow streets.
Samuel W. Davies, Merchant,
    211 West Third street.
Lewis B. Gunckel, Lawyer,
    6 North Main street.
Horace A. Irvin, Manufacturer,
    213 Boulevard.
John G. Lowe, Lawyer,
    127 South Main street.
William H. McKinney.
Harry E. Mead, Manufacturer,
    Runnymede.
Claudius N. Mitchell, Manufacturer,
    112 East First street.
John H. Patterson, Coal Merchant,
    First and Ludlow streets.
S. J. Patterson, Coal Merchant,
    Sixth and Ludlow streets.
Edward L. Rowe, Lawyer,
    134 West Fifth street.
Robert C. Schenck, Manufacturer,
    305 West Second street.
George W. Shaw, Manufacturer,
    Third and Perry streets.
Clarence E. Shook, Solicitor,
    Care, "Times—News."
William H. Simms, Banker,
    Care, Dayton National Bank.
James M. Smith, Farmer.
John W. Stoddard, Manufacturer,
    Dayton View.
Walter L. Tobey, Journalist,
    1438 West Third street.
Isaac VanAusdal, Merchant,
    Dayton View.
Herbert H. Weakley, Journalist,
    337 West Second street.
Harry Weidner, Journalist,
    28 East Garden street.
Perry W. Weidner, Book-keeper,
    Ware Block.
A. G. Wilson, Lawyer.

COULTERSVILLE.
Robert C. Hamilton, Physician.

EATON.
William H. Bonner, Merchant.
Charles F. Brookins, Student.
Henry H. Farr, Merchant.
Elam Fisher, Lawyer.
George E. Gowdy, Minister.
Walter C. Harris, Student.

Robert A. Hiestand, Student.
A. E. Hubbard, Banker.
James E. Lough, Teacher.
William H. Lough, Farmer.
Alfred A. Lovett, Physician.
James L. Quinn, Physician.
Walter G. Shannon, Life Insurance.
Frank G. Thompson, Lawyer.

ECKMANSVILLE.
John M. Lockhart, Physician.

FAIR HAVEN.
Abdallah M. Howe, Physician.

FARMERSVILLE.
Christian A. Coler, Farmer.

FERNBANK.
Abraham Brower, Lawyer.

FINCASTLE.
Jesse L. Baird, Physician.

FINDLAY.
Robert H. Holliday, Minister.
James L. McLain, Physician.

FOSTERS.
James Davis, Farmer.

FRANKLIN.
William A. Hutchison, Minister.

FREDERICKSBURG.
Brownhill T. Sheeley, Minister.

FREDERICKTOWN.
John W. Lindley, Farmer.

FREMONT.
William E. Findley, Architect.

GEORGETOWN.
John R. Moore, Lawyer.

GLENDALE.
Joseph Cox, Lawyer.
James R. Patterson, Merchant.

GRATIS.
Kearney Prugh, Teacher.

GREENFIELD.
Fay Baldwin, Banker.
Hugh P. Jackson, Minister.
Albert M. Mackerley, Lawyer.
Francis L. Wilson, Physician.

GREENVILLE.
James C. Elliott, Lawyer.

MIAMI UNIVERSITY.

Isaac N. Gard, Physician.
John R. Knox, Lawyer.
John F. Martin, Lawyer.

HAMILTON.

William Beckett, Manufacturer,
    Fifth and Dayton streets.
Philip G. Berry, Lawyer.
William R. Cochran, Lawyer,
    South B street.
Pierson C. Conklin, Lawyer,
    27 B street.
Stephen Crane, Lawyer.
Cyrus Falconer, Physician.
Orlando B. Finch, Teacher.
Charles W. Gath, Undertaker.
William S. Giffen, Lawyer,
    Reily Block.
Alexander F. Hume, Lawyer.
Edward H. Jones, Lawyer.
Charles I. Keely, Dentist.
Lawrence M. Larsh, Official.
Joseph J. McMaken, Lawyer.
Thomas Millikin, Lawyer,
    113 South Second street.
James W. Moore, Agent.
Thomas W. Moore, Lawyer.
Henry Lee Morey, Lawyer.
Jamea E. Morey, Lawyer.
Oakey V. Parrish, Insurance.
Isaac Robertson, Lawyer.
Elihu C. Simpson, Minister.
Culbertson J. Smith, Lawyer.
Benjamin F. Thomas, Lawyer.
Samuel V. Wasson, Farmer.

HARTWELL.
J. Edward Baker, Physician.

HILLSBORO.
Livy B. Boyd, Coal Merchant.
Joseph M. Hibben, Merchant.
Hugh S. Fullerton, Physician.
William J. McSurely, Minister.
Jacob J. Pugsley, Lawyer.
Samuel P. Scott, Lawyer.
John A. Smith, Lawyer.
Kirby Smith, Lawyer.

JAMESTOWN.
John M. Heron, Minister.

JOHNSVILLE.
Peter Drayer, Merchant.

KING'S MILLS.
Algernon S. Stevens, Physician.

LANCASTER.
Philemon B. Ewing, Lawyer.

LEBANON.
William F. Eltzroth, Lawyer.

Joseph Morrow, Lawyer.
John K. O'Neal, Lawyer.
Edward B. Stevens, Physician.
Isaac N. Walker, Lawyer.

LIMA.
Calvin S. Brice, Lawyer.
Peter H. Brooks, Physician.
Jonathan B. Vail, Physician.

LOCKLAND.
Lutellus Hussey, Physician.

LOGAN.
David R. Moore, Minister.

LONDON.
Bruce P. Jones, Lawyer.

LYNDON.
John Barrett, Minister.
Samuel C. Kerr, Minister.

LYTLE.
Jeremiah M. Hunt, Physician.

MCCOMB.
Daniel W. Cooper, Minister.

MAPLEWOOD.
Benjamin Le Fevre, Lawyer.

MASON.
John M. VanDyke, Physician.

MIDDLE POINT.
David Johnston.

MIDDLETOWN.
Richard Corson, Teacher.
John McClellan, Lawyer.
William V. Shaffer, Physician.
Joseph L. Thornton, Manufacturer.

MILFORD.
Arch Longworth.

MILLVILLE.
Walter D. Hancock, Physician.

MORNING SUN.
Robert J. Brown, Farmer.
Ebenezer N. Elliott, Minister.

MORROW.
Adolphus Dudley, Minister.
Thomas L. Pendery, Farmer.

NEWARK.
Henry C. Johnson, Minister.
James W. Owens, Lawyer.

NORWICH.
Richard C. Wyatt, Minister.

OBERLIN.
Mark Williams, Minister.

OXFORD.
Daniel P. Beaton, Agent.
Lazarus N. Bonham, Agriculturist.
Benjamin H. Brown, Farmer.
Waldo F. Brown, Farmer.
Robert H. Cook, Student.
Elmer B. Finch, Photographer.
Edward H. Greer, Salesman.
Wilbur J. Greer, Teacher.
David W. Guy, Lawyer.
Robert M. L. Huston, Farmer.
George Kramer, Farmer.
Theodore R. Kumler, Stock Raiser.
Walter S. Kumler.
Abraham S. Lee, Retired.
George M. Lee, Merchant.
Joseph L. Molyneaux, Farmer.
John S. Muddell, Clerk.
James B. Porter, Physician.
Sutton C. Richey, Banker.
Willam J. Rusk, Lawyer.
Orange W. Schultz, Merchant.
Caleb A. Shera, Banker.
John H. Smith, Student.
Palmer W. Smith, Lawyer.
James R. Spivey, Druggist.
William Stewart, Teacher.
Faye Walker, Minister.
Thomas J. Woodruff, Farmer.

PAULDING.
Thomas J. Dague, Minister.

PIQUA.
John M. Layman, Minister.

PLEASANT RIDGE.
Josiah E. Brown, Real Estate Broker.

PORTSMOUTH.
Charles P. Dennis, Dentist.
Nelson W. Evans, Lawyer.
John A. Lowes, Teacher.
David S. Tappen, Minister-

RED OAK.
ames H. Cooper, Minister.

REILY.
Joseph Urmston.

ROSS.
Franklin F. Scott, Merchant.
Nehemiah Wade, Farmer.

ROXABELL.
James N. Jamison, Farmer.
John M. Jamison, Farmer.

SANDUSKY.
Ulysses T. Curran, Lawyer.

SEVEN MILE.
David C. Scott, Farmer.
Wilson B. Smith, Farmer.

SIDNEY.
Thomas B. Marshall, Book-keeper.
Walter L. Spence, Teacher.

SILVERTON.
Samuel B. Halley, Merchant.

SOUTH CHARLESTON.
James K. Gibson, Minister.
Thomas Mattinson, Civil Engineer.

SPRINGFIELD.
Enoch G. Dial, Lawyer.
Alexander Dunlap, Physician.
George H. Fullerton, Minister.
Israel H. Kelley, Manufacturer.
John H. Rodgers, Physician.
William C. Smith, Com'l Traveller.

STEUBENVILLE.
Elisha P. Potter, Merchant.

TOLEDO.
Augustus W. Eckert, Lawyer.
James R. Linn, Lawyer,
                   3 Trinity Block.
James A. P. McGaw, Minister.
                1828 Adams street.
Benjamin F. Miller, Lawyer.
Nathan E. Warwick, Lawyer,
                609 Madison street.

TORONTO.
Homer Sheeley, Minister.

TROY.
Ahijah R. Byrkett, Lawyer.
Isaac E. Craig, Lawyer.
John R. Evans, Physician.
John W. Morris, Lawyer.
Walter S. Thomas, Lawyer.

URBANA.
Frank Chance, Lawyer.
George W. McCracken, Lawyer.
David W. Todd, Lawyer.
Charles S. Wood, Minister.

WAKEFIELD.
H. M. Sargeant.

WASHINGTON C. H.
George F. Robinson, Merchant.
John N. Van Deman, Lawyer.

WEST ALEXANDRIA.
Robert D. Huggins, Physician.

WEST CHESTER.
James Belch.
John S. Cox, Merchant.

WOODS.
Sam Stephenson, Lawyer.
John M. Trembly, Physician.

WYOMING.
William E. Allen, Farmer.
Jere M. Cochran, Journalist.

XENIA.
Clark M. Galloway, Physician.
James E. Galloway, Merchant.
John T. Harbine, Manufacturer.
William C. Hutchison, Merchant.
Clark Kendall, Minister.
David MacDill, Teacher.
Edmund H. Munger, Lawyer.
James P. Townsley, Merchant.
Thomas P. Townsley, Merchant.

YOUNGSTOWN.
Daniel H. Evans, Minister.

ZANESVILLE.
Silas F. Edgar, Physician.
John S. Holderman, Physician.
Martin V. Kennedy, Merchant.

OKLAHOMA TERRITORY.

OKLAHOMA CITY.
James Lyman Brown, Lawyer.

OREGON.

BAKER CITY.
George A. Hutchison, Minister.

DALLAS.
Thomas C. Bell, Teacher.

PORTLAND.
William A. Charles, Insurance,
    P. O. Box, 453.
Harry C. Hume, Civil Engineer.
Edward H. Miller, Merchant,
    Care, Knapp, Burrell & Co.
William W. Page, Lawyer.
Harlan P. Ustick, Oculist.

SALEM.
George Knox Sheil, Lawyer.

PENNSYLVANIA.

ALLEGHENY.
Eben S. McKitrick, Minister,
    34 Beech street.
David M. Ure, Minister,
    25 Esplanade street.
Walter Ure, Physician,
    176 Federal street.

BRIDGEVILLE.
Virgil G. Sheeley, Minister.

BRISTOL.
Edward Patrick Shields, Minister.

EASTON.
Charles Stewart, Manufacturer,
    123 North Second street.

MOUNT JOY.
James P. Ziegler, Physician.

NEW ALEXANDRIA.
James R. Johnston, Farmer.

NEW WILMINGTON.
Mitchell M. Brown, Minister.

PHILADELPHIA.
George Junkin, Lawyer,
    1334 Chestnut street.
Samuel T. Lowrie, Minister,
    2104 Pine street.
Woodhull S. Schenck, Navy Officer,
    216 South Second street.
David Steele, Minister,
    2102 Spring Garden street.
Thomas Williams, Lawyer,
    128 South Nineteenth street.
James Avery Worden, Minister,
    1334 Chestnut street.

PITTSBURG.
Jeremiah P. E. Kumler, Minister,
    413 Highland avenue.

STANTON.
Joseph McFarland, Farmer.

WASHINGTON.
Abraham Brower Lowes, Minister.

SOUTH CAROLINA.

CHARLESTON.
James D. Kirkpatrick, Cotton Factor.

TENNESSEE.

AUSTIN.
Persius Barnet Calhoun, Farmer.

CHATTANOOGA.
Archibald S. Dunlap, Physician.

COLUMBIA.
David McCaw, Farmer.

MEMPHIS.
Calvin F. Vance, Lawyer,
    250 Second street.

NASHVILLE.
Gates P. Thruston, Lawyer,
    318 N. High street.
Charles A. Wilson, Teacher.

SHERMAN HEIGHTS.
James H. Garvin, Minister.

SMYRNA.
Theophilus C. Hibbett, Engineer.

SWEET WATER.
Perry W. Jenkins, Teacher.

TEXAS.

AUSTIN.
Paul F. Thornton, Lawyer.
    1909 August street.
John A. Webb, Merchant.

CORSICANA.
John C. Young, Lawyer.

CROCKETT.
John B. Smith, Minister.

DALLAS.
Abner S. Lathrop, Lawyer,
    240 Main street.

HOUSTON.
John H. Duncan, Lawyer.
Lewis D. Watson, Banker.

SAN ANTONIO.
Joseph S. O'Connor, Lawyer.

WACO.
Robert M. Loughridge, Minister.

UTAH.

RANSFORD SMITH.
Ransford Smith, Lawyer.

VIRGINIA.

BEDFORD CITY.
Henry B. Colburn, Real Estate.

LYNCHBURG.
Albert M. Doyle, Real Estate.

WASHINGTON.

PORT TOWNSEND.
John N. Scott, Lawyer.

SPOKANE.
John W. Feighan, Lawyer,
    1803 Second avenue.
James Z. Moore, Lawyer,
    2209 Fourth street.

TACOMA.
Frank Allyn, Lawyer.
Benjamin Sheeks, Lawyer.

WEST VIRGINIA.

CHARLESTON.
William E. Truslow, Banker.

CROWN POINT.
Holway B. Smith, Superintendent.

FORT GAY.
Newton R. Kirkpatrick, Minister.

PARKERSBURG.
William M. Trevor, Officer.

WISCONSIN.

MERRILL.
Henry L. Brown, Minister.

WYOMING.

CHEYENNE.
John M. Davidson, Lawyer.

FOREIGN.

BRAZIL.

PARA.
Juan D. P. Damasceno, Engineer.

NEW BRUNSWICK.

ST. JOHN.
Armour J. McFarland, Minister.
    25 Peel street.

SANDWICH ISLANDS.

HONOLULU.
Robert W. Andrews, Civil Engineer.

ADDENDA.

DAVID T. WOODROW, of the class of 1834, died at Cincinnati, Ohio, in May, 1892.

REV. JOHN A. ANDERSON, of the class of 1853, died at London, England, May 18, 1892, while enroute from Egypt to the United States.

GEN. BEN PRATT RUNKLE, of the class of 1857, is now located at San Jose, California.

JOHN F. MARTIN, of the class of 1873, is practicing law in Greenville, Ohio, and not in Cincinnati, as erroneously printed in the Alumni.

WALTER L. TOBEY, of the class of 1891, and the editor of the catalogue of Alumni and Former Students of Miami University, was elected managing editor of the "Hamilton Daily Republican" and "Butler County Republican" at Hamilton, Ohio, June 2, 1892.

REV. DR. THEOPHILUS A. WYLIE, professor of mathematics in Miami University from 1845 to 1852, is now living at Bloomington, Indiana. Mr. Charles Hruby, professor of Modern Languages in Miami University from 1852 to 1857, is erroneously printed as being a teacher at Bloomington, Indiana. His present address is unknown.